THE *COMPLETE* BOOK OF
GAME
FISHING

THE *COMPLETE* BOOK OF
GAME
FISHING

INTRODUCTION BY PETER GATHERCOLE

CollinsWillow
An Imprint of HarperCollins*Publishers*

First published in 1994 by
Collins Willow
an imprint of HarperCollins Publishers
London

Based on The Art of Fishing
© Eaglemoss Publications Ltd 1994

A CIP catalogue record for this book is
available from the British Library

ISBN 0 00 218515 6

Printed and bound in Hong Kong

Contents

Introduction

Trying to catch game fish can be a frustrating experience. At times, dealing with linked factors like weather, season, water height and which fly pattern or lure to use can tax the patience of even the most seasoned angler. However, much of this frustration can be eliminated by following the solid, commonsense advice in *The Complete Book of Game Fishing*.

Your decisions about tackle affect your chances of success, so the first chapter, Choosing Tackle, deals with the often bewildering task of selecting the right equipment for the job in hand.

Faced with the grey expanse of a large lake or the power of a broad salmon river, it can be difficult to know just where to begin. The next two chapters, Stillwater Tactics and River Tactics, cover all the major water types, from the tiniest upland brook to the mightiest salmon river, from the smallest pond to the largest 'concrete-bowl' reservoir or Scottish loch. Just what goes on beneath the surface has always been one of the major fascinations of angling, and the cross-section illustrations offer real insight into the importance of underwater ledges, weed beds and other spots where the fish lie and where their food is found.

Next, Know Your Fish looks in depth at our main game species. A profile of the native brown trout — its habitat, feeding patterns and how to locate it — provides a vital key to catching this wily fish. Similarly detailed coverage is given to the majestic salmon, sea trout, grayling, char, various whitefish species, and the rainbow trout, a North American import which has become an important species for Britain's stillwater trout anglers.

Flies, Lures and Spinners explores the game fisher's dazzling array of flies and artificial lures. The whole aim of fly fishing is to fool a fish into taking an imitation of a real fly, and to many people, mimicking a specific insect in this way is the pinnacle of game fishing. Traditional wet flies, dry flies and nymphs are all covered, as well as modern reservoir lures and spinners.

After a section dedicated to the tools and materials you will need, the final chapter, Fly Tying, shows you the art of transforming ▶

fur, feather, wool and tinsel into effective artificial flies. The patterns discussed range from the simple Black Pennell, through the Pheasant Tail Nymph and the Adams dry fly, up to deadly monstrosities such as the Booby, Muddler and Dalberg Diver.

Learning to tie these key patterns gives you a range of skills enabling you to create hundreds of other flies. Tying your own flies is not strictly necessary, but there is something special about catching a fish on a fly you have tied yourself. Fly tying is more than just an enjoyable pastime in itself, for trying out new ideas and developing your own patterns allows you to play an active role in the constant evolution of fly fishing — and will most likely help you catch more fish too!

Few anglers truly understand every facet of game fishing. But, by distilling the knowledge of many of Britain's leading trout, salmon and grayling specialists, *The Complete Book of Game Fishing* lets you in on the secrets of the most effective techniques, traditional and modern. Whatever your level of expertise, its information-packed features written by top names such as Bob Church, Peter Cockwill, Charles Jardine, Jeremy Herrmann, John Roberts, Stan Headley and Jon Beer, are bound to extend your abilities. Each author has been closely involved in the development of modern game fishing, but while one of them prefers to cast a line for lake or reservoir trout, another finds the allure of salmon or small hill-stream brown trout irresistible.

As a result, this book is crammed with up-to-date information and advice on a wide range of methods, fly patterns and baits. In addition, it is illustrated with high-quality colour photos and illustrations designed to help you get the best out of your game fishing. For the most important thing is to put this wealth of expert advice to work where it really counts — out on the water.

Peter Gathercole

CHAPTER ONE

CHOOSING TACKLE

The basic fly kit

Trout fisheries are now so common in Britain that many die-hard coarse anglers are giving fly fishing a try. Peter Cockwill lists everything you need to enjoy some great sport.

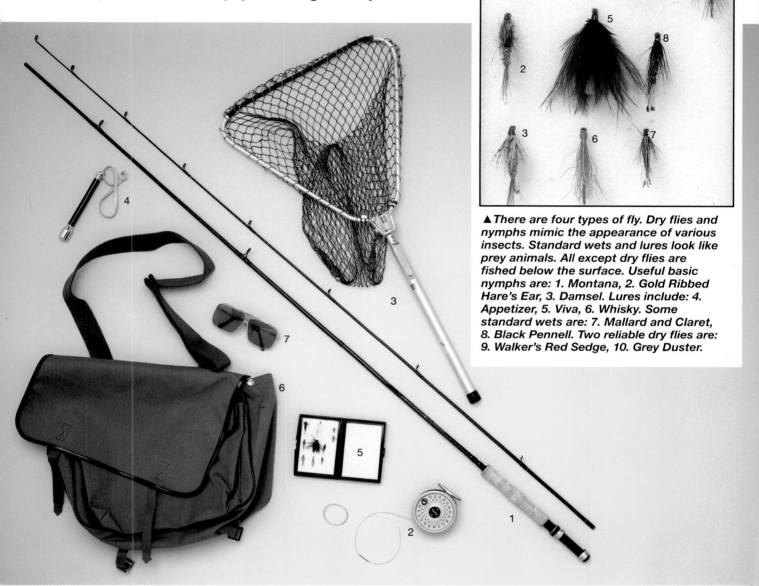

▲ *There are four types of fly. Dry flies and nymphs mimic the appearance of various insects. Standard wets and lures look like prey animals. All except dry flies are fished below the surface. Useful basic nymphs are: 1. Montana, 2. Gold Ribbed Hare's Ear, 3. Damsel. Lures include: 4. Appetizer, 5. Viva, 6. Whisky. Some standard wets are: 7. Mallard and Claret, 8. Black Pennell. Two reliable dry flies are: 9. Walker's Red Sedge, 10. Grey Duster.*

Key

1. Fly rod Two piece carbon fibre.
2. Fly reel, fly line, backing and leader.
3. Landing net This model folds away.
4. Priest Used to kill the fish quickly.
5. Fly box and flies This selection covers most situations.
6. Tackle bag to carry your equipment and catch.
7. Polarising sunglasses Essential to cut out reflected glare.

The fly fisherman is trying to tempt the fish into taking a hook dressed with fur, feathers and tinsel to represent its food. This is the fly and it is the only piece of terminal tackle used.

The fly weighs almost nothing and, because there are no other weights attached to the line, it is the line itself that is heavy. At the heart of fly fishing is the use of this special heavy line to cast the fly out into the water.

To start fly fishing you need a rod, a reel, fly line, some nylon, flies and a few accessories. As fly line is central to casting, you first need to know which type of line to choose.

Line and AFTM numbers

Line weights range from 1-15 (light lines have low numbers, whereas heavier lines, for long distance casting, have higher numbers) and this rating is referred to as the AFTM number. A number 7 is the most useful to the inexperienced angler.

In addition, lines come in a range of different densities – which allows them to float, or to sink at different rates. Lines also taper as an aid to casting – either from one end or from the middle towards both ends.

A floating double taper line is useful for most purposes and is marked DT7F (double taper 7 floating). A length of 27m (30yd) is all you need.

Matching rod to line

For fishing small still waters you need a 9-9½ft (2.70-2.85m) rod, with a crisp action, rated for a number 6-7 line. The rod is marked with this rating, either as AFTM 6/7 or simply as number 6/7. Carbon fibre rods are light and good value for money.

Filling the reel

Fly reels are centrepins with a heavy ratchet and sometimes a drag mechanism to help slow down the flight of a running fish. Ask your tackle dealer for a simple lightweight reel that balances your rod.

Before you fill your reel with line, load at least 27m (30yd) of 25lb (11.3kg) backing line (nylon monofilament). This allows a large trout to run further without taking all your line. It also ensures that your fly line is not wound too tightly on the reel, which can cause casting problems. Tie the backing to the reel with a tucked half blood knot and to the fly line with an Albright knot.

Choosing flies

There are literally thousands of fly patterns and this can be very confusing at first. You need about ten to cover most situations on small trout lakes and you will quickly discover your own favourites. Ask other anglers which flies they have found effective on the waters you are going to fish. A small fly box keeps your flies safe and organized when you are not using them.

Because fly line is thick, which puts the fish off, the fly must be tied to a length of nylon, called a leader. This should be at least as long as the rod and about 5lb (2.3kg) breaking strain. It is tied to the main fly line by means of a loop. Any good tackle dealer will attach a short loop of 10lb (4.5kg) line to the fly line. You can also buy braided loops which you glue to the fly line. Tie the leader to the loop using a loop knot.

Accessories

Most waters require the use of a landing net. Stocked fisheries usually insist that you kill every trout you catch. A small cosh called a priest is best for this. You will need a bag to carry your tackle and a pair of polarising sunglasses to protect your eyes from glare and enable you to see where the fish are below the surface of the water. With all the correct tackle you are now equipped to try your hand at fly fishing.

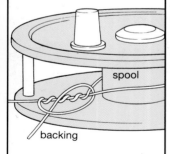

Tying your line

Attaching a braided loop

braided loop   fly line

at least 5cm

Cut the end of the fly line to a point and insert it into the braided loop. A drop of instant glue will hold it in place.

rubber sleeve

Seal the end, either with a rubber sleeve or by whipping it in place.

Albright knot

backing   fly line

This is to attach the fly line to the backing. Tighten the knot gently.

Tucked half blood knot

spool

backing

This knot can also be used for tying fly to leader by threading the main loop through the hook's eye.

▶ *Fly fishing for trout is often an active sport, involving a constant search for feeding fish. These two fine specimens fell for fly fishing tactics – the top fish is a brown trout, the bottom one a rainbow.*

Fly lines

Peter Cockwill – stillwater specialist and tackle dealer – sorts through the welter of colour and design to explain fly lines.

Since an artificial fly weighs so little, the main fly line must be heavy enough to allow the whole set-up to be cast out over the water. Lines come in a range of densities – some float, while others sink at any one of a wide variety of rates. There is also a complex range of tapers for specific types of fly fishing.

Originally made of silk dressed in oils, fly lines today are high-tech items. Modern lines consist of a braided Terylene core coated with PVC to repel water and give slickness for casting. Lines are now also being made of polymers over a core of Kevlar, or something similar. They offer improved slickness and lower stretch but some anglers prefer the slight stretchiness of the older, PVC-coated lines.

The AFTMA rating

All fly lines are graded in a range of 1-15 on a scale calculated by the Association of Fishing Tackle Manufacturers of America (AFTMA). The first 35ft (10.7m) of line is weighed, regardless of density or taper, and given a number on that basis. A number 1 line is the lightest and thinnest and a number 15 the heaviest. In Britain, the most commonly used lines are in the range AFTMA 5-8.

Fly rods are designed to work at their best with 35ft (10.7m) of a particular AFTMA-rated line out beyond the tip ring. The butt of each rod carries the rating of the line it is designed to cast. A number 7 rod would carry the mark AFTMA 7 or #7.

For casts of longer than 35ft (10.7m), this same length is aerialized (in the air beyond the top rod ring during the cast) and the

▲ *Floating line should be clearly visible to you on the surface – so you can spot bites. The colour does not usually deter the trout.*

Tip Daily stretch

Before each fishing trip, stretch the line in short sections. This removes reel memory (those springy coils of line), making casting easier.

▼ *At a big reservoir – this is Fewston near Harrogate – you often need a long cast. This angler is using weight forward line and a style of casting known as double hauling to gain extra yards.*

A FLY LINE FOR EVERY SITUATION

▲ The codes for fly lines are common sense. Here, the top right line is marked WF-7-F and is a Weight Forward Floating line rated AFTMA 7. The other line (DT11F/S) is a Double Taper Floating line with a Sinking tip (F/S = floating/sinking) rated AFTMA 11.

✗ Even hand

It is not difficult to fill the reel evenly, yet many anglers still tend to forget. Every time you wind line on to the spool, avoid unevenness and loose coils or you'll have problems casting and playing fish. Also, at the end of a day's fishing, the finer nylon of the leader can fall between these loose turns of fly line, causing the reel to jam solidly the next time you come to use it.

rest of the line is pulled through the tip ring by the momentum of the 35ft (10.7m) used in the cast.

Which taper?

While it is still possible to buy fly line which is the same thickness along its whole length (known as level line), this has generally been replaced by line which tapers to help casting or presentation of the fly. Three main tapers are used in fly fishing although there are many variations on the basic themes.

A double taper line is thickest in the middle, tapering to a finer diameter at each end. It is generally the best line for delicate work at short range, such as dry fly fishing on running water or small still waters. It

▲ *Dry fly fishing on fast-flowing rivers is one of the most enjoyable ways to catch trout. Floating double taper line is the usual choice for this type of fishing. The taper allows you to cast a fly with great accuracy and to present it delicately.*

Tip Feet of clay

Try to keep your line as clean as possible while fishing, especially if the banks are clay based. The dirt your line picks up can wear through wire rod rings and reel fittings and can mess up your tackle. A line basket worn around your waist keeps it all cleaner. It also makes it impossible for you to stand on the line and helps to prevent it getting tangled – both of which can be disastrous when playing any fish of a decent size.

also has the advantage that you can reverse it if one end gets damaged at the waterside. This is an emergency measure only, because the undamaged end of the line tends to have a high reel memory. Replace any line which you're using like this as soon as you can.

A forward taper line (weight forward) has its main bulk concentrated in the first 35ft (10.7m). The rest of the line consists of a narrow, level section – so that it slips easily through the rod rings after the main section for casts of more than the 35ft (10.7m). It is used to gain greater distances than are usually possible with a double taper.

A shooting taper is essentially a weight forward line with nylon backing replacing the narrow section of fly line. The backing follows this shooting head even more easily – giving still more distance. However, using a shooting taper does involve a certain loss of accuracy and presentation.

Fly lines are commonly 27yd (25m) long though shooting heads are only about 35ft (10.7m) and some specialized makes and profiles can be up to 40yd (37m) long. In most cases it is best to learn to cast with a double taper, so that you gain good

control and presentation before moving on to forward and shooting tapers. The line you choose depends on the water you intend to fish, the distance you have to cast and how delicate your presentation needs to be.

To float or not to float

Fly lines not only taper to help casting, they also float or sink to get your fly right to the depth at which the fish are feeding. Lines which float are the obvious choice for dry fly fishing, but they are also useful when you want to fish your fly quite close under the surface. Using floating line, you can get your fly down as deep as the length of a sinking leader. This versatility makes floating line best for the beginner.

Floating lines come in a staggering range of colours, some of which seem guaranteed to drive fish screaming to the other end of any water. However, you must remember that fish see line that floats as a silhouette against the sky – a dark outline – rather than, for example, a shocking pink strand. The colours simply help you detect any movement that might mean a bite. Choose a line that is visible against both glare and dark water.

Sinking lines are usually a more sombre colour, such as green or brown. They have different densities, allowing you to search for fish at varying depths. On a small still-water, an intermediate or slow sink line is often the most useful. If you want to fish deeper waters, such as reservoirs, lead-cored lines are often the order of the day to get the fly down deep enough.

Sink-tip lines are floating lines with an end section which sinks. These are popular with anglers fishing rivers for migratory fish (mainly salmon and sea trout). Once again, the density of the tip can vary enormously, allowing you to achieve the sinking rate you require.

Having learnt to cast competently you are then in a position to start thinking

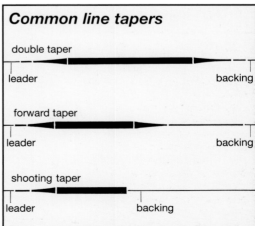

Common line tapers

double taper

leader   backing

forward taper

leader   backing

shooting taper

leader   backing

These are the three most common types of line taper or profile. The actual lengths of the various sections of line depend on the particular manufacturer.

about the presentation of the fly. Only then are you able to choose from the different lines available – and to use them to find the fish and tempt them into taking. A choice of lines at the bankside (on spare spools or different reels) can be invaluable to cope with varying conditions.

Care and maintainance

All PVC lines gradually deteriorate as the plasticizers used to keep them supple leak out of the coating. This leads to stiffness and eventually causes the line to crack. You can prolong the life of line by washing it in mildly soapy water and treating it with plasticizing agents. Keeping the spooled line out of strong sunlight and heat helps, but even so it won't last forever. A good floater lasts about two or three years.

Poor casting technique is the biggest single factor in line deterioration. It causes the line to flex excessively over a short length, hastening the cracking of the PVC. Stepping on your line is another short-cut on the road to ruin.

Fly lines vary widely in price and generally what you pay for is what you get. Expensive lines are more supple and slicker with smoother tapers – increasing casting efficiency. However, there is little point buying the best as a beginner,

because you won't be able to appreciate the difference. Move on to quality when you have command over the elements of casting. Whichever line you buy, make sure you choose the right AFTMA rating, taper and density for the type of fishing you plan to spend your time on.

The needle knot

fly line

nylon leader

1 Push the needle up the core and through the PVC after about 6mm (1/4in). Heat the needle, removing it after a few seconds. Thread the leader through the hole narrow end first.
2 Wrap the thick end of nylon leader round the fly line as shown forming coils **(a)**. Wrap the length of leader **(b)** round the fly line and leader **(c)**. The coils are now used to create the actual loops **(d)** of the knot.
3 Continue wrapping leader **(b)** around **(c)** forming loops **(d)**, unwinding all the original coils as you do so.
4 Pull tight and trim.

▼ *Late in the season at Rutland Water, big rainbows like this one can be caught on fry-imitating lures. Lead-cored lines are often required to get your fly down to the depth at which the fish are feeding.*

Looking after fly lines

No fly line lasts forever. But regular 'tune-ups' ensure that it stays in top condition for a long, healthy working life.

It's a pleasure to cast a new fly line and see it slip effortlessly through the rod rings towards a rising trout. Admittedly, a quality line is expensive, but it is one piece of equipment you shouldn't skimp on. By maintaining the line – cleaning, plasticising and treating regularly – you can keep it in tip-top condition and save money by getting several seasons of use from it.

Cleaning your line
During day-to-day use the number one enemy of a fly line is dirt. Mud and sand are highly abrasive. In no time at all they remove the slick surface of the line. Microscopic particles of dirt (and even algae) can cling to the surface of a floating line, adding weight and causing it to sink.

When the line does get dirty, wash it regularly. Add a drop or two of washing-up liquid to a basin of warm water, and leave it to soak for three minutes or so. Then run the line through a cotton cloth, applying pressure with your fingers. Do this several times for heavily stained areas.

Applying plasticiser
Fly lines such as the Scientific Anglers' range have a PVC (polyvinyl chloride) coating. This coating is hard and brittle on its own, so at the time of manufacture PVC lines receive a suitable softening agent or plasticiser, but this is lost as you use the line. In time, if the plasticiser isn't replaced, the coating hardens and can crack.

If your PVC line is showing signs of wear – if the coating is hard and worn after a season of fishing, for example – there are several plasticisers you can buy in tackle shops. Permaplas is a one of the most popular brands.

One word of warning about plasticisers – you must follow the manufacturer's directions carefully. If you don't, you could per-

Key to products

1. Mucilin
2. Permaplas Plasticiser
3. Line grease
4. Mastercare line conditioner
5. Xink tippet sink
6. Fly floatants

▼ *A bank angler on Fewston Reservoir in North Yorkshire blasts out a team of nymphs.*
   Keeping your fly line slick and healthy helps to reach those trout feeding a long way out.

Tip   *Give it a good stretch*

Fly line which has not been used for a while (or new line) may require a good stretch (above left) to eliminate line memory. At the venue you're fishing, simply wrap one end around a pole or tree (above right) and stretch the line for 10-30 seconds or until the memory is gone.

Before using a shooting head, it's essential to stretch the 20-30lb (9-13kg) mono backing to reduce tangling.

---

manently damage the coating of the line and have a serious 'meltdown'.

Not all lines require plasticising: there are some available (such as the Airflo series) which aren't PVC coated but use a polymer covering on Kevlar-core backing. So they don't suffer from cracking in the same way as PVC lines.

Slick as ice

PVC and non-PVC lines both require a treatment or conditioner to ensure that they retain their silky feel.

Generally, you can buy the manufacturer's own brand of line treatment. But for PVC lines, car-upholstery protectant (such as Armour All or Vista) works very well.

▼ *Plasticising restores the suppleness to the coating of a PVC line, helping to reduce the likelihood of cracking.*

Here, the top line has been maintained properly and as a result is in good shape. The bottom line is so severely worn that it must be thrown away.

Simply wipe on the solution, wait a moment then wipe off. Most auto shops have these products. Russ Peak Line Dressing and 303 Protectant – available at fly fishing tackle shops – also do the job.

Use regularly for best results – some anglers apply protectant after every fishing session!

If you're not sure which plasticisers or protectants are suitable for your line, write to the manufacturer for details, or ask experienced fly fishing tackle dealers for advice.

Permanent loop for PVC lines

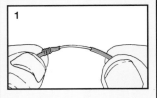

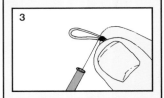

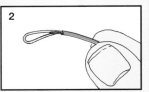

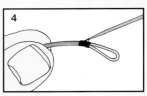

Although a fly line needs to be looked after, a permanent leader loop – made properly – doesn't.

1. Strip away the fly line's PVC coating.
2. Make a loop and secure it with instant glue.
3. To reinforce the glued area further, whip over it with micro thread.
4. Coat the thread with waterproof glue.

◄ *Many anglers apply conditioner to their PVC lines before fishing for maximum 'shootability'.*

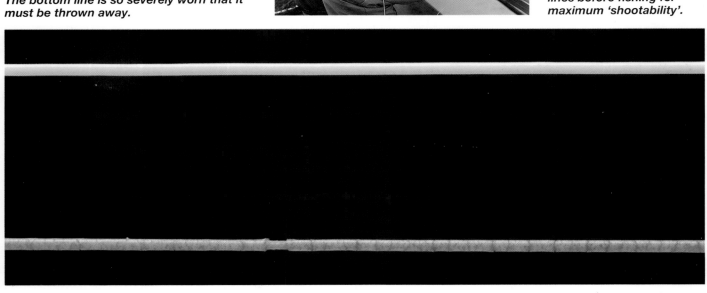

Fly rods for trout

Tackle manufacturer and England International Bob Church recommends a selection of different fly rods for fishing brooks, streams, rivers and reservoirs.

◀ *Taking great care not to be rash or impatient, this angler gently persuades a fine lip-hooked rainbow into the net. This way the fish can be returned unharmed.*

There are three main materials for fly rods: split cane, glass-fibre and carbon fibre. Split cane, even though it is costly and rather heavy, has an enthusiastic following among stream and river anglers. Glass-fibre rods are now quite rare and virtually outdated.

Since its introduction in 1973, carbon fibre has revolutionized rod building. It is much stiffer and lighter than either split cane or glass-fibre. This means that a carbon blank can be much thinner than the alternatives, with more of a tip-action for distance casting. Other materials are often added to the carbon fibre, such as silicon carbide, kevlar and boron, which change the action of the finished rod.

Fly rods vary enormously in length — from a 6ft (1.8m) brook or small stream rod, through a 12ft (3.6m) loch style rod to a 18ft (5.5m) 'dapping' rod.

Just as a fly line is given an AFTMA rating according to the weight of the first 10.7m (35ft), so rods are rated by the line they are designed to cast. However, even rods of equal length with identical AFTMA ratings can feel quite different. This is because actions can vary. They range from all-through to tip-action.

There are many options in material, length, action and style to catch trout. Here Bob Church looks at the batch of rods he keeps for his own use. They cover all aspects of fly fishing in the UK.

Small stream rods

Bob's 6ft (1.8m) split cane rod is perfect with AFTMA 3 line. He uses it on small streams or chalk streams where long casting isn't necessary and where the fish aren't too big. The rod is a pleasure to use – and it can flip a tiny fly under an overhanging branch with great delicacy.

Short rods like this one are essential if you plan to fly fish streams with heavily overgrown banks where overhead casting might prove difficult. An all-through action lets you feel the fight of a small brownie more than a tip-action rod. Bob also has a crisp tip-actioned 8ft (2.4m) cane rod for dry fly fishing on chalk streams where accuracy and power are vital.

The AFTMA rating

AFTMA (the Association of Fishing Tackle Manufacturers of America) grades all fly lines in a scale from 1 to 15. The first 10.7m (35ft) of line is weighed, regardless of density or taper, and given a number. A number 1 line is the lightest and thinnest, a 15 the heaviest.

Fly rods at a glance

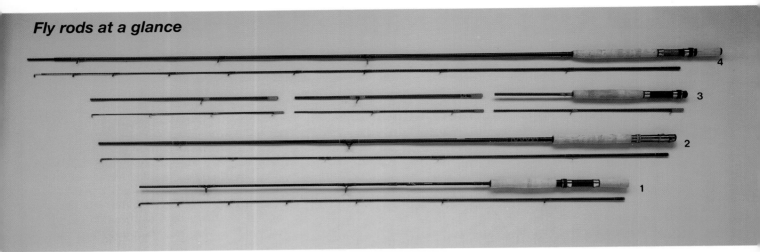

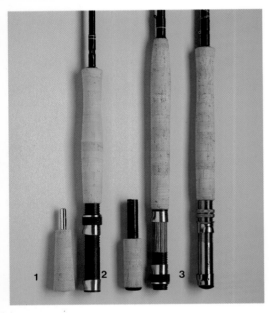

▲ *Most reel seats nowadays are screw fitting. They come in a variety of materials – mainly plastic (1), hardwood (2) or metal (3). Rod handles come in a variety of shapes such as the cigar (2) and half well (1 and 3). Some rods also have small extension butts to help keep the reel away from your body when playing large fish.*

Look after it

All rods, no matter how well made, need to be looked after properly. Never put the rod away wet – wipe it down carefully before storing it. Keep the joints clean and rub them down occasionally with wax, and check the rod rings regularly for signs of wear.

▲ *A brook or stream rod (1) is usually between 6ft (1.8m) and 8ft (2.4m) in length. It needs to be short so that you can cast in very tight places along the bank.*

Small fishery and river rods (2 and 3) are generally from 8½-9½ft (2.6-2.9m) long. Small fishery rods are stiffer to handle the big fish and often include materials such as kevlar or boron in the blank. Multi-piece rods are convenient and easily stowed away.

Although long (up to 12ft/3.6m), reservoir boat rods (4) for fishing loch style often have a softish, all-through action. Shore anglers need a stiffer middle-to-tip action to punch the flies a long way out.

River rods

A high modulus carbon rod of 8-9½ft (2.4-2.9m) with a middle-to-tip action (AFTMA 4-6) is suitable for many river situations. It is ideal for roll casting on a river lined with trees and bushes. It casts weighted nymphs very well and is good for various wet fly styles. An excellent all-round rod, it can be used at a pinch in any circumstances you are likely to encounter on the river.

When chest wading, working your way upstream, it can also be useful to have a 10½ft (3.2m) rod with a soft, all-through action. It is perfect for single Spey casting

▶ *Carbon fibre rods now dominate the scene as the best all-round rod material, but split cane rods like these are still held in high esteem although they are heavier than carbon.*

on wide rivers where there's not enough room to use the overhead cast or when it's necessary to handle long lines.

Small fishery scene

Generally, it's not necessary to cast a long way on small still waters, but often you need a powerful rod to cast heavily weighted flies and to fight very large fish which may be well over 10lb (4.5kg).

A middle-to-tip action with plenty of power in the butt is the preferred rod for fishing small fisheries, and here the high modulus carbons dominate because they are light, stiff and reasonably priced. Bob recommends a rod of about 9-9½ft (2.7-2.9m) – rated for AFTMA 5-8 line.

Big reservoirs

One of the most important aspects of reservoir rods is weight – the rod needs to be light enough so you aren't worn out after a few casts. Buy a light carbon rod if you plan casting at full bore for a whole day. For large reservoirs you need several rods to cover every eventuality.

Fishing from the bank or in a boat at anchor early in the year, you need to be able to cast great distances. Length, power and a stiffish action are essential. To handle the shooting head lines and large lures so often used for this, Bob suggests you use a rod about 10-11½ ft (3-3.5m) long with ratings of AFTMA 8 or 9.

Loch-style fishing (a team of three flies cast a fairly short distance and worked back to the drifting boat) is becoming more popular. Because distance casting is less important, an all-through action is common on rods for this type of fishing.

Rods with a stiffened mid section and a

▲ *A semi-stiff 10-10½ft (3-3.2m) middle-to-tip action rod is ideal for many kinds of boat fishing since it allows you to cast a long way and to control hooked fish easily.*

soft tip are also gaining in popularity for fishing loch-style. They give you greater control over hooked fish, especially close to the boat. Whichever action you choose, the rod needs to be 11-12ft (3.4-3.6m) long, both to control the flies on the retrieve and to handle hooked fish.

You also need a long, powerful rod when using lead-core lines to fish at great depths. The rods need to be tremendously strong and stiff, quantities which tend to stifle the feel of a hooked fish. Nonetheless, they are essential for this style of fishing.

▲ *Rod rings are either wire snake rings (top) – or lined with a smooth, hard-wearing substance like aluminium oxide, silicon carbide or ceramics (centre and bottom). Snake rings are popular but wear out fast.*

New style for old

One of the beauties of split cane is that its hexagonal cross-section structure resists twist and distortion. The round cross-section of carbon rods twists more easily.

But now some top of the range carbon rods simulate split cane in both looks and structure. The exterior of the blank is hexagonal and reinforced for extra strength – helping the rod resist twist and distortion.

Finally there is the art of dapping, in which a very long rod – as much as 18ft (5.5m) long – is needed to dangle or dap a natural or artificial fly on the water surface. The use of a special 'blowline' allows you to control the fly accurately in front of a drifting boat. A long rod and a light to moderate breeze are essential to float the flies out to where they're needed. Because this style does not involve casting, any long, light rod will do.

Right rod, right place

There are many different types of fly rod – each suitable for a particular fishing situation. You can't cover every situation properly with just one rod. Whatever type of fishing you do – whether casting 30m (33yd) or 3m (10ft), playing double-figure rainbows or small wild brownies – you need a rod to suit. Carbon is by far the best general choice because it offers better casting potential, helps you strike more effectively – and even the cheaper ones are excellent value.

◀ *Bob Church with a small-fishery rainbow. Use an AFTMA 5-8 rated rod at these waters.*

▼ *On a windy day at Coldingham Loch on the Scottish Borders, this angler has a stiff rod to power out his fly line. For shore fishing Bob Church recommends middle-to-tip action rods of about 10-11ft (3-3.4m) long with AFTMA rating from 8 to 10.*

Fly reels

Jon Beer, an enemy of unnecessary gear, discusses fly reels and boils down the unending list of accessories to the basics.

▼ *Reels with a wide spool of small diameter tend to store line in tight coils. The line needs a good stretch to remove 'memory' before you begin fishing.*

There is cheap tackle and there is expensive tackle. Nowhere is this price range wider than in fly reels – from under £15 to several thousand. However, pretty well all – even the cheapest reels – should do the job.

A word about bags

"My own choice," says Jon, "is practical – even if idiosyncratic. It is a leather tool pouch adapted to carry fly-box, clippers, spools of nylon, pliers, torch – and a folded landing net."

▼ *Stillwater fly fishing in Sussex. If he valued his eyes he would have added a pair of polarized sunglasses to his fishing equipment.*

A reservoir

A reel – an encumbrance on your rod – should be as small and light as possible, provided it can hold your line and backing without fouling the frame of the reel.

Fly lines are bulky. Reels are usually rated for the size of line they hold, but a low density floating line may be a size or two bulkier than an ordinary floater or a sinking line.

Spools can be narrow with a large diameter, or wide with a small diameter. The large diameter reels retrieve line quicker – each turn brings in more line – and the line is stored in looser coils, so it isn't stiff and full of 'memory'.

Giving out line

All reels have some form of brake or drag to stop the spool revolving freely. This prevents the spool from over-running as line is pulled off when you cast and when a fish runs. It also tires the fish. At its simplest, the drag is a spring-loaded pawl; at its most sophisticated it can be an adjustable thrust-bearing or disc brake. The value of such sophistication in trout fishing is debatable.

Retrieving line

Most British reels are simple winches. This has two advantages. First, there is little to go wrong in the reel itself, and second, an angler is in direct contact with the fish. The disadvantage is the slow speed of retrieve. It can take some time to wind loose line on to the reel. And *two* hands are needed to

A range of fly fishing equipment

Several fly reels

Key to equipment

There are stacks of accessories with dozens of variations and myriad variations on these.

Above are a few pieces of suggested gear. But keep it simple.

Going clockwise, starting at about 9 o'clock, these items are: Thigh boots, wellies, a multi-pocket waistcoat, a trout bag, a bass bag for storing fish, waterproofs, a hat with a decent brim to shade your eyes from the sun, polarized sunglasses, floatants and a leader-sink agent, fly boxes, fly reels, a priest and a landing net.

▶ The 'compleat' fisherman – with hat, waistcoat (with mounted scissors and fly patch), boots, net and River Avon brown trout.

An array of reels

Some popular fly reels – going left to right, top row first, they are: System Two 56L (river), Silstar FG7 (river), an extra spool for the System Two 56L, Shakespeare Beaulite 2873 (still water), Shakespeare Fly 2629 (still water).

reel in the fish. In fact, you really need a *third* hand to hold the landing net. But there are ways round this.

Geared reels increase the speed of retrieve. Many Continental anglers use single-handed automatic reels which rewind by a clockwork spring or an electric motor. Inevitably, though, these reels are heavy.

A good compromise, rarely seen in Britain but found everywhere in Europe, is the semi-automatic. Line is wound on by pumping a lever with one finger of the rod hand. This reel is fast, very light and single-handed.

Other equipment

There is much innocent pleasure to be had in accumulating fishing tackle. But beware: when you buy yourself a super fly-fishing waistcoat with thirty-six pockets, you'll find thirty-six things to fill them. It's best to fish light.

Fly boxes Dry flies are best kept loose in small compartments to avoid distorting the hackles. If these compartments have separate lids a malicious wind cannot empty the whole box in one gust. Wet flies can be stuck into flat or ridged foam containers. Avoid using metal clips or springs: they can blunt the hook point. It is a good idea to have large boxes to stock and organize your collection – and a small box for a working selection at the water.

Floatants Dry floatants come in aerosols, powders, liquids and grease. To carry less gear when fishing, soak the dry flies in a permanent floatant for a couple days. Then they'll float all season long. Leaders can be treated to sink or float, to reduce their visibility or to keep a nymph just below the surface.

Clippers If your teeth won't do, you'll need something to trim excess nylon: small clips are safer than scissors, but it is easy to drop these. Attach them to your jacket on a spring-loaded reel. *Always* carry a small pair of side-cutting pliers. These can save a trip to the hospital if you get a fly embedded in some part of your anatomy. Push the barbed point through and out and snip it off: then withdraw the hook. You can also use the pliers to flatten hook barbs for catch-and-release.

A torch If you want to fish after dark or

▲ *A plump rainbow is returned to the water. Whether you're fishing on stillwaters or rivers, take a minimum amount of gear, so you can move around freely without encumbrance.*

▶ *Extendible nets are used most on stillwaters. Some nets have ultra-fine mesh which, if returning trout, won't damage the fish.*

Tools to go?

For the self-confessed accessory addict, there is the portable 'match the hatch' kit – a set of fly-tying tools (usually enclosed in a compact folding pouch) which allows you to tie flies by the waterside. But hauling the feathers and fur is an unforeseen burden.

even into the dusk a small torch is invaluable. It can be clipped to the jacket, or you can hold it in your mouth to leave both hands free.

Nets To all but a boat fisherman a landing net is an inconvenience for most of the time. Occasionally it's an essential item for the river fisherman. The best river nets have a rim of collapsing spring steel and are housed in a holster to keep them away from brambles and barbed wire. Stillwater nets should have long handles and a wide, fixed rim.

Thigh boots and chest waders These are invaluable for the river fisherman. A wading angler can keep low and manoeuvre into the best positions to cast. Even ashore waders keep your legs dry from a dripping jacket and dew-covered foliage.

Whether you purchase chest or thigh waders depends on the depth of water you usually fish. The best investment in the long run is to get stocking waders of both sorts with separate wading boots. Underwater surfaces – rocks especially – can be very slippery: always buy either studded or felt-soled waders – or get a really good insurance policy.

Sunglasses These are eye-protectors first, fish-finders second. The lenses should be polarized to reduce reflected glare and as pale as possible to transmit maximum subsurface light.

Bags All this equipment must be carried in something. The traditional bag or creel is fine for the boat fisherman for whom weight is no object. For the river fisherman the

modern fly fishing waistcoat can carry everything you need in the numerous pockets and D-rings. But as with the traditional bag, the weight is carried on your shoulders which can tire you during a long day's fishing. A practical alternative is a fisherman's 'bum bag' which is worn around the waist.

So when boat fishing on stillwaters, you can take a mountain of gear. When you are river fishing, however, remember that it's best to carry as little equipment as possible – the minimalistic philosophy is of vital importance.

▲ *Deceived by a wet fly, a wild Lough Corrib (Republic of Ireland) brown trout lies in a standard, wide rimmed boat-fishing net.*

▼ *To some anglers trout bags are an unwelcome, extra weight to carry around. Others, however, make ample use of the space, packing sandwiches and a small flask for a mid-afternoon break.*

Fly leaders for trout

Charles Jardine explains what you need to know about the leader, the vital link between the fly line and fly. Success in deceiving a trout may depend upon choosing the correct type.

▼ *In the heart of the Yorkshire Dales, an angler fly fishes on the River Wharfe downstream of Bolton Abbey.*

Hot weather, bright conditions and low water all mean you'll need to use very light tippets of no more than 1½lb (0.68kg).

You can design a range of fly leaders simply by using various lengths of nylon in their many shapes, diameters and make-ups.

Balanced leaders

It's unwise to connect knotted lengths of monofilament which differ drastically in breaking strain (for example, 10lb/4.5kg line to 4lb/1.8kg). The step down from the heavier to the lighter line is too steep and unbalances the leader when you cast. As a result the fly lands abruptly. In short, an unbalanced leader hinders presentation – which affects a trout's response to your fly.

For proper 'turnover' – transferring the unfurling or unrolling motion of the fly line as you're casting to the leader and tippet – construct a tapered leader with staggered line weights (for example from 10lb/4.5kg to 8lb/3.6kg to 6lb/2.7kg to 4lb/1.8kg). Alternatively, buy a knotless tapered brand.

Types of nylon

The different kinds of nylon affect how both the leader and the fly behave. Nylon can be categorized into stiff, semi-stiff, limp and low diameter types.

Stiff nylons are a boon when it comes to making butt sections – the junction between fly line and the working leader. Stiff lines also help to hold droppers at right angles.

Semi-stiff nylons are the most useful, filling many leader functions from mid-sections to droppers.

Soft or limp nylons are best suited to making tippets. Soft nylon is pliable, allowing the fly to move freely and naturally in the current.

Low diameter (extra strength) nylons can be of enormous benefit if they are used correctly. The wariest of fish can be deceived.

Most of the nylons are shiny. It's a good idea to apply a liberal coating of sink mixture (fuller's earth and glycerine) to create a matt finish and also to help the line cut through the surface film.

Line colour

The colour of nylon (like fly lines) is a bone of contention among anglers. One thing, however, is certain: a clear line is less visible in a greater range of water conditions. Green nylon in green-tinged water works exceptionally well, as does brown line in the peat-stained water of Scottish lochs and spate rivers. If the colour is wrong, your catch rate may drop.

Fly size and line weight

Another factor concerning leaders in gen-

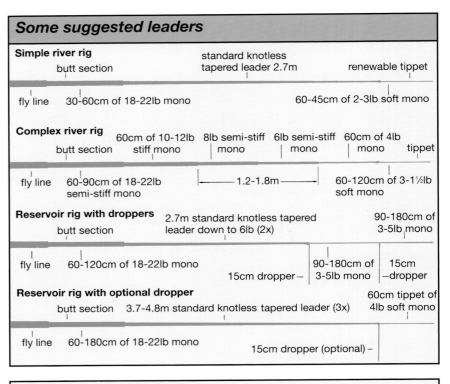

Some suggested leaders

Simple river rig

butt section	standard knotless tapered leader 2.7m	renewable tippet
fly line — 30-60cm of 18-22lb mono		60-45cm of 2-3lb soft mono

Complex river rig

butt section	60cm of 10-12lb stiff mono	8lb semi-stiff mono	6lb semi-stiff mono	60cm of 4lb mono	tippet
fly line — 60-90cm of 18-22lb semi-stiff mono		1.2-1.8m		60-120cm of 3-1½lb soft mono	

Reservoir rig with droppers

butt section	2.7m standard knotless tapered leader down to 6lb (2x)		90-180cm of 3-5lb mono
fly line — 60-120cm of 18-22lb mono		90-180cm of 3-5lb mono	15cm dropper
	15cm dropper —		

Reservoir rig with optional dropper

butt section	3.7-4.8m standard knotless tapered leader (3x)	60cm tippet of 4lb soft mono
fly line — 60-180cm of 18-22lb mono	15cm dropper (optional) –	

Leader materials

This is a selection of different brands of braided leaders, lines and strike indicators. **1.** Braided leaders; **2.** Braided leaders; **3.** Shop-bought knotless tapered leaders; **4.** Monofilament leader spools; **5.** Strike indicators; **6.** Braided leaders.

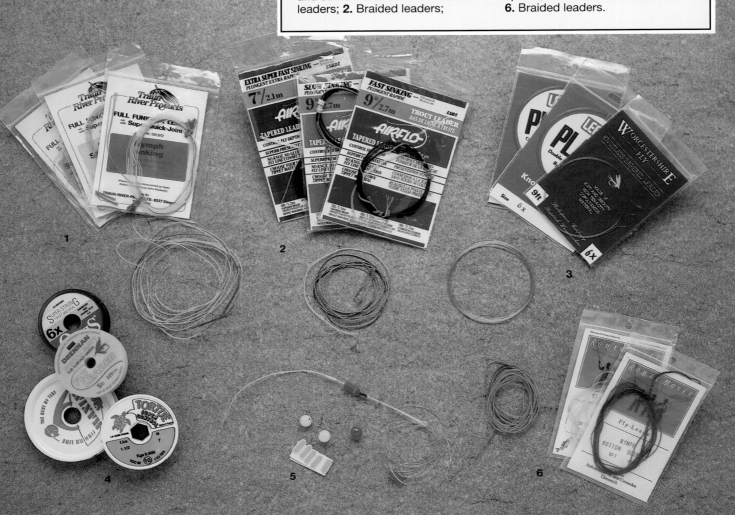

eral is the importance of matching the fly size to the correct diameter of line. A good match ensures that the artificial behaves as naturally as possible. A size 20 Black Gnat on a 5lb (2.3kg) point resembles a piece of thistledown tethered to a section of wire. As a general guide, hook sizes 18-20 require 1½-2lb (0.7-0.9kg) line. You may need 3-4lb (1.4-1.8kg) line for hook sizes 12-16.

Leaded patterns in sizes 4-10 need line of 5-10lb (2.3-4.5kg). Connecting a leaded pattern to a 3lb (1.4kg) tippet is asking for trouble. The hinging movement as you're casting creates leader fatigue, weakening the nylon. The fly simply doesn't fish well when retrieved.

River leaders

A combination of accuracy and delicacy is the criterion for fishing chalk streams or freestone rivers. The longer the leader is, the less accurate casting becomes. However, delicacy increases when the leader is lengthened, and the potentially fish-scaring fly line is distanced from the fly.

A widely used type of leader is the 'Ritz' formula, created by Charles Ritz – in which as many as five or six nylon sections step down in decreasing breaking strains to the

Tip Feeding zone

The aim is to get your fly into the trout's feeding zone. There are various ways of doing this. One is to use a heavy fly so that it sinks quickly to the trout's level.

Casting far enough upstream of the trout also allows the artificial to sink in time.

In slow or medium currents casting upstream is practical, but if the water proves too fast, try a heavier fly, split shot or extra fast sinking braided leader.

▶ **Under the hand of a watchful angler, a brown trout is almost secure.**
A 10½ft (3.2m) leader with a 1½ft (45cm) tippet section of 2 or 3lb (0.9 or 1.3kg) is recommended for river fishing.

tippet. Using many double grinner or four-turn water knots may appear clumsy and unsound, but most river fly fishing is done 'dead drift'. Small knots along your leader can aid turnover when casting across or downwind. You also have the ease and economy of using large spools of various diameter nylons for knotting leaders yourself.

Alternatively, use standard 9ft (2.7m) knotless shop-bought tapered leaders. The weight or diameter is rated in 'x' numbers from 0x (9lb/4.1kg at the tip) to 8x (¾-1¾lb/0.34-0.79kg). You can extend their life by adding butt or tippet lengths. The added sections can be re-tied when they become either too short or damaged – proving to be an economical and practical move.

When you are fishing the dry fly, emerger and even the sub-surface nymph, the length of the leader need not be over 12ft (3.7m). A length of 9½-10ft (2.9-3m) is ideal for general fishing on medium or large rivers, and 8ft (2.4m) for brooks and streams. Using a leader any shorter is likely to lead to poor, splashy presentations. Sometimes when it's windy, however, you may need to shorten the leader. A longer leader length of 14-16ft (4.3-4.8m) is difficult to control and may cause tangles and inaccurate casts.

Tapered braided leaders (floating, sinking, extra fast sinking) are an effective alternative for river fishing. All you have to

◀ **The water seethes as a wild brown trout is brought to the surface.**
Long leaders are a must when fishing in flat, calm water.

Tip Greasing your fly line

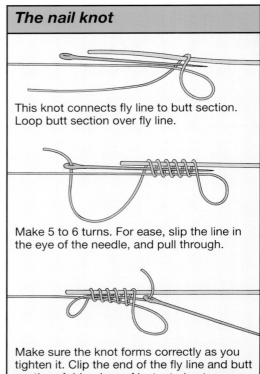

Apply grease to your fly line and first few feet of leader every ten or so casts, so they float. This is important on fast water, where they need help to stay on the water's surface.

▼ *A plump, fully finned and beautifully marked 7lb (3.2kg) brown trout like this one can make up for those occasional fishless sessions.*

do is increase or decrease the tippet diameter and length to suit the various conditions.

Because they are supple, braided leaders help to transfer energy from the fly line to the leader to the tippet better than straight mono. This aids presentation. They aren't recommended for casting long distances, though, because they don't cut through the air well.

When nymph fishing from mid-water down to the river bed, ensure that your leader is over depth, and make allowances for your angle of entry and the river's rate of flow.

Problems arise, however, when trout are feeding in fast currents or deep water. Try attaching a fast or extra fast sinking braided leader, weighted pattern and suitable tippet.

Leaders for stillwaters

A long leader is crucial in stillwater fly fishing since it separates the fly line from

The nail knot

This knot connects fly line to butt section. Loop butt section over fly line.

Make 5 to 6 turns. For ease, slip the line in the eye of the needle, and pull through.

Make sure the knot forms correctly as you tighten it. Clip the end of the fly line and butt section. Add a drop of instant glue to secure the knot.

the fly. Bulky flies and a floating fly line tend to create wake when retrieved – especially in flat conditions. On days where there are waves, this isn't as important.

On many occasions when using a floating line, the depths you want to reach may be more than 9-10½ft (2.7-3.2m), the length of the standard leader with a tippet section added on. In order to fish a depth of 12ft (3.6m), for example, you need an 18ft (5.4m) leader. There comes a point (over 24ft/7m) where a leader simply becomes unmanageable. Consider alternative solutions such as using a sinking fly line.

You can buy a 12ft (3.6m) knotless tapered leader and add on a tippet or butt section. There are even 15-16ft (4.6-4.9m) lengths available, perfect for stillwater nymph and lure fishing.

The knots in the Ritz formula for river fishing can be detrimental on stillwaters, creating disturbances when using a floating line as you pull the line over the surface of the water.

Experiment with the distance between the droppers. In general, spacing nymphs or lures 3-4ft (1-1.2m) apart is appropriate. Dropper lengths should never be much longer than 6in (15cm).

Even level leaders (straight 6lb/2.7kg mono, for instance) have a purpose, for example when loch-style fishing or using large lures, tandems or tubes for fry-feeding trout. It is rare to use line much lighter than 6lb (2.7kg) when casting with lures.

There is without question still a world of exploration in leaders!

A fly leader kit

Too many anglers are concerned with rods, reels and fly lines, ignoring leaders – the vital link between the fly and fly line.

▲ Rain-fed rivers call for a repertoire of fly fishing styles and tactics which a leader kit can help you perform.

▼ A leader kit should include the following: (1) two braided fly line connectors with a sleeve; (2) a 12in (30cm) and a 24in (60cm) mini lead-head; (3) a 5ft (1.5m) and an 8ft (2.4m) braided tapered leader; and (4) a selection of 4ft (1.2m) tippets. This is the ready-made Orvis kit.

A daptability is important in fly fishing, especially on rivers – one moment you need to drag the depths where a big, golden-bellied brown lurks, while a little farther downstream a long, weedy glide requires you to fish a dry fly for trout keyed in to small upwings. A leader kit saves time and trouble and may also help you enhance your casting and presentation.

Four part make-up

A well-balanced leader kit contains the following items.

1. Fly line connectors Needle and nail knots have been more or less superseded by braided line connectors. The looped connectors eliminate the need for fiddly, permanent butt sections of stiff, heavy mono. They allow you to change leaders quickly by simply connecting the looped ends.

2. Lead-core lines Two sections of lead-core line – one short and one long – help your fly get to the bottom. A 12in (30cm)

off. However, the braided leaders are harder to cast into the wind.

A 5ft (1.5m) and an 8ft (2.4m) braided tapered leader cover most styles of river fly fishing.

4. Tippets There are several ready-made 1.2m (4ft) tippets available in various diameters – from 3x to 7x. A braided leader with the added 4ft (1.2m) tippet makes the total length – 9ft (2.7m) and 12ft (3.6m). Alternatively, you can make your own tippets of straight mono to suit the conditions you are fishing.

It's possible to purchase these items individually, but modifying lead-core lines can be tricky. The Orvis Company has come up with the entire leader kit which folds in a compact wallet and comes in two sizes (one for 3-5 weight fly lines and one for 6-7 weight lines).

▶ ▲ *A section of lead-core line can help you reach the bottom of fast water (right) and help you catch more superb brown trout such as this one (above).*

section of lead-core or fast sinking braided leader works like a split shot, helping your fly and tippet to fish along the bottom. But you can cast the fly line easier than with split shot along the leader – no more 'chuck and duck' fly fishing.

A longer length of lead-core line (24in/60cm) transforms your floating fly line into an effective, working sink tip. So there's no need to change from reel spool to spool – with the loop to loop connectors the job takes only a moment or so. And even the longer length of lead core lines doesn't hamper your casting.

3. Braided tapered leaders offer two distinct advantages over tapered or straight monofilament leaders. They transfer the unrolling action of the fly line much better, helping to present your fly more delicately. Secondly, they stretch easily. When you strike into a fish, the leader absorbs some of the shock, reducing the chances of breaking

Some suggested leaders for river fishing

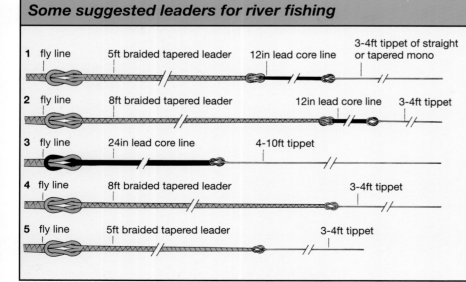

1. This set-up allows you to fish along the bottom of glides and runs and even riffles generally under 1.2m (4ft) deep. Getting your fly to the bottom depends on the speed of the current and the angle of the cast.
2. The longer braided leader may prove more efficient for fishing in deep pools (up to 3m/10ft). The strike indicator won't be pulled under.
3. To make your floating line into a sink tip, loop the 24in (60cm) mini lead-head to the fly line on one end and on the other a length of straight mono.
4. The 12ft (3.6m) leader is needed for fishing in low, clear water – where trout can be spooked by the fly line.
5. Use the standard 9ft (2.7m) leader for dry fly or nymph work.

Fly boxes

With so many quality fly boxes available today to help you organize your flies, you can spend more time searching the water for trout instead of searching your boxes for that special fly.

W ith the quantity and range of fly fishing tackle available today, it's easy to understand a beginner turning up at the river bank with five chest-like wooden fly boxes, each stuffed and ready to burst like an over-packed suitcase.

Many anglers new to fly fishing often buy too many boxes of the wrong type. If you're a river angler, you simply don't need to be weighed down with box after box of flies. It's far more sensible to have a large central resource box and and take one or two smaller ones with you on the day. (Reservoir boat anglers, of course, don't

have to carry their gear; they can take as much as they want, stowing it safely away at the bottom of the boat.)

More than just a box

Made of plastic, wood, aluminium and even leather, fly boxes come in a range of sizes and colours. Far from being just hold-alls,

▲ *A good box protects your flies and helps you to find the right one quickly – if the flies are arranged in a neat, orderly fashion and not strewn all over the place.*

A selection of standard fly boxes

These are some of the various styles of fly boxes available today.
1) Multi-tier boxes
2) Folding aluminium boxes
3) Leather fly wallet
4) Compartmented dry fly boxes

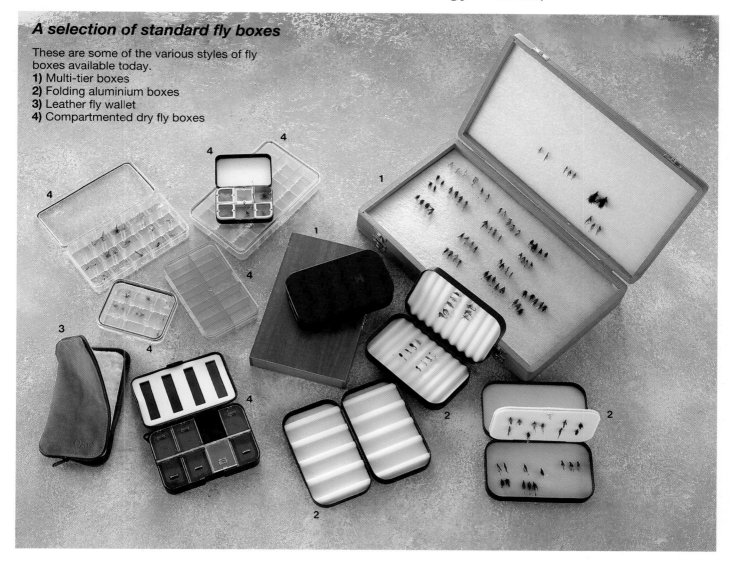

► *If you have many fly boxes, selecting the right fly for the day isn't always easy. But expertise comes with experience.*

good boxes protect the flies and allow you to manage your stocks so that you pick the right fly quickly without spending five minutes racking your brain trying to find it.

Important considerations when buying fly boxes include how many flies they can hold, whether they are waterproof or not and how strong the hinges and clips are. But perhaps the most important aspects are the weight of the box and the *types* of flies they are designed for.

1. Multi-tier boxes hold absolutely stacks of flies. Very popular with reservoir anglers – especially boat anglers – and river anglers as a central resource box, they are sturdy, take a beating and offer maximum protection to your flies. The metal hinges on these boxes are strong and last a long time. However, they are not waterproof, so keep them in a waterproof bag.

Multi-tier boxes are suitable for lures (including large ones), wet flies and modern dries. The hackles on some dry flies, however, can become distorted when pinned against the foam.

2. Folding aluminium boxes Lined with closed-cell foam, these offer effective security and durability even though they aren't waterproof. The rippled bottom is especially useful for holding dry flies, giving the hackles plenty of room. You can store lures, wets and dries in them, and since they are slim and usually only 15cm (6in) or so long, they are the perfect choice for the river angler.

Some come in flat foam with a swinging panel which increases the surface area of the box but cuts down on the size of flies which it can hold. This type isn't suitable for holding large lures but it is, nevertheless, a good nymph/wet fly box.

▼ *Rainbows can't resist lures – keep many colours in your box to find the right one for the day.*

3. Leather fly wallet More of a way to store flies than a practical, working device, this wallet holds about 20 salmon flies and can also store lures just as easily. It isn't recommended for taking along on a day's fishing because the soft leather doesn't support the flies and can be moved about. Hair wings or marabou fibres may be distorted or even damaged in a wallet.

4. Compartmented dry fly boxes come in plastic and metal versions. Usually the plastic boxes are inexpensive and have one lid covering every compartment. When using these boxes, be careful that the wind doesn't empty out the entire contents. Some plastic ones, however, have small separate covers over each compartment which solves the wind problem.

The hinges and front clips on the plastic boxes are rather weak: many times they break after using for just a short time. Some of these boxes have the advantage of a lined lid, making them waterproof.

The metal boxes also have compartments with lids on them, but they tend to be spring-loaded, which makes them rather more expensive.

CHAPTER TWO

STILLWATER TACTICS

The overhead cast

You can't get a fly into the water without casting, so you need to learn to cast properly before you start fishing. Peter Cockwill shows you how.

Casting styles

The overhead cast is not the only way to throw a fly line. Later you may wish to use other styles including the roll and side casts for cramped conditions, and the single and double-haul casts for when you need to fish at longer distances.

C asting requires timing and technique, not muscle, so an hour spent with a qualified instructor could save a lot of frustration. Some of the better venues provide tuition and very often let novices fish free of charge until the first fish is landed.

With or without professional instruction, the only way to perfect your casting style in safety is to practise with a leader but without a fly. The best place for this is in your garden or an empty field, not at a water.

Two casts in one
Casting a fly is done in two stages – a back cast and a forward cast. The rod is designed to work best with about 10-12m (11-13yd) of line worked through the rod rings on to the ground in front of you.

In the first stage – the back cast – you lift the line off the ground and swing out through the air, behind your head. In the second stage – the forward cast – you throw the line on to the ground, leaving your fly about 12m (13yd) from where you are standing. Ideally both the fly and fly line should land softly, so that it won't cause much of a splash when you come to cast on to water.

Recasting
After you have slowly retrieved some of the line to give fish the chance to bite, you have to recast. It's a good idea to practise this on dry land. The procedure is similar to before except that now you have 4m (13ft) of fly

Teaching organisations

You can get details of casting instructors from the fly fishing press and from some tackle shops (particularly those that specialise in game fishing tackle). You can also contact the Association of Professional Game Angling Instructors direct.

● The Association of Professional Game Angling Instructors,
c/o Mr D Downs,
The Mead,
Hosey, Westerham, Kent, TN16 1TA.

▶ *Good casting technique is more important than many anglers realize. It allows you to present a fly to wary fish in a natural way.*

line in a pile at your feet.

Make the back cast, holding the line below the first rod ring with your free hand to prevent the spare line slipping. As the line is travelling out in front of you in the forward cast, release the spare to slip through the rod rings. In this way you recast the full length. This is known as 'shooting' the line. Also try casting on a windy day at various angles to the wind.

You'll often have to cope with this when fishing and it can make a difference to where the fly ends up. This will stand you in good stead when you get down to the water, as it is rarely completely windless.

Practise these basic techniques until they feel natural. Don't make your first ever cast at the water's edge and expect to catch fish. You'll be too busy untangling your line from nearby trees.

Practising the overhead cast

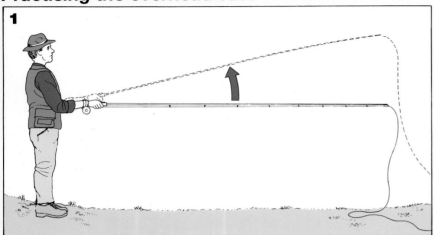

1. Work about 10-12m (11-13yd) of line through the rod rings on to the ground, or water, in front of you. Starting with the rod in the horizontal position, raise your forearm until it reaches the vertical, keeping your wrist stiff and straight. Accelerate smoothly through this movement and the line will lift off the ground to stream out behind you, over your shoulder.

2. Stop the rod in the upright position – don't allow it to drift back past the vertical. Loop an elasticated sweat band round your wrist and rod butt (as shown) to stop you cocking your wrist. This stops the rod going too far back which would throw the line downwards.

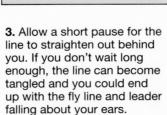

3. Allow a short pause for the line to straighten out behind you. If you don't wait long enough, the line can become tangled and you could end up with the fly line and leader falling about your ears.

4. Lower your arm until the rod is horizontal, keeping your wrist rigid. The rod action flicks the line out in front of you to land gently on the ground or water. If the line lands with a thud (or splash) you have lowered your arm too fast or too far. All your movements should be smooth and use the minimum force required to get the line where you want it. If you are too jerky or violent, you'll get tangles, or cause the fly to 'crack off' (which is exactly what it sounds like). The timing of these steps will come with practice.

Rainbow trout: strategies for success

In 1884 the wild rainbow trout was imported to Europe from the USA. In Britain you can find rainbow trout in most if not all fisheries.

Compared with the native European brown trout, rainbows are easier to rear and are able to stand higher water temperatures and lower water quality. Rainbow trout also rise more readily than browns and, as anyone who has hooked one knows full well, make many fanatical, often unstoppable, bids for freedom.

Fishing for rainbows

There are only a few places in Britain where rainbow trout reproduce naturally, the River Wye in Derbyshire being the most noted example. Almost all small fisheries, however, breed or buy-in rainbows.

You should begin your apprenticeship on small stillwaters, for you stand a far better chance of seeing and catching rainbows than on reservoirs or even large gravel pits.

Nymph fishing – using imitations of immature aquatic insects – is probably the most common method of catching trout on small stillwaters. Attach a Black Buzzer, Hare's Ear (variant), Pheasant Tail Nymph or goldhead nymph and then cast to cruising trout. It's a good idea to experiment with the retrieval speeds to see what's working on the day.

Use the countdown method to explore all depths. Cast out and, before you begin to

▶ *An early winter's day on Leominstead Lake (Hampshire) pays off as a rainbow trout comes to the net. On many small stillwaters you can fish for rainbow trout all year round – there's no close season.*

retrieve, count to ten (for example). Repeat the process adding on ten or so seconds after each cast. If you hook a trout, remember the number at which you stopped counting and began retrieving, and repeat the process.

Lure fishing There are imitative lures which represent coarse fish fry and brightly coloured ones which provoke aggression and curiosity. Some fisheries may ban certain types; check before you go. On the bank use the same procedure as with nymphs, experimenting with retrieval speeds and a

◀ *If you are new to the sport, it's a good idea to let someone experienced net your first trout.*

Tip *Gear up*

Watching the rainbows continually pass up your offering – be it nymphs, lures or dry flies – is frustrating, to say the least. This, however, is part of stillwater angling. What can be done?

Lengthen your leader and reduce the breaking strain of the tippet. Try to cast directly in front of the trout and use the induced-take method.

If that fails, cast out and retrieve your nymph with a very slow figure-of-eight retrieve (1in/2.5cm per second).

variety of different depths.

The dry fly Using an artificial fly that floats on the surface of the water is an underrated method of catching stillwater rainbows. Though simple, it requires a bit of patience.

In most stillwaters trout have specific patrol routes. On some waters you can actually see them cruising along the margins. Attach a dry fly such as a Hare's Ear Emerger or White Wulff and cast about 1m (1yd) in front of the trout – then wait. When casting, make sure you don't slap the water with your line.

You'll be able to see the trout take the fly. A word of warning, however: don't strike immediately. Wait until the fish has taken the fly and turned down into the water. Then lift the rod firmly. As a general guideline, wait about three seconds after the trout surfaces.

Dry fly fishing is effective even if you can't see the trout patrolling the water. Sometimes you may have to wait up to ten minutes without recasting.

If it's windy, cast straight out towards the middle of the water, and allow the wind to sweep the fly in an arc to the margins. Repeat the process. If you get impatient, retrieve the fly very slowly.

Alternatively, give the fly an occasional twitch by quickly lifting your rod. (The trout can sense the surface vibrations very well.) Overall, dry fly fishing on stillwaters is successful if you have the patience to allow it to work.

Once you catch a rainbow you'll soon see why it's a furious fighter. A word of advice – don't attempt to bring the fish in too quickly, or it may break off. Allow the trout to take line, but keep constant tension on the line. You won't lose too many fish if you play them patiently and have suitable monofilament line. Don't attempt to use 2lb (0.9kg) nylon. As a minimum, use 5lb (2.3kg) b.s. line. Enjoy the battle.

▼ *Many anglers reckon that the fighting abilities of stillwater rainbows (such as this specimen) are second only to salmon.*

Five stillwater patterns

A selection of stillwater flies which should catch in most circumstances. From left to right: Hare's Ear Emerger (variant), goldhead nymph, Gold Ribbed Hare's Ear, Buzzer, Pheasant Tail Nymph.

Targeting stillwater brown trout

Many reservoirs around Britain contain both rainbow and brown trout, yet browns, very different in character, aren't caught nearly as often as rainbows. Tony Blakeman explains.

▶ *An angler used a Cat's Whisker, fished on a Hi-D, to catch this Grafham brown which was feeding along the bottom on roach.*

Both the native brown trout and the imported rainbow are reared in stew ponds and stocked into Britain's rivers, ponds, lakes and reservoirs from 8oz to 20lb (0.23-9kg) or more. But unlike nomadic rainbows, browns are very territorial, establish particular feeding habits and live in deep water, rarely making their presence known to anglers.

Catching recently stocked browns (or rainbows for that matter) is easy. The fish tend to stay in the area where they were stocked until they adjust to their new surroundings and become familar with the available food. The stocked browns which aren't caught probably move out to deep water, though obviously it is difficult to know that for sure.

▼ *One of the most popular venues for brown trout, Blagdon Water in Avon, has plenty of fly life to produce some excellent grown-on fish.*

Where there is a concentration of fry or even sizeable coarse fish, a large brown will almost certainly be lurking, following the prey and waiting to pounce. A brown of over 5lb (2.3kg) won't hesitate to take a 12oz (0.34kg) roach, for example. One or two of these fish each day may keep the trout content in summer for quite a while, giving it plenty of time to ignore your imitations. A good hatch of fly can also tempt browns to the surface to feed.

▲ *Bank anglers fish the deep water off the dam wall on Grafham Water. Low light levels give the brown trout security to venture towards the bank in search of food – this is especially true when deep water is located close in.*

Fishing from the bank

Before beginning, always have a look at the catch returns and, more importantly, talk to local anglers for up-to-date advice about the best fishing areas.

Some of the most notable general areas are boat jetties, which always attract fry. These in turn draw fry-feeding rainbows and browns. Keep a lookout for seagulls wheeling in the air and plunging into the water for fry. The chances are brown trout are harrying their prey from below just as the gulls are from above.

Sunken islands with deep water nearby and valve towers are other good areas to locate browns.

Methods Your best chance of taking a big brown trout from the bank of a reservoir is early in the season or at the end of the season. Of the two, the early season is better, because the banks have been rested all winter long, and the trout can patrol very close to the bank.

Cover as much water as possible. Start by fishing close in and then and only then should you bang out a long line. A stiff rod with a WF or ST (shooting head) 7-9 is ideal. Floating, intermediate, Wet Cel II (medium-fast sinking) and Hi-D lines are essential.

It's hard to beat a floating line and a team

Imitative flies aren't the only ones which catch browns. Jeremy Herrmann prepares to land a brown caught on a Pink Tadpole from Blagdon Water.

of nymphs or buzzers for brown trout all season round. Because they aren't as aggressive as rainbows, you're far likelier to succeed with the imitative approach. Hare's Ear and Damsel Nymphs in sizes 8-12 as well as Pearly Buzzers and Thorpe Buzzers in sizes 10-14 work well.

With the wind blowing from left to right (assuming that you're right-handed) cast out perpendicular to the waves and allow the wind to swing the line around. When fishing flat water, use a slow strip or figure-of-eight retrieve. The count-down method enables your flies to explore all depths.

If that fails try fishing in deep water with a Wet Cel II and a marabou lure, experimenting with different colours – but especially black and green. Vary the retrieves – slow figure-of-eight, long, slow strips interrupted by the occasional quick jerk or hand-over-hand which is one of the best ways to fish big lures these days.

Using a Booby on a Hi-D is a very effective way of fishing the bottom without constantly getting hung up on weed or debris. Alter the leader length from 15cm (6in) to 3m (10ft). With a short leader, retrieve slowly so that the fly doesn't dive and pick up weed. You can fish the fly much more erratically with a longer leader. Many big browns fall for the Booby each season.

For the boat angler

Boat anglers should also give attention to deep water marks, sunken islands and shallow plains. Where bank fishing is prohibited or inaccessible, boat anglers can target browns undisturbed near the shoreline.

A brown trout from Colliford Reservoir in Cornwall crashes on the surface. Browns are better known for their deep, dogged style of fighting, rather than surface-crashing style.

Anglers fish loch-style on Grafham Water. This method, which catches both browns and rainbows, allows you to cover a lot of fish-holding water.

▲ Tony Blakeman hoists aboard a good trout from Draycote Water. Some days large lures are most successful; other times you can catch browns on the dry fly, and sometimes you can't catch at all! They follow but won't take.

▼ Superb browns such as this 3½ lb (1.6kg) grown-on fish don't come too often. That makes catching them all the more a special occasion.

sedge imitations work well too.

Floating and Hi-D Along with a floating line and nymphs, anglers often catch browns using a Hi-D line and large marabou lures such as tandems or tube flies. These attractors can be over 15cm (6in) long and tied in bright colours to irritate the fish or in white and grey to imitate coarse fish.

One of the most popular boat methods for covering a large area of water is the rudder (see *Drift fishing for big stillwater trout*, pages 57-60, for more information). Check that it's legal before beginning. The rudder allows the boat to move in and out of bays and follow the contours of the bank. Again blast out a lure as far as you can to allow the line to sink and to produce a sufficient arc. Browns usually hit as the fly speeds up when coming around the arc.

The tactics and retrieves when boat fishing aren't a great deal different from bank fishing styles. One advantage of boat fishing is that you can hang the flies at the end of a retrieve – this often results in many last-second takes.

Patchy sport

Brown trout fishing can be very frustrating, to say the least. You may have days when big trout follow but just won't take. The fish just play games with you. Sometimes two fish follow the same fly. A noted area can be fished hard all day and might only result in follows. The same place the next day may well fish its head off.

It's also hard to say that the fish you'll catch will be a brown trout. When fishing big established reservoirs, you never really know what's going to grab your offering – it could be a big pike, a rainbow or a brown. Unless you see your quarry there's no way of telling. This is why big browns always hit the angling headlines.

Loch-style Welsh, Scottish and Irish waters contain wild browns used to eating insects at all levels of the water, but especially just below the surface and in the surface film. Small wets and dries fished on floating or intermediate lines are the order of the day. A 3lb (1.4kg) brown from such waters is an excellent trout.

Useful flies for these regions are mainly palmered. Bibio, Zulu, Soldier Palmer and Bumbles are excellent bob flies. Small wets such as Butcher, Wickham's Fancy, Greenwell's Glory and Black and Peacock Spider all take trout. Dry flies such as Daddy Longlegs and various mayfly and

Retrieving the line

Fly patterns receive too much attention these days – at the expense of how to present them, says top fly matchman Jeremy Herrmann.

Numerous books have been written on fly patterns and how to dress them. Indeed, at the waterside the standard question the unsuccessful angler asks the successful one is, "What fly did you get your trout on?"

While fly patterns are part and parcel of the magic of fly fishing, they are, sadly, not as important as the way you present the flies to the fish. Fly pattern is nearly always secondary to presentation. The more appropriate question the unsuccessful angler should ask is, "At what depth and what speed did you get the trout?"

Often you'll see anglers along the banks of reservoirs or in boats casting and retrieving mechanically. They do catch fish from time to time, but as you'd expect, thoughtful retrieving always puts more fish in the bag.

There are several different ways of retrieving, but here are three of the most common, and a lesser known fourth which can be devastatingly effective.

The strip

This is the easiest retrieve to do (and the most used, for that matter). Simply put, a right-handed angler holds the rod with his right hand, traps the line with the index finger of that hand and pulls it with the left hand (the other way round if you are left handed, of course).

▲ *The Booby is THE early and late season lure. Couple it with a Hi-D line and slow figure-of-eight retrieve, and cracking concrete bowl rainbows such as this find the lure hard to pass up.*

▶ *During the early season, when the trout are subjected to a 'ho-hum' barrage of boring retrieves, it pays spotted, pink-striped, rod-bending dividends to use a little FTA (Fooling Them About).*

 **Tip** **Get as close as you can**

Casting from a boat to rising fish on large waters requires you to spot the fish, figure out which way they're moving and present your flies (not fly line) to them. A near miss is no good. You need to cast just in front of them, moving your flies with either a strip or a fast figure-of-eight.

difficulty in catching the fly. The slow strip is also useful for moving nymphs and wets from the bank or from an anchored boat.

The fast strip is at its best in high summer, and its uses are mainly associated with fit, daphnia-feeding rainbows which stay high in the water, close to the surface. Flies such as Muddlers and Peach Dolls are very effective when stripped back quickly; they bring out the aggression in the super-fit summer rainbows. Indeed, when using flies at this time of year, you cannot move them too fast! The fast strip is also effective for imitating the quick darting movement of damsel nymphs.

The figure-of-eight

This is probably the second commonest retrieve. Holding the rod with your right hand, trap the line with the right index

▲ ▶ The strip is the easiest style of retrieve. To begin (above) hold the rod with your right hand (vice versa if you are left handed); trap the line with the index or middle finger of that hand and pull the line (right) with your left hand.

You can pull the line at a variety of speeds. Some examples of how you might use the strip are slowly and steadily with wets, quickly for lures and erratically with nymphs.

A slow strip is the most effective way of catching fresh stockies, especially if combined with a lead-headed fly such as a Tadpole. The reason for this is that stock fish are used to food which either falls vertically through the water or floats. They are not used to chasing. The slow strip is a predictable way to move the fly and usually results in firm takes, for the fish have no

The hand-over-hand retrieve   Step one

The hand-over-hand style of retrieve enables you to move your fly in many ways. Since you use both hands when retrieving, your fly moves in a smooth, level path and not in the up-down presentation that the strip produces.

1. Secure the end of the rod and reel under your right arm. Support the rod by propping the top of the handle on your upper forearm or in the crook of the arm.

2 & 3. The left hand pulls line down while the right hand holds the line. After the left hand has gone down as far as possible, continue to pull with the right hand while the left comes up again to make another cycle. (Easily done, but complicated to describe.)

If a fish taps your lure, keep pulling. To strike, don't lift the rod up vertically. Swing it around to the right (if you are right-handed and vice versa if left-handed). This keeps constant tension on your line.

The figure-of-eight retrieve

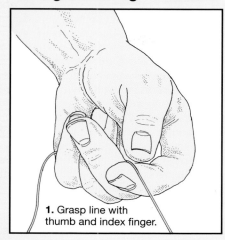

1. Grasp line with thumb and index finger.

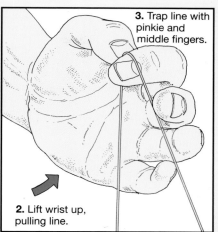

2. Lift wrist up, pulling line.

3. Trap line with pinkie and middle fingers.

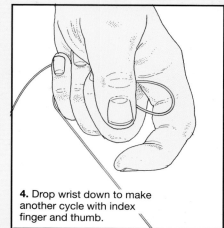

4. Drop wrist down to make another cycle with index finger and thumb.

1. Grasp the line with your thumb and index finger, making sure the line is lying in your hand.

2. Lift your wrist up and bring your middle fingers and little finger towards the fly line or backing.

3. Trap the line against your palm, and then grasp it with your thumb and index finger to make a cycle.

finger. Instead of stripping the line you bunch it into your left hand. (See *The figure-of-eight retrieve* on this page.) Some anglers drop the line after each cycle, but the choice is yours.

Use the figure-of-eight with imitative flies. From the banks of large stillwaters or from an anchored boat, try casting across the wind and taking up the slack using this form of retrieve: the flies drift with the wind-induced currents.

From a drifting boat, the figure-of-eight is an effective way to fish imitative patterns such as Pheasant Tails, Buzzers or dry flies such as Hoppers or Shipman's Buzzers. Make a long cast downwind – then use the figure-of-eight to take up the slack line or inch the flies along by retrieving them slightly faster than the moving boat.

The figure-of-eight retrieve is deadly when you're using a Booby fished on a Hi-D line and short leader.

On small stillwaters and even slow-moving rivers use a fast, erratic figure-of-eight to imitate freshwater shrimps and a slow one for buzzers.

Hand-over-hand

This method produces a constant motion in the fly and can be devastating. Many anglers, fishing in one spot for an hour without seeing any action, have had savage takes when reeling in to move.

To begin, trap the rod under your right arm and support it with the crook of your elbow or your forearm. Retrieve using both hands in turn, so you achieve a constant motion. This is an excellent way of retrieving lures, especially in hard-fished waters where the trout have seen many flies being

Tip *Warp nine?*

If you are using imitative flies, ensure that the retrieval speed corresponds to the natural insect's movement. It's useless to put on a team of size 14 Buzzers, for example, and rip them back at the speed of light.

As a general guideline, freshwater shrimps have a stop-start style of movement: short strips do the job here. Damsels dart: long fast strips work well. Buzzers barely move: the slow figure-of-eight is the key to this one.

Step two

Step three

▼ **The figure-of-eight and strip are useful when fishing pools and glides on rain-fed rivers such as the Cumbrian Derwent.**

stripped or inched back with the figure-of-eight style.

Some anglers complain that it's difficult to hook fish with this style of retrieve. The trick to successful and consistent hooking is to keep pulling when a fish plucks at your fly and, when the trout does commit itself, to swing your rod around horizontally – to the right.

If you strike in the same plane in which the line is moving (by swinging the rod to the right), you maintain the line contact and won't lose fish. But if you try to raise the rod, you'll momentarily lose line contact – and probably the trout.

FTA – Fool Them About

It's a widely known fact that trout are very aggressive. A somewhat lesser known fact is that they also have a fairly good short-term memory. This may be the reason that a fly can be so effective one week, and then useless the next.

Most people retrieve lures in the same methodical way day in and day out all season long. A trout which has followed a stripped lure, taken it and then escaped, is naturally going to be wary of any pattern moving in a similar way.

For this reason when you are fishing attractor patterns, it sometimes pays to retrieve your fly in a way in which no trout could possibly have seen before – enter FTA, Fooling Them About. This style of retrieve is often successful when others fail.

Fooling Them About basically involves permutations and combinations of all the above mentioned retrieves. Trying to put FTA into an exact formula defeats the point of the method, for the essence of it is variety.

A good example is to start the retrieve with a figure-of-eight, pause for a second, give two sharp strips, one long slow pull, pause, figure-of-eight for a few metres, strip three times as fast as you can, pause, then slow strip, fast strip – and while watching the line carefully lift your flies off slowly.

Expect to get takes either at the beginning of the retrieve, during the speed-ups, pauses or at the end of the retrieve. Always stop and watch the line before the fly comes into view. Sometimes when you lift off, the trout thinks its prey is getting away and nails it at the last moment, metres from your feet.

This way you'll catch a high percentage of those trout which follow and swirl away at the end of a retrieve at the last moment.

Fly fishing from reservoir banks

You don't always need to go out in a boat to catch reservoir trout. They often come within casting distance to feast on fry, buzzers and margin-dwelling corixae. Reservoir specialist Tom Saville explains.

To enjoy bank-fishing to the full, you need the appropriate tackle and the correct strategies as the seasons change.

Proper equipment

A 10-10½ft (3-3.2m) carbon fly rod (rated AFTMA 7-8) is powerful enough to cast 25m (27yd) of line and reach trout which are holding well out. Don't attempt to fish a reservoir with a short rod because you won't have the leverage to hook a fish at a distance.

It's easier to cast weight forward lines than straight or double-taper ones because

▲ *Early in the season brown and rainbow trout are reluctant to venture into the cold shallow water (under 3m/10ft deep) along the reservoir margins.*

◄ *This is what bank fishing is all about – reading the water, selecting the right flies, casting effectively and, finally, safely landing big trout.*

Line stress

Try not to aerialize more than the tapered section when false casting with WF lines. The line hinges in mid-air, breaking down the coating at the point where the tapered section joins the level section.

the weight is concentrated in the first 3m (10ft). A 7 or 8 is ideal for bank fishing.

Floating lines are used most of the time – the fast sinker or Hi-D is reserved for fishing deep water. Attach the fly line to 75m (82yd) of backing, and use a needle or nail knot to connect a 30cm (12in) butt section of 25lb (11.3kg) stiff mono to the fly line. Tie a loop in the butt section so that you can change leaders quickly.

For most work on reservoirs, fish with the longest leader you can manage – ideally, twice the length of the rod, with two 10cm (4in) droppers at 1.2m (4ft) intervals from the tip. The overall leader length should not be less than 5m (16ft).

A popular nylon strength for most reservoir work is 6lb (2.7kg). Learn to tie the blood loop or double grinner knot for making droppers. You can help to avoid tangles by attaching the heaviest fly on the point and the bulkiest fly on the top dropper.

In addition to good waterproof clothing, thigh waders and a large landing net, other

This well-marked brown trout, taken from the shore of a Midland reservoir, fell for a size 12 nymph fished on a long leader.

essential equipment includes a fly fisher's waistcoat (with plenty of pockets to hold tackle), scissor-pliers, priest, fly box, polarized sunglasses, an assortment of nymphs and lures and a bag to keep your catch fresh.

Seasonal tactics

It goes without saying that you need to adjust your approach as the seasons change.

In April most reservoirs open for fishing. The water is still cold after months of winter temperatures, and the trout are fairly lethargic. Unless a hatch of flies (midge pupae or buzzers) brings the trout to the surface, they swim near the bottom and can be tempted to take a slow-moving weighted black lure. Lures such as the Viva, Tadpole or Cat's Whisker with their mobile marabou tails or wings are best. With the lure on the point, put a Black Buzzer Nymph on the middle dropper and a Black Zulu on the top dropper. Size 10 hooks for all three are suitable.

Using your floating line, cast out, and then wait until the flies sink well down. Retrieve slowly with the rod tip about 20cm (8in) above the surface to keep in direct contact with the line and flies – this increases

---

The double haul

1. When you need to punch out a lot of line, use the double haul, a cast which dramatically increases the line speed.

The angler begins by holding the rod level with the water. With his left hand he grasps the line. There's about 10-15m (11-16yd) of line extended in a straight line.

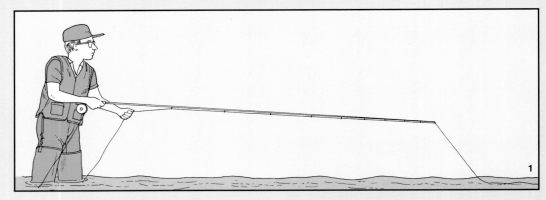

2. With the fly line still held in one hand, the angler lifts up quickly on the rod as if he were making a normal cast. Notice his left hand; it is near the top of his head as he brings the rod up.

3. On the rear power stroke, just **when the butt of the rod is at about a 90° angle** to the water, the angler pulls the fly line down 30cm (1ft). This is the first 'haul'.

Hi-D strategies

When used with a Hi-D line and a short leader, the Booby (far right) dives and bobs, pulsing the mobile marabou.

You can make floating fry (right) dive enticingly and then rise to the surface. All that surface action brings rainbows from afar.

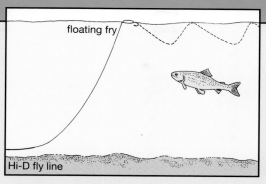

floating fry

Hi-D fly line

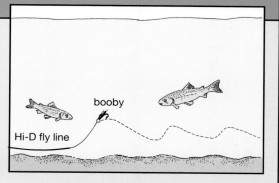

booby

Hi-D fly line

your chances of hooking a trout.

Early in the season the best places to fish are the dam walls and gently shelving banks where the depth is about 3m (10ft) at a comfortable casting distance.

Don't fish with a wind coming directly behind you because the water temperature is then at its coldest. Fish near the downwind shore with the wind blowing from the direction opposite to your casting arm. For example, if you're right-handed, fish with the wind blowing from left to right.

For deep water, use fast sinking line. Loop about 50cm (20in) of 7lb (3.2kg) nylon to your 25lb (11.3kg) butt section, and attach a buoyant Black Booby. Cast as far as you can, and again wait until the line sinks to the bottom.

The Booby is now suspended just above the bottom. Leave it static, keeping a good hold of your fly line, or you can retrieve it slowly.

In May and June prolific hatches of buzzers usually occur. As the year progresses the water gets warmer, and the trout become more active. Try a Pheasant Tail Nymph or a Gold Ribbed Hare's Ear Nymph on the point, with Buzzer Nymphs on the droppers. If you see adult midges on the surface, attach a winged wet fly, similar

Tip Casting well

Though you can learn the casts yourself, personal casting tuition from an expert helps to iron out any problems that you may have and provides you with many helpful insights.

Some waters have resident casting instructors. It is advisable to book well in advance.

4. The line begins to unroll during the backcast, and the angler again brings his left hand up near his head and pauses briefly.

5. The angler then pulls the line down about 60cm (2ft) just **as he begins the forward power stroke.** This is the second 'haul'.

If you memorize what the angler is doing when he makes each pull, you'll have an easier time practising on your own and can save yourself a lot of frustration.

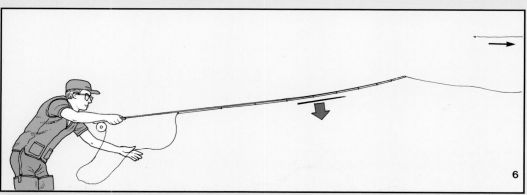

6. The angler releases the fly line and lowers the rod so that it's almost parallel with the water. The line shoots out in a tight loop, and the leader unfurls perfectly over a rise 25m (27yd) away. The line jerks away suddenly. He waits and then lifts the rod... got 'im!

Tip *Wind and wave*

How fast does a nymph move in the water? The answer is very slowly. Many anglers are guilty of retrieving their lines much too quickly.

One way to overcome this is to let the wind and waves move the flies. Cast out, and allow the floating line to cover a wide area. Watch your line: takes can sometimes be hard to see.

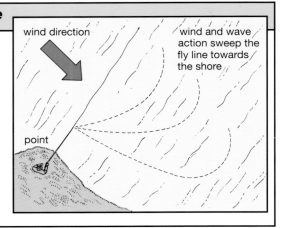

wind direction

wind and wave action sweep the fly line towards the shore

point

in colour and size, to the top dropper.

If trout are rising regularly, ensure that your flies hang just below the surface of the water by applying grease to your leader. If there's no surface activity, try a weighted Stickfly or Montana Nymph on the point; let it sink well down, and retrieve slowly.

In late June and early July there are many hatches of sedge flies, especially in the evenings, and the trout feed enthusiastically on them. Popular sedge imitations that you can try are Invicta, Green Peter, Wickham's Fancy and Fiery Brown.

Buzzers are still on the trout's menu, and the fish are now likely to be tempted by imitations of hatching flies emerging at the surface. Offer 'dry fly' patterns such as the Shipman Buzzer or Hopper – both treated with floatant – but again make sure the leader sinks. Allow the flies to drift around without retrieving. When your fly is taken, wait a few seconds before striking.

In August the weather can be very warm – but as you probably know, trout don't like

Back off!

Don't get too close to another angler – even if he's catching fish. It's courteous to stay at least 50m (55yd) away. You can still see what he's doing and learn from him.

warm water. The coolest water is found along the shore from which the wind is blowing (with the wind at your back). So choose your location accordingly.

Trout often feed on coarse fry in mid-season. You usually see big splashes around marginal weedbeds as the trout slash into the shoals. Such is the force of the attack that some fry are stunned and float to the surface. The trout return to pick them off. You can catch these trout by offering them a floating Ethafoam Fry. Just cast it out near the activity: resist any temptation to move it! The trout takes it like a dry fly. It's vital to wait a couple of seconds before striking, or you won't hook the fish very well.

As autumn approaches, wet and humid weather encourages hordes of craneflies to appear in the surrounding grassland. Some of these are blown on to the water and prove an irresistible mouthful for trout.

Experiment how far out to fish the fly. If there's no response close in, use the wind from the windward shore to drift the floating 'Daddy' a long way out. When you get a take, don't strike immediately: let the fish take the fly down first.

◄ *Cracking rainbow trout such as this one are often the target of the bank angler early in May and June – times when distance casting isn't essential.*

▼ *The lure of the bank at dusk: moving to shallow water to hunt for roach and perch fry, brown trout come well within casting range.*

Stone-sided reservoirs

Appearing featureless on the surface, concrete bowl reservoirs hide a wealth of underwater features, says Mickey Bewick, fishery manager of Berkshire's Queen Mother Reservoir.

 The bottom or what?

Using a medium fast sinking line (and not a high-density, super fast sinking line) and then waiting until it sinks is not a very effective way to fish along the reservoir bed. Slow and medium sinking lines aren't very dense: as you retrieve, the line rides up off the bottom, and your fly fishes at mid level which isn't where you want it.

Many anglers claim the weight forward high density lines fish the bottom better than the shooting head types simply because almost the entire length of the WF line lies along the bottom. The monofilament section connected to the shooting head tends to ride up in the water.

The rainbow and brown trout from concrete bowl reservoirs are virtually wild and very wary. They are by no means easy to fool – but their size, condition and fighting abilities are more than worth the effort.

Get beneath the surface

If the wind direction is your only guide to where you choose a mark, you'll probably have a long, fishless session. But concrete bowl reservoirs have some important fish-attracting features to look out for.

Level platforms The sides of the reservoir don't descend straight to the bottom at an uninterrupted angle. A series of level platforms about 1m (3ft) wide line the bowl, forming rings. Depending upon the reservoir, these shelves are spaced anywhere from 1.5-4.6m (5-15ft) apart. Silt and debris collect over the platforms, providing ideal insect habitat and attracting coarse fish such as perch and ruffe (which in turn attract trout).

Since there are shelves near the shore, you don't have to fish as far out as possible, for the trout sometimes come in close to feed – especially when the water has a slight chop (which helps to diffuse light). If you're not careful and observant, you can overcast.

Slipways are diagonal indentations (or platforms on some reservoirs) along the side of the bowl. Situated near the shallow ends of most reservoirs, they are used to launch sailboats and fishing boats.

Large amounts of silt settle in the slipways, and where there's mud, insects aren't too far away.

Towers The inflow and draw-off towers are located in the deep part of the reservoir. Some draw-off towers have spiral staircases which descend to the reservoir bed. Big trout hover off the silt-covered stairs in the early season, picking off bloodworms and caddis larvae.

In the heat of summer, trout need cool, well-oxygenated water – 10°C (50°F) is their preferred temperature. Most reservoirs and small stillwaters have high levels of oxygen near the surface and in bright light. Trout won't feed if there aren't cool

▶*Casting platforms provide a stable and level base for you to cast – even though you are more visible to trout.*

FLY-FISHING A CONCRETE BOWL

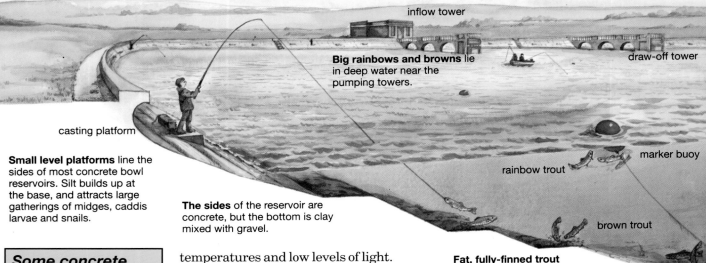

Most concrete bowl reservoirs are built with a sloping bottom, so deep water is always near the pumping and inflow towers.

inflow tower

draw-off tower

Big rainbows and browns lie in deep water near the pumping towers.

marker buoy

rainbow trout

brown trout

casting platform

Small level platforms line the sides of most concrete bowl reservoirs. Silt builds up at the base, and attracts large gatherings of midges, caddis larvae and snails.

The sides of the reservoir are concrete, but the bottom is clay mixed with gravel.

Fat, fully-finned trout are common in concrete bowl reservoirs.

Some concrete bowl reservoirs

- **Queen Mother Reservoir,** Horton Road, Horton, Berkshire (tel 0753 683605).
- **Eglwys Nunydd Reservoir,** Margam, Port Talbot, South Wales (tel. 0639 871111, ext 3368).
- **Farmoor Reservoir (no. 2)** Oxfordshire (tel 0865 863033).
- **Toft Newton Reservoir,** Lincolnshire (tel 0673 7453).

temperatures and low levels of light.

Many concrete bowl reservoirs, however, have aerators in the inflow towers that oxygenate the water. So trout have the security and comfort of deep, oxygenated water and may be persuaded to feed much more readily.

Weeds Some reservoirs have weed growth – especially when the sun warms the water in summer. Obvious insect and fry-attracting features, weeds grow along the bottom as far down as light penetrates.

Jetties or piers Coarse fish, the staple diet of large trout, congregate around these structures. Any feature which offers shelter usually holds fry. You can fish these areas effectively with a boat using a team of small, fry-imitating lures.

Food sources

Since the water quality is excellent in concrete bowls, trout are often fat and healthy, feasting on a variety of aquatic animals.

Snails mainly feed on algae, insect larvae and even fish eggs and are an important food group. You can find them near weeds or in silty areas.

▼ *At first sight reservoirs such as this – the Queen Mother – look pretty bleak and featureless. But learn what to look for and your catch rate should improve greatly.*

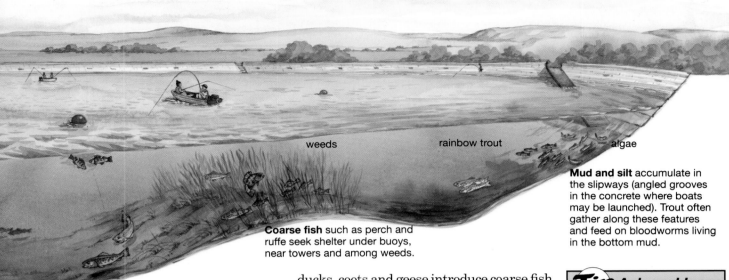

weeds   rainbow trout   algae

Coarse fish such as perch and ruffe seek shelter under buoys, near towers and among weeds.

Mud and silt accumulate in the slipways (angled grooves in the concrete where boats may be launched). Trout often gather along these features and feed on bloodworms living in the bottom mud.

Daphnia (or water fleas) are extremely important in the food chain. Big and small trout feed greedily on these protein-packed creatures. Daphnia are small (3mm long) but immensely prolific – especially in mid summer.

Since they don't like bright light, they descend to the deep areas of the reservoir in mid-afternoon and move up closer to the surface as light intensity decreases. More than other food items, daphnia are responsible for producing some really big, fighting-fit rainbow trout.

Midges (chironomids) are second only to daphnia in importance for supporting a large head of trout. Once the end of the season comes, you can spoon a fish and find it's packed with bloodworms (midge larvae).

At Queen Mother Reservoir, for example, there's a big buzzer hatch in April, and then from May to June things are a bit sparse. Midge hatches increase between July and October – the water seething with buzzers in the evenings.

Hoglice are a good food source for trout at the beginning and end of the season – when insect activity is slow. They can be found along the bottom of the reservoir and among weeds or any debris.

Coarse fish Sticklebacks, ruffe, perch and miller's thumbs (bullheads) are abundant in most reservoirs – even though they aren't stocked.

Fish eggs become trapped in the feathers of waterfowl. Flying from water to water,

ducks, coots and geese introduce coarse fish into many reservoirs and rivers. In winter and early spring trout especially rely on these fish.

Concrete tactics

These suggestions may help you catch more fish from concrete bowl reservoirs.

Early season If the winter has been really cold, the overwintered trout as well as the stockies move to the deep, warmer water. Fish the deep water – 12m (40ft) or so. But when fishing along the bottom in deep water, you must remember to think about *how long it takes your line to sink*. This is something too many anglers fail to do. Always present your fly or lure at the

Tip Ask and learn

Don't just begin fishing without talking to the fishery manager. It's part of his job to describe the features of the reservoir and provide you with tips.

▼ *For results such as this 2lb (0.9kg) rainbow trout in mid summer, fish deep marks with a boat, and allow your line plenty of time to sink all the way to the bottom.*

level where the trout are. It's best to use a watch, or count.

If, for example, your high-density line sinks 15cm (6in) a second and if you are fishing in 12m (40ft) of water, it takes your line one minute twenty seconds to sink to the bottom. When fishing over deep areas (over 12m/40ft) anchor the boat.

If the winter has been fairly mild and the water temperature isn't too cold, you'll still find a good number of fish in depths from 12m (40ft) right to the bank – the overwintered fish are usually in the deepest areas, hovering off the bottom and feeding on bloodworms, hoglice and fry.

Typical tactics include using high-density line with small lures such as boobies fished along the bed.

Mid season Use floating line, a long leader (15ft/4.6m) and a nymph. The main food items eaten by trout at this time are daphnia, and midge and sedge pupae.

A blowing wind can concentrate daphnia and midge pupae in one area of the reservoir. Casting with the wind at your back is undoubtedly much easier than battling against the steady onslaught of a gusty southwesterly. But the rewards of casting into the wind – catching trout – are well worth the labour.

Late season The reservoir bank fishes well – especially when trout herd the fry against the sides of the concrete bowl.

Once the first frosts come, however, the trout seek the sanctuary of deep, warm water. Most anglers put their rods away at the end of September. But for a regular angler at a concrete bowl reservoir, this is complete folly. The reservoir is like a giant vacuum flask: warm water stays warm for a long time and cold water stays cold for a long time.

▲ *Landing trout from the banks of a concrete bowl isn't easy – remember not to walk too close to the slippery green edge.*

▼ *Flawless specimen overwintered rainbows like this one are what attract fly fishermen to concrete bowl reservoirs.*

Drift-fishing for big stillwater trout

If the thought of hooking a big reservoir trout is one that fills you with a sense of longing, then drift-fishing could be for you, says stillwater specialist Peter Gathercole.

Catching specimen trout, especially from a vast reservoir such as Rutland Water, is not easy. It calls for a range of methods designed to shorten the odds of what would otherwise be a hit-and-miss affair.

Large brown trout, not rainbows, are the main quarry because they're predictable and can often be found along specific deep-water marks for most of the season. Big rainbows of over 5lb (2.3kg) are all but impossible to locate in numbers. They are far more elusive and occur much more randomly – though you can still catch them when drift-fishing.

▼ *After blasting his big fly out to the side of the boat on Rutland Water, Jeremy Herrmann pays out line to sink the fly to the required depth.*

Where to begin?

Confronted by a vast area of open water, you may wonder where to start. Begin with a map of the stillwater, and locate landmarks such as towers in deep water. If there are two towers on a piece of water, they are often connected by a pipe allowing the transfer of water. This lies just off the lake bed and is an attractive fish-gathering feature, offering shelter and working in much the same way as a reef draws marine fish. Other good features include dam walls, holes in the lake bed or points with deep water nearby.

Point-first drifting

Once you decide on likely fish-holding areas, you need a way to present the fly at the correct depth. Although anchoring is a good way of getting the imitation down to the fish, a more effective technique is to allow the boat to drift with the breeze. This enables you to cover large areas of water at a reasonable pace.

Chasing big brown trout is often a frustrating game – but it's made a little easier if you can drift over as much fish-holding water as possible.

When you are drifting side-on to the wind in the classic loch-style technique, the boat's movement is usually quite slow (in moderate winds). For this type of drift-fishing to be consistently effective, you must

move quickly. With the point of the boat travelling downwind, you can achieve good speeds. However, even if you begin drifting in the correct position, the boat will quickly swing side-on.

So, to give adequate torque to alter the boat's course, a rudder with a large blade is essential. Most of the boats available for hire on the reservoirs have outboard motors without rudders – you have to provide your own. You can either buy one or make your own. (See *The rudder* on page 60.)

'Flies' for big browns

To be fair the term fly is somewhat inexact. What you need for big reservoir trout is something really meaty. Although normal longshank or leadhead lures can succeed, large tandems are particularly effective when the trout are hitting coarse fish. Tube flies up to 10cm (4in) long are also hard to beat. They may be tied either with a wing of feather or scintillating mobile tinsels such as Flashabou (in gold or silver) or Crystal Hair.

One contentious but deadly pattern for big brown trout is the Waggy. Developed by big fish specialist Fred Wagstaffe, the lure uses the seductive wiggle of an artificial sandeel added to the back of a tinsel-winged tandem. This 'fly' has taken a great many double-figure brown trout. Remember, attach *a minimum* of 10lb (4.5kg) b.s. leader to whichever fly you use.

Lines to tame the depths

Virtually all the techniques for catching a monster brown trout require the use of various sinking lines. If the fish are down deep, a heavily weighted fly and floating line just won't reach them.

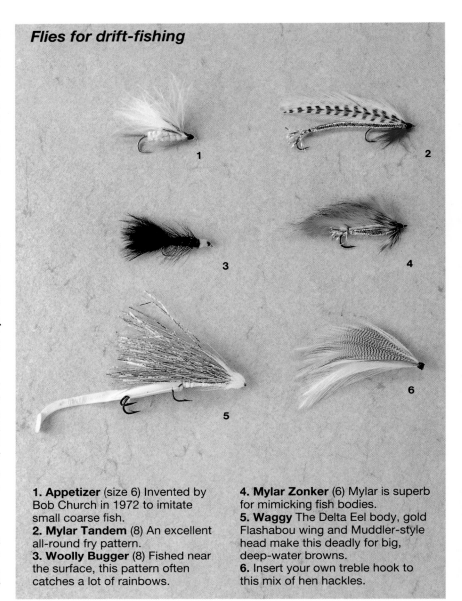

Flies for drift-fishing

1. Appetizer (size 6) Invented by Bob Church in 1972 to imitate small coarse fish.
2. Mylar Tandem (8) An excellent all-round fry pattern.
3. Woolly Bugger (8) Fished near the surface, this pattern often catches a lot of rainbows.
4. Mylar Zonker (6) Mylar is superb for mimicking fish bodies.
5. Waggy The Delta Eel body, gold Flashabou wing and Muddler-style head make this deadly for big, deep-water browns.
6. Insert your own treble hook to this mix of hen hackles.

For fishing mid water to the surface, Wet Cel II is the standard choice. This dark green line was once the main fast sinker for boat anglers, but with the development of higher density, faster sinking lines, game anglers now consider it to be only a medium-fast sinker. We now have the Hi-Speed Hi-D, Di line and lead-impregnated lines which sink fast enough to fish water up to 9m (30ft) deep.

For very deep water you can even try lines with a lead core. Though rather unresponsive to use, they sink extremely fast – perfect for getting down to the effective level quickly and staying there to keep your fly in the 'killing-zone' as long as possible.

Lead core lines, originally developed for trolling the Great Lakes in the USA, come in 90m (100yd) lengths. They are THE lines to use when the fish are hard on the bottom, and they may be used whole or in shorter sections. A favourite method is to make the lead-core line into a 9m (10yd) shooting head. This allows you to cast a long way.

Which line do you use? There are two points to consider. The first is the level at

Fishing the curve

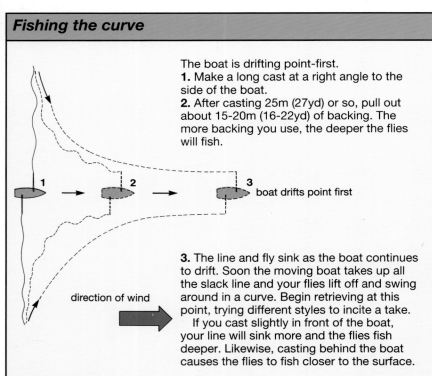

The boat is drifting point-first.
1. Make a long cast at a right angle to the side of the boat.
2. After casting 25m (27yd) or so, pull out about 15-20m (16-22yd) of backing. The more backing you use, the deeper the flies will fish.

boat drifts point first

direction of wind

3. The line and fly sink as the boat continues to drift. Soon the moving boat takes up all the slack line and your flies lift off and swing around in a curve. Begin retrieving at this point, trying different styles to incite a take.
If you cast slightly in front of the boat, your line will sink more and the flies fish deeper. Likewise, casting behind the boat causes the flies to fish closer to the surface.

The lead-core pay-out

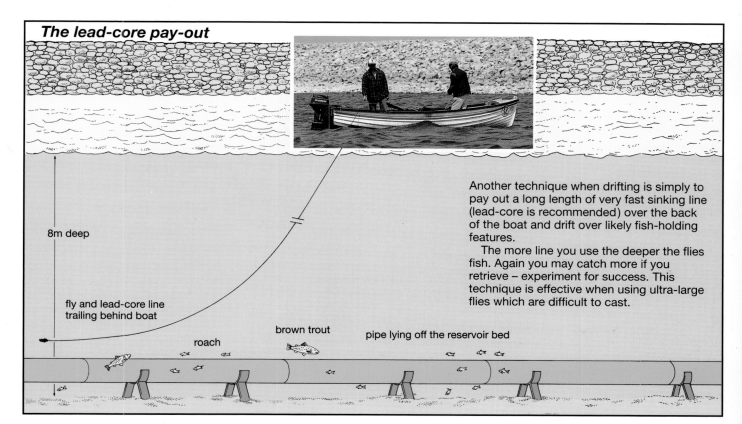

8m deep

fly and lead-core line
trailing behind boat

roach

brown trout

pipe lying off the reservoir bed

Another technique when drifting is simply to pay out a long length of very fast sinking line (lead-core is recommended) over the back of the boat and drift over likely fish-holding features.

The more line you use the deeper the flies fish. Again you may catch more if you retrieve – experiment for success. This technique is effective when using ultra-large flies which are difficult to cast.

▶ ▲ *A large Rutland brown trout, taken near the North Tower, surfaces by the boat (right).*

This is the most critical time – panic and you may lose the fish of a lifetime.

A Gold Tandem (inset above) deceived this big brown. Grown-on trout like this feed almost exclusively on roach and perch fry.

which the fish are lying – and this can only be determined by experimenting or from experience. The second, and perhaps less obvious, is the speed at which the boat is drifting. The stronger the wind, the faster the boat drifts. And the quicker the boat moves, the higher the line is pulled in the water. Moving quickly is great for covering large areas of water, but it does mean that you need to use faster sinking lines than when there isn't too much wind.

Two techniques to try

There are two main ways of drift-fishing using the rudder. Both of them are suited

Restricted use

Rutland, Draycote, Farmoor, Foremark, Eyebrook and Kielder Reservoirs allow drift-fishing with a rudder.

Reservoirs such as Grafham, Bewl and Chew do not. If you aren't sure whether the method is permitted, ask before you go. This will save you a lot of hassle.

for fishing alone or with a partner. (Of course, it always helps to have a partner to help manage the boat.)

The curve This is a deadly technique for both rainbow and brown trout at all depths. To allow the line to sink freely while the boat is drifting, cast at a right angle to the boat and then pay out some 10-20m (11-22yd) of backing. Your partner should do likewise on the other side of the boat. (Shooting heads are perfect for this style because you can cast a long way to produce an effective curve.)

The lure covers a 30m (33yd) curve either side of the boat – which causes the fly to swing, then lift in the water as the line tightens. A good comparison is the classic down-and-across wet-fly method used on rivers. Rather than the current moving the flies, the drifting boat causes the flies to swing around.

The pay-out The other method to fish really deep water – and keep the flies there – is simply to pay out lengths of ultra-fast sinking line. Some anglers use lead-core trolling line (which changes colour every 9m/10yd to show how much is out). Others use two 25m (27yd) lengths of high density fly lines spliced together. Obviously lines such as these cannot be cast; they are merely put out over the back of the boat while drifting.

Retrieving the line

A final consideration is retrieval rate. It may be as varied as you want – indeed it's a

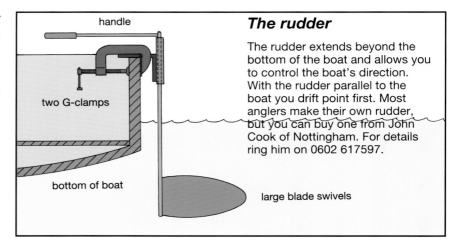

The rudder

The rudder extends beyond the bottom of the boat and allows you to control the boat's direction. With the rudder parallel to the boat you drift point first. Most anglers make their own rudder, but you can buy one from John Cook of Nottingham. For details ring him on 0602 617597.

handle

two G-clamps

bottom of boat

large blade swivels

▼ *Get it right on the day and you could be in for a haul such as this, taken over two days.*

The biggest brown trout taken on this trip weighed 7lb 3oz (3.3kg).

good idea to alter the speed and vary the pauses until you find a method which works for you on the day.

Big browns are fickle creatures – what works one day may well be totally useless the next. Try a slow, steady series of pulls followed by three or four quick ones, or long strips as fast as you can pull. This speeds up the lure, and a response may come suprisingly quickly. Be versatile – browns get used to a particular style quite quickly and it pays to ring the changes.

Who knows, you could easily find yourself connected to one of those lovely big, tackle-testing browns.

▼ *Catching specimen brown trout is no easy feat, but drift-fishing allows you to cover a lot of water quickly.*

Boat fishing on reservoirs for trout

Early season trout are not always the easiest fish to find – but they're there. Bob Church, Britain's best known reservoir fly fisherman, shows you where they lurk.

▼ *Some reservoirs, like Rutland Water (below), are huge and can be quite daunting to an angler used to smaller waters. Drifting – as these anglers are doing – can often be an excellent way to locate and catch trout. A short cast is often more successful than a long one as you don't scare fish which are close to the boat by casting over them.*

Although there are a number of small reservoirs in Britain of 60-100 acres, most are around 300 acres with some, such as Rutland Water, covering more than ten times this area. On these 'inland seas' a boat can help you get the best of the sport – as long as you know how to handle it and where to position it.

Most reservoirs are not the featureless places that some people imagine them to be. There are bays and headlands, valve pumping towers, submerged islands and many other features. These areas fish well at different times of the day and in different seasons – using various techniques. Taking a boat out means you can fish any of these places – and if the action's slow, it's easy and quick to move to another spot.

Using a boat can be dangerous, so fish with someone else unless you are highly experienced. Before you and your partner set out from the jetty, make sure that your boat has all the essential equipment.

You'll need an anchor – the kedge-type is best because it holds bottom firmly without being very heavy. (It has blades which dig in when you pay out enough line.)

If the boat has an outboard motor, and most do, make sure there are a pair of oars under the seats for emergencies. Nothing is guaranteed to ruin your day more effectively than being adrift in 3000 acres of water waiting for a rescue boat.

Check the rowlocks aren't damaged and that there is a life jacket or a buoyancy aid for you and your fishing partner. There should also be a bailer beneath the seat to get rid of the water you bring into the boat with your wet tackle and, with any luck, your fish.

For control over your drifting speed, a drogue (a small parachute dropped in the water and used to slow the rate of drift) is essential. One of 130cm (50in) square is just right. Obviously this is only useful for fishing on the drift.

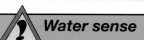

Water sense

Bob Church recommends that you wear a buoyancy aid whenever you're afloat, no matter how well you swim. You may never need it, but too often anglers using boats drown unnecessarily.

▲ *The start of the day at Llyn Brenig in North Wales – time to make sure everything you need is there, and stowed away tidily.*

Tip Using the anchor

When fishing at anchor, you must avoid any noise which may scare off the fish. Drift or paddle to your intended anchorage from upwind, have the anchor rope untangled and ready to drop, and drop it *quietly*.

▲ *Landing fish in a boat shouldn't be any harder than it is from the bank. Just draw the trout over the net.*

Spring sport

Early in the season, the water is beginning to warm up and weeds are starting to grow in the shallower water. These weeds are a haven for insects and fish fry which attract the bigger fish. Areas of shallow water accessible only by boat are usually great places to find early season trout.

Headlands often continue underwater for

A WINDY SPRING DAY ON A RESERVOIR

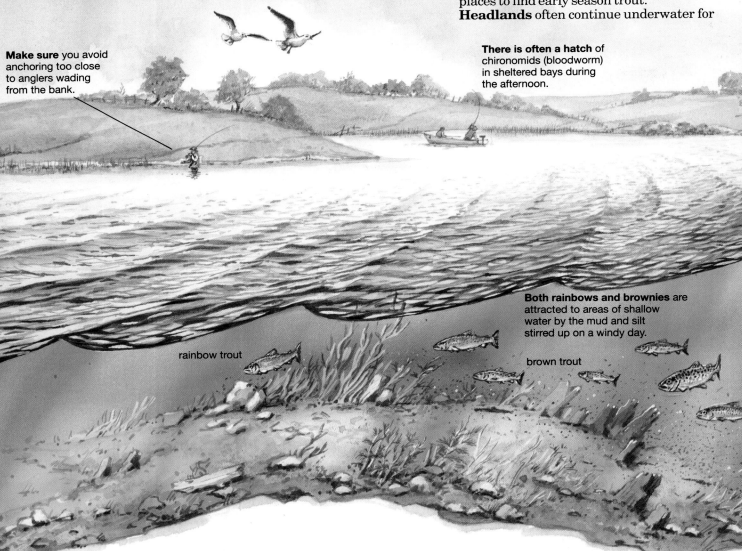

Make sure you avoid anchoring too close to anglers wading from the bank.

There is often a hatch of chironomids (bloodworm) in sheltered bays during the afternoon.

Both rainbows and brownies are attracted to areas of shallow water by the mud and silt stirred up on a windy day.

rainbow trout

brown trout

hundreds of yards, providing areas of shallow water. This type of feature produces some prime fishing from April to mid-May. The weedy ridge provides food and shelter for the trout and many can be caught before sport tails off in late summer. Approach the ridge downwind – to avoid scaring the fish you want to catch – and drop anchor about 60-80m (66-87yd) from the shore and 20m (22yd) upwind of the ridge. The fish lie close to the bottom, over and around the ridge.

In a light to medium wind, drop the anchor out from the central stern position – this stops the boat swinging about. In a higher wind with waves of 60cm (2ft) or more, tie up from the bows to reduce risk of capsizing. Some anglers tie up from the central rowlock, leaving the boat broadside to the wind. If you do this, then even if you stay right way up, the extra area presented to the wind can cause the anchor to drag along the bottom over the ridge – spoiling the fishing.

Submerged islands provide very similar opportunities in mid to late spring. The shallow water over these areas also encourages weed growth and provides shelter for trout. Both types of hotspot fish well with a wave of 60cm (2ft). This can stir up the water, colouring it slightly over ridges and

▲*A good wind producing waves like these often makes for the best trout catching conditions in the early season. These anglers afloat on Berkshire's Queen Mother Reservoir have anchored near the dam wall to fish deep. Fish often wait for food swept in by the waves.*

Boat handling

Fishing from a boat offers you the freedom of the water, but with it goes a certain amount of responsibility – both to other users of the water, and to yourself. Here are some simple rules which you should follow whenever you step into a boat to help you fish safely and with consideration.
● Most waters insist on your wearing a buoyancy aid. Though these tend to be brightly coloured, presumably to aid rescue, they won't put the fish off as long as you don't stand up making yourself visible to trout for miles around.
● Standing up is a bad idea in any case as small boats are not very stable.

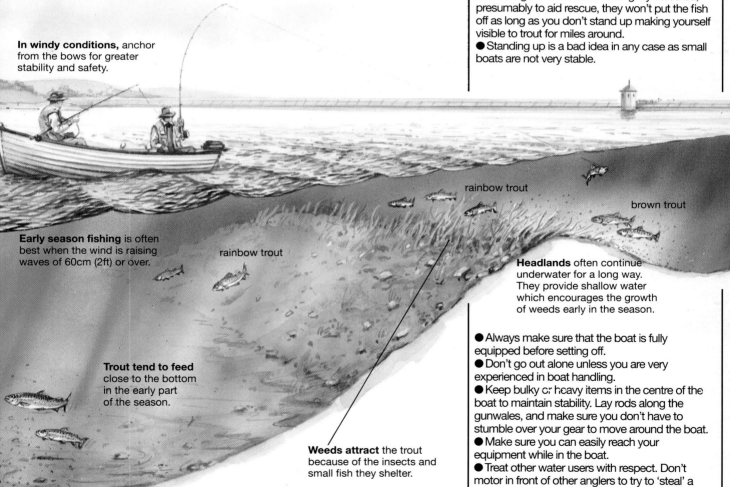

In windy conditions, anchor from the bows for greater stability and safety.

Early season fishing is often best when the wind is raising waves of 60cm (2ft) or over.

rainbow trout

rainbow trout

brown trout

Headlands often continue underwater for a long way. They provide shallow water which encourages the growth of weeds early in the season.

Trout tend to feed close to the bottom in the early part of the season.

Weeds attract the trout because of the insects and small fish they shelter.

● Always make sure that the boat is fully equipped before setting off.
● Don't go out alone unless you are very experienced in boat handling.
● Keep bulky or heavy items in the centre of the boat to maintain stability. Lay rods along the gunwales, and make sure you don't have to stumble over your gear to move around the boat.
● Make sure you can easily reach your equipment while in the boat.
● Treat other water users with respect. Don't motor in front of other anglers to try to 'steal' a good fishing position, and always leave at least 50m (55yd) between you and the nearest angler.

▲ *Late afternoon to dusk is traditionally a good time for hatches of insects that prompt trout to feed.*

islands and creating a trail of colour downwind. Such a trail acts rather like groundbait and can attract fish from quite some distance.

Other styles

Sometimes the obvious hotspots fail to produce, and that's when you must search for your fish. In a mild spring, you can try drifting. This is most effective in 2.4-4.6m (8-15ft) of water, with the fish tending to lie near the bottom. Always use the drogue except in the lightest of breezes. Without it, you'll find yourself drifting too rapidly towards your flies.

At the end of a drift, pull in the drogue and motor back upwind to start another from a new position to the left or right. That way you cover a large area of water. When you find a fish or two, use the same drift-line until you stop catching. Don't motor over the area down which you're going to drift or you'll scatter the fish. Use the deep water at the middle of the reservoir for this, and make sure you steer well clear of other anglers' lines of drift. Etiquette on the water is more than just politeness – if everyone simply motored wherever they wanted, there would be more accidents and fewer trout caught.

In the sheltered, tree-lined margins of the reservoir there is often a hatch of chironomids in the late afternoon. This is another good place to hunt for trout in late spring. Anchor far enough away from the shore to avoid scaring the fish you want to catch – but not so far that you can't cast to them. If you see trout rising, they are probably taking the emerging pupae trapped in the surface film of the water. Etiquette again demands that you anchor no closer than 50m (55yd) to the nearest boat – and watch out for anglers wading from the bank.

◀ *The frayed tail of the brown trout (top) shows that it has been recently stocked, whereas the rainbow is full-finned and wild.*

Loch-style fishing

▲ *Two anglers fish loch-style for brown trout on Tal-y-llyn in North Wales, their only companions being the fearsome mountains and cold September wind.*

As its name suggests, loch-style fishing originated in Scotland. An angler in a boat drifts broadside with the wind and, using three flies, makes short casts downwind to intercept surface-feeding trout. Bruce Vaughan explains.

Loch-style fishing using traditional wet flies is a method for the summer months when the water has warmed and the trout search for food in the surface layers. The great advantage of this method is that you continually cover new, unfished areas of the reservoir or loch.

Trout tend to work upwind when feeding at this time of year, taking hatching insects in the surface film as well as terrestrials blown on to the water.

The first key: equipment
Loch-style fishing requires a certain range of equipment for success.

The rods With a long rod (10-11ft/3-3.4m), you can control the flies more effectively during the retrieve than with a short one. A long rod also makes the handling of hard-running rainbows much easier. Since you don't need to cast very far, a softish rod with an all-through action is recommended – but buy a *lightweight* one to save your casting arm.

The line The best choice is a WF6 – heavier lines make a splash on landing; this could scare fish near the surface (especially in calm lanes).

Although sinking lines are sometimes used, the traditional way to fish loch-style is with a floating line and a long leader with three wet flies (or nymphs).

When trout are not showing at the surface, however, you might want to try a slow-sinking line to fish the flies a few feet below the surface film.

The leader and flies Especially useful are extra-strength nylon leaders which combine clarity and high breaking strain with a low diameter.

The correct construction of a leader helps to reduce tangles. The length between the fly line and the bob fly (first one) should be 1.8-3m (6-10ft) of 10lb (4.5kg) mono. The farther the flies are from the fly line, the

Double grinner

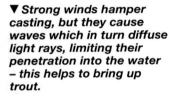

This is a strong knot for making droppers. Leave the end pointing *towards* the fly about 10cm (4in) long.

▼ *Strong winds hamper casting, but they cause waves which in turn diffuse light rays, limiting their penetration into the water – this helps to bring up trout.*

Loch-style fishing – at a glance

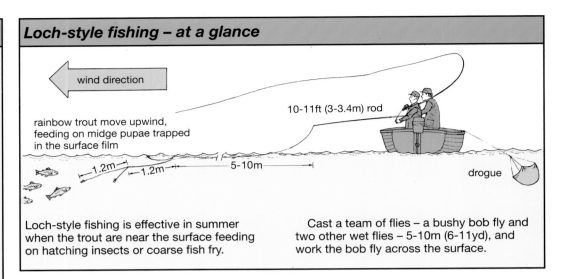

wind direction

rainbow trout move upwind, feeding on midge pupae trapped in the surface film

10-11ft (3-3.4m) rod

1.2m 1.2m 5-10m

drogue

Loch-style fishing is effective in summer when the trout are near the surface feeding on hatching insects or coarse fish fry.

Cast a team of flies – a bushy bob fly and two other wet flies – 5-10m (6-11yd), and work the bob fly across the surface.

less likely trout are to be spooked by the line, and the more confident the take.

From the bob fly to the middle fly, use 1.2m (4ft) of 7lb (3.2kg) line. From the middle fly to the point fly, attach 1.2m (4ft) of 6lb (2.7kg) mono. Each line length is reduced or stepped down in breaking strain to help the whole leader turn over better during the process of casting.

Connect the sections (and also create droppers – short lengths of mono on to which the bob fly and middle fly are tied) with proven knots such as the double grinner (see diagram on this page) or the four-turn water knot. Droppers about 10cm (4in) in length help reduce tangles, yet they are long enough for you to change your flies once or so.

Even with short casts tangles inevitably

occur; it's just a fact of life when using three flies. But by fishing with a slightly heavier – and perhaps larger – fly on the end (point) of the leader, you can reduce tangles greatly. The extra weight turns over the leader better and helps to keep the trio of flies apart.

Flies can climb up and down large waves in windy conditions, and trout may not see them. Fish something heavier on the point – a weighted pattern or a fly tied on a twin-pointed hook.

The second key: retrieve

The most important aspect of loch-style fishing is to bring 'life' to the bob fly: to imitate an insect struggling to escape from the surface film – not to mention hungry trout. Choose a bushy fly and work it *across the*

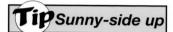

Tip Sunny-side up

Fishing in sunny conditions, use patterns with silver or gold bodies (such as Bloody Butcher, Silver Invicta or Teal and Silver); they can be more effective than dark bodies in bringing trout up.

▼ *An early-season rainbow thrashes about on the surface, stubbornly refusing to be beaten. Notice the huge landing net correctly positioned.*

surface back towards the boat. As you retrieve line, gradually lift the rod from a horizontal position to a vertical one.

Trout have good eyesight and will move a long way to intercept a well-worked bob fly. In some cases, though, they are attracted by the movement of the bob fly but take one of the other flies in the team – particularly the point fly which fishes deeper than the bob fly and is frequently the first one the trout will in fact encounter.

When the flies reach the boat, pause for five or so seconds before recasting – for unseen trout which have been following the team sometimes erupt through the surface to engulf a fly, believing it's about to make a last-second escape.

Another trick which may convince reluctant trout is to experiment with the speed of the retrieve. Sometimes trout chase flies

Tip Serial drifts

Trout may not be evenly spread out throughout a large stillwater, so it pays to keep moving around until you locate them. Once you find a trout-holding area, make successive drifts over it until the trout become wary and move down to deep water.

Give the area you intend to fish a wide berth when making your way back to the top of your drift – you can't motor over fish and then expect to find them still feeding at the surface.

▼ *Wild brown trout such as these – taken from a Scottish loch on wet flies – are high on the agenda of many game anglers. Silver-sided, stew-pond pellet feeders cannot be compared with the slim, wary and distinctively marked wild trout.*

stripped back fast. Other times, however, trout take them only when retrieved slowly. The behaviour of fish can change even during the course of the day, and not just from day to day.

Third key: the drift

Some of the best times to use this method are on grey, overcast days and in the mornings and evenings when the light isn't too intense. Trout are less wary and feel more confident to come near the surface in low levels of light.

When drifting always be on the look-out for rising trout. If you're drifting too fast, use a drogue to slow things down. On many southern reservoirs drogues are used almost all the time – except when conditions are very placid.

Fish activity at the surface may not always consist of a swirl followed by ever-widening rings. Often you see a fin or a back cutting through the surface in waves. Sometimes it's a tiny dimple rise. No matter how insignificant a disturbance on the water, always cast your flies at it. It's amazing to see lazily feeding rainbows hovering near the surface suddenly become transformed into highly aggressive predators as a team of artificial flies is pulled past their noses.

Rainbow trout seem to possess an in-built shoaling instinct, and very often when a rising rainbow is encountered, others are also in the vicinity. If one angler in the boat hooks a fish, the other should continue to fish, looking very hard for any signs of activity.

Fourth key: calm lanes

Obstructions on the bank – a clump of trees, a barn or a draw-off tower – block or divert the wind, forming calm, alley-like lanes. But sometimes there's no apparent reason for their formation. Concentrations of drowned and trapped flies can rapidly build up in the lanes. Some insects tend to find it difficult to escape from the surface film in calm water. Trout are quick to take full advantage of the abundance. On good days you can see trout working upwind along the calm lanes, and you can make some fine catches.

Often it is better to cast to the edge of the lane into the ripple where the leader and flies are less likely to make a disturbance. The fly line and leader can look all too obvious right in the flat, placid lane.

Loch-style fishing is probably the most demanding style of trout fishing. Frequent casting and effective working of the flies have to be combined with constant alertness at all times. Even so, watching a trout shoot through the surface of the water to engulf your bob fly or other flies is more than enough compensation.

Trout strategy on small stillwaters

Stillwater trout supremo Peter Cockwill sheds light on his sporting and successful method for a mighty popular angling discipline.

Stillwater trout anglers are spoiled for choice these days. There are dozens of small fisheries in most areas that offer varied sport with small stockies, fine brownies and mammoth rainbows. All you have to do is get down to your local fishery with some gear, a method and a few ideas.

▶ Good casting technique is vital for achieving glory on small stillwaters. Aim for a smooth turnover of the leader and delicate accuracy – particularly if casting to rising fish.

You can divide small stillwaters into two main groups: those where the water is clear, and those where it is not. With some of the clear ones you don't have the problem of working out where the fish are – you can see them. If you don't have the luxury of clear water then you'll have to study the activity of insects such as water midges (chironomids) to aid location. You should also take into account water depth and wind speed and direction.

Once you've found the trout you'll discover they react to artificial flies in much the same way – whether the water is clear or not. The trick is to present your fly so the fish think it's an item of food or strike it out of aggression.

Strip search

If fish are feeding in or very near the surface, use a floating line to fish either dry or unweighted flies in the surface layers. There are times, however, when the wake created by a floating line can spook fish. When this happens, try a very slow sinking line to counteract the problem.

You can't always be sure at what depth the fish are feeding, but you can home in on them if you're methodical in your approach. fish a weighted pattern such as a Walker's Mayfly Nymph on the end of a leader of at least 15ft (4.5m) long. Aim to cover the mark by fishing at different depths – retrieving the fly in successively shallower zones or strips until you find fish.

On your first cast let the fly sink down to the bottom before retrieving steadily. If there are no takes, fish a little higher up next time – don't wait as long for the fly to

◀ An angler plays a fish from a casting platform at Rooksbury Mill, Hampshire. Many stillwaters have platforms and some even have boats to reach awkward spots.

sink before you retrieve. As you fish higher and higher you cover the water strip by strip. As long as the fly travels in a more or less steady path you will hook into fish sooner or later.

If your retrieve rate is slow the weighted fly stays down at the required level and travels in an even path. As soon as you speed up, the fly is forced upwards as the water pressure acts on it. This can be to your advantage if you want to lift the fly to avoid an obstacle. But when you want the fly to follow a level path, stick to a slow retrieve. Even if you do this, wind pressure on the line or surface drift can cause the fly to rise. To counteract it use a slow sinking line. Usually known as intermediate or neutral density lines, these are probably the most useful for small stillwaters.

Help yourself
You can do a number of things to step up your rate of attracting trout and recognizing a take when using a sinking line.

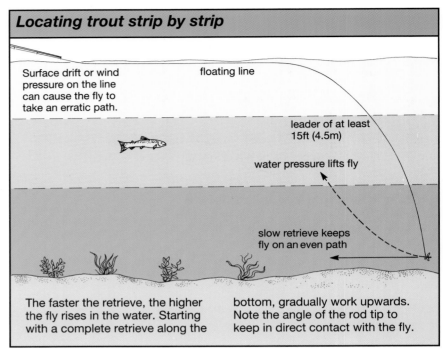

Locating trout strip by strip

Surface drift or wind pressure on the line can cause the fly to take an erratic path.

floating line

leader of at least 15ft (4.5m)

water pressure lifts fly

slow retrieve keeps fly on an even path

The faster the retrieve, the higher the fly rises in the water. Starting with a complete retrieve along the bottom, gradually work upwards. Note the angle of the rod tip to keep in direct contact with the fly.

Casting and retrieving A good casting technique is vital to achieve a smooth turnover of your leader. The more practice you get the better. In still conditions, especially when stalking fish, you need delicate, spot-on deliveries.

If the leader unfolds well it means you are in direct contact with the fly as soon as you start to retrieve. Tapered leaders help the presentation – braided leaders also achieve good turnover.

There are several different ways you can retrieve a fly. Try experimenting with a variety – long, smooth pulls, short fast, short slow, steady figure-of-eight or fast figure-of-eight retrieves – before you think about changing flies.

◀ *A large rainbow's final and futile dive for freedom is revealed in the clear water of Dever Springs, Hampshire.*

A stillwater fly selection

1. Gold Head Nymph
2. Damsel Nymph
3. Walker's Mayfly Nymph
4. Cat's Whisker
5. Corixa
6. Freshwater Shrimp
7. Peach Doll
8. Buzzer

Choose a reasonable mix of flies for small stillwaters. Lures might fool stockies but some fish shun them.

Nymphs and flies that suggest food are more likely to appeal to trout. There can be hatches too. Then it's worth trying to match the hatch and turn to fishing dries on the surface.

Tip angle Keep your rod tip very close to the water surface so that you are in direct contact with the line and you can feel the slightest touch.

Last minute Imagine a fish is following your flies at all times. Trout often follow a fly a long way and can sometimes be induced to take at the very end of the retrieve.

Avoid snatching the fly out of the water and going straight into a backcast. Often a swirl on the surface indicates a following fish desperately searching for the titbit that has just been whipped out of its clutches. It is far better to lift up the rod at the end of a retrieve so the fly accelerates towards the surface, inducing the fish to take as it thinks the fly is escaping.

Balanced action The action of the fly in the water is partly influenced by the diameter of the tippet material. A 16 tied to heavy 6lb (2.7kg) line just isn't as enticing as when it is tied to 3lb (1.4kg) line. At the other extreme you risk breakage if you fish a size 8 weighted lure on 3lb (1.4kg) tippet.

Behaviour study

Good technique almost always helps you pick up extra fish – especially on those hard days when you might only get an occasional offer, and it's vital to translate it into a hooked fish.

If you get the opportunity to fish clear stillwaters where you can observe individual fish, spend some time watching how fish react to your fly. When you come to fish

► *Many trout stillwaters provide good sport with lots of fish in the 1-4lb (0.45-1.8kg) range and the odd bigger trout. Some waters are known for very large fish, such as this 12lb (5.4kg) beauty.*

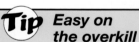
Tip Easy on the overkill

Don't keep plugging away with large flies when sport is slow – you're far likelier to succeed with a small pattern. When you're struggling, try fishing a small black fly as slowly as possible. Black is probably the all time favourite colour for a trout fly. It doesn't spook the fish and a small fly stands repeated presentation without arousing any suspicion.

◄ *Trevor Housby collects a trout in a breezy corner at one end of a stillwater. Trout are often found in areas where wind-blown food collects.*

Tip Ring of confidence

If the area of fish activity is fairly compact, fish your fly around the margins of the concentration rather than right in the middle of it.

This way you reduce the risk of spooking – and losing – the whole lot. Remember that it's very much easier to catch a fish that is unafraid and feeding confidently.

► *With delightful scenery and well stocked waters, it's no wonder some small stillwaters are very popular. It's wise to book your venue well in advance.*

murkier waters, use this experience to help you. In clear waters you soon notice that when a trout takes an interest in your fly and starts to follow, it loses interest and turns away if you stop the retrieve or slow it down. Always maintain continuity of retrieve to keep the fish's interest. All too often anglers get a small initial tweak from a following fish and instantly stop or slow the retrieve. This is a passion killer to trout. Increasing the retrieve rate is more likely to

induce the fish to take positively.

When you feel you have worked an area sufficiently at different depths, try somewhere else. There are hotspots on a fishery but that doesn't mean the fish are always to be found there. Sometimes it pays to try an area where not many anglers fish. There may be fewer trout but there's a chance they'll be feeding more confidently and be more inclined to take than trout receiving a hammering in the hotspots.

▼ *Rainbow trout are the mainstay of many stillwater fisheries, but brownies, such as this sizeable beauty in Peter Cockwill's net, are a splendid bonus.*

Variations of technique – a change of retrieve, line or leader, or anything which alters your presentation to the fish – can tip the odds in your favour.

Gravel pit fisheries

Gravel pit fishing has become a dominant part of the UK trout angling scene as more waters become available to suit the needs of anglers discovering fly fishing, says Peter Cockwill.

▼ *Clean, clear water and a variety of habitat which includes islands, ridges, shelves, shallows, holes and sudden drop-offs, combine to make gravel pit fisheries first-class trout venues.*

Very different from purpose-built fishery waters, gravel pits are created by flooding when gravel extraction has finished. They are also generally much larger and have sharply defined deep and shallow areas. Although they have no dam, they possess a vast array of underwater features which make for some fascinating fishing.

The other main feature of such fisheries is the quality of the water: it is almost always superb. Alkaline, clear and pure, the water in gravel pits supports abundant insect life and weed growth, creating perfect conditions for stillwater trout.

Follow the features

Gravel pit fisheries can range from just a few acres to several hundred, but typically they cover 15-30 acres with depths up to 6m (20ft). In some places they can be very exposed until planted trees and bushes become established – or until a range of wild plants takes hold. The main tree to colonize the margins is willow, with alder a close second. They often need regular maintenance work to keep them in check.

The variety of bottom contours – ridges, shelves, holes, sharp drop-offs, islands, deep margins, shallows – gives an immense

range of habitats in a fairly small area. Look for these and you'll soon build up a picture of fish-holding areas and lies.

Most gravel pit fisheries have an area set aside as a nature reserve; this is usually brought in as part of the planning requirement even before the gravel is extracted. It is an excellent idea from the angler's point of view as it leaves an area where fish can live unmolested and put on weight. Because of the rich feeding available you often come across fish which have evaded capture and grown on to make first class specimens. This is particularly true of brown trout.

◄ *Rainbows, like this beauty, are the main target in gravel pits. Brownies are there, but they are much harder to catch.*

A mixed menu

You can see the whole spectrum of trout feeding behaviour on these fisheries. There are excellent hatches of buzzers and sedges, as well as tremendous damselfly populations, and very often there is the bonus of a mayfly hatch. As gravel pit fisheries almost always support a coarse fish population, you can also see the trout engaged in late season fry bashing.

It is, in fact, quite hard to know which style of fly fishing to use on some gravel pit fisheries since virtually any method from dry fly to lure stripping can work.

The secret is to be versatile and aware of what is happening on the day you are fishing. With such rich populations of insects it often happens that the fish become preoccupied with a particular style of feeding. While early morning may see good feeding on buzzers, it is quite possible that as the sun climbs higher in the sky the damsels start to hatch and the fish change to feeding on the emerging insects.

A GRAVEL PIT TROUT FISHERY

willows

alder trees

island

The downwind side of an island is a prime lie for trout during the day.

reeds

Deep water often holds big grown-on brown trout, lying in between gravel ridges.

trout

Large, sharply defined areas of deep and shallow water are typical of gravel pit trout fisheries.

gravel bottom

ridges

ridges

reeds

The variety of bottom contours undulations, points, drop-offs, flat gravel beds – leads to an immense range of habitats within a relatively small area.

Weed growth is prolific in gravel pits and helps to support many aquatic insects such as damsels, buzzers, sedges and even mayflies – all important food for trout.

► *A trout comes to the net at Langford Fishery, near Salisbury in Wiltshire. This venue has two waters – one of 7 acres and one of 15 acres – and both are stocked with rainbows and brownies. Langford is open all year round.*

weeds

What fish where?

Rainbow trout are the usual stock in gravel pit fisheries. In addition to being easier and cheaper to breed and rear, their wandering habit makes them more prone to being caught. The territorial brown trout can be a difficult fish to catch and hence is of small benefit to the fishery manager.

However, where a percentage of browns are stocked it may pay to seek them out since they can and do grow to a considerable size, remaining undetected for years in the deeper areas. These long-term residents sometimes make mistakes during fry time at the end of the summer or perhaps on very windy, wild days when they seem to lose their caution. On such days try fishing a large Muddler Minnow for an hour or so through the waves on a slow sinking line (but make sure you use a strong leader as takes are sudden and hard).

Among the weed In gravel pits the weed is the angler's ally – normally the presence of weed beds greatly assists in locating trout. Fishing along the edge of beds you can usually find feeding trout. Look on weed beds as being the natural larder for the trout and don't be afraid to fish in and around them rather than keeping to clear areas where the fish are not so numerous.

► *A 5lb (2.3kg) brown trout caught on a dry fly. This method can be excellent on gravel pits since the clear water and abundance of insect life encourage the fish to feed at the surface. Great accuracy of casting is essential for success, though.*

Pits to fish

- **Chigborough Fisheries,** Maldon, Essex. Day tickets. Tel 0621 857368.
- **Church Hill Farm,** Bucks. Two waters. Day tickets. Tel 0296 720524.
- **Dorset Springs Trout Lakes,** Dorset. Open all year. Tel 0258 857653.
- **Langford Fisheries,** Steeple Langford, near Salisbury, Wilts. Open all year. Tel 0722 790770.
- **Newbury Trout Lakes,** near Reading, Berkshire. Day tickets. Tel 0635 38280.
- **Rooksbury Mill Trout Fishery,** near Andover, Hants. Day tickets. Tel 0264 352921.

▲▶ Since fisheries are created by flooding gravel pits when they have been worked out, they can look pretty bleak at first. This is Kingsbridge Trout Lake, Poole, Dorset at an early stage of development (above) and later on (right) when trees and bushes have grown large enough to provide a windbreak.

In the winter Even in winter, when the water can look grey and lifeless, there are always fish over the remains of weed beds. If you know where they are then you can score. Winter rainbows fight hard and often the best of the sport can be had in the colder months when the fish are at their physical best and fewer anglers are around.

Fighting fit Gravel pit trout are known for their strong fighting ability and long runs are quite normal for even modest-sized fish. The clear water and good feeding soon naturalize newly introduced stock and they become quite silvery and behave like the fish in large reservoirs. Many anglers hold the fish too hard when playing them and broken leaders are not unusual, especially as it's often necessary to fish quite fine in order to get a take.

Make use of the wind

The effect of wind can be the dominant factor in a day's fishing, and while logic usually says that you should fish on the downwind bank where, unfortunately, it is the most uncomfortable, this is not necessarily true for some pits.

Where the bottom consists of extensive ridges the wind may not turn over the water layers in so pronounced a way as usual, and the fish don't move around as much as they would on a pit with a more even bottom contour. Bear in mind that surface-feeding fish usually follow the wind and concentrate more on the downwind shore.

Tip Peter's four top tips

- **Be observant** – look for signs of feeding fish or areas where insects are hatching.
- **Fish on the downwind** bank if you are new to a water and don't know the lie of the land.
- **Begin fishing** with small nymphs (eg. the Pheasant Tail nymph) or dry flies (such as the Grey Wulff).
- **Search the deep gullies** for large resident brown trout which may be hiding there.

Always search the *downwind* side of islands for fish feeding on the surface. There are calm pockets of water immediately downwind of islands. Land-borne insects which fall from trees and shrubs can sometimes accumulate there.

Don't ignore the dry fly

Dry fly fishing on gravel pits can be the absolute cream of the sport. The clear water and abundant natural life encourage the fish to be surface feeders, and the emerger style of flies can be a tremendous method of catching if you can place the fly accurately in the path of a cruising fish. If you can't see any feeding fish, a Daddy-Long-Legs fished either static on the surface or slowly retrieved just sub-surface will bring fish up from quite deep down.

Paul Canning used a roll cast on the island to avoid snagging in the trees behind him. Don't always fish along the well-trodden trail – trout may be closer to the bank than you think.

Fishing for winter rainbow trout

Many trout fisheries now offer winter fishing for rainbows. England International Paul Canning tells you where to look for cold-water trout at Lakedown Fishery in East Sussex.

With over 20 acres of water to explore, Lakedown is large enough to cater to dozens of anglers, but few dare to brave the wintry weather.

Admittedly, some winter conditions pose problems for prospective trout anglers. On very cold, windy, rainy days under 2°C (35°F) or so the fish are down deep and reluctant to move. Pulling a fly past their noses brings little response. Your chances of catching in these conditions are slim.

Yet on a mild, sunny day it's not unusual to see trout up in the surface layers of the water looking for hatching midges. The fish may respond to imitative nymphs, lures and even dries. Winter fly fishing is never easy – even at a stocked fishery. But to increase your chances of catching, fish on the warmish days. The trout are much more active then.

Mobility is the key

"People bring a bag and a second rod with them when fishing places such as Lakedown," says Paul, "and they set up camp in one spot instead of coming prepared to walk. To get the most out of a fishery I think you've got to travel light and walk around a lot." And that's exactly what he does, as he begins looking for signs of life on and beneath the surface of the lakes.

"On a still, misty day such as this, I'm looking for trout feeding on small dark midges. Hatches mainly occur during the

On Lake Four use the high vantage point to look for fish moving on top. Only if no fish are topping start to explore the features – the island, the point and so on.

▲ *In winter the trout may come close to the banks in search of shrimps, corixas, midges or fry. Stand back from the water's edge, and begin fishing the margins. Slowly work your way out towards deeper water.*

warmest part of the day – usually in the early afternoon. And if there wasn't a sharp frost the night before you'll probably have a good chance of seeing plenty of flies."

Is the imitative approach necessary at a trout fishery? "Trout seem to acclimatize very quickly. They take advantage of food items a few days after going in, and they usually get into a pattern. Obviously you can catch trout on lures, but that's not my choice. I prefer to use small nymphs or even dries."

Midges, shrimps and nymphs are the dominant food items at this time of year. The trout may also feed on corixas in the margins or among decaying weeds, and fry also feature in their diet.

The clarity of Lake Four

Recent rain has drowned the countryside – Lakes One, Two and Three are coloured, making it difficult for the trout to spot the flies. For this reason, Paul decides to try the last lake which has remained much clearer than the others.

The back-end flats At the far end of the lake there is a large open area of water where Paul spotted a few trout breaking the glassy surface to take hatching midges. The depth tapers gradually to reach about 2.4m (8ft) or so at 15m (16yd) out.

This is where he starts fishing. He says that some trout mount cyclical patrols at regular intervals and may come close to the weedy, reedy margins in search of food.

Most anglers tend to cast out thoughtlessly to the middle of the lake instead of trying the margins first. "Fish just off the bank; if anglers haven't disturbed it too much, the trout will be cruising just along the sides.

"As the days and weeks go by the trout get used to anglers fishing on one side of the

THE NORTH POINT OF LAKEDOWN'S LAKE FOUR IN WINTER

island

casting platform

point

brown trout

rainbow trout

fry

lake, and during the day they move over to the quieter side."

The island Paul crosses a wooden bridge which provides access to the small tree-covered island (there's a well-worn path surrounding the feature). Fishing off the island allows you to cast to areas too far to reach from the banks. The trout may also hold near the bank in the deep water off the north-west side.

According to Paul, if nothing is moving, the island is a good mark to fish from – a short cast puts your flies over water 3-4m (10-13ft) deep.

"Very often you'll find people fishing where access is easy and comfortable – the open end of the island, for example. They can set up camp in an obstruction-free area and use the overhead cast for maximum distance. Picking a difficult spot, such as near the trees on the northwest side, may mean you'll have to roll cast and fish close in, but little fishing pressure generally

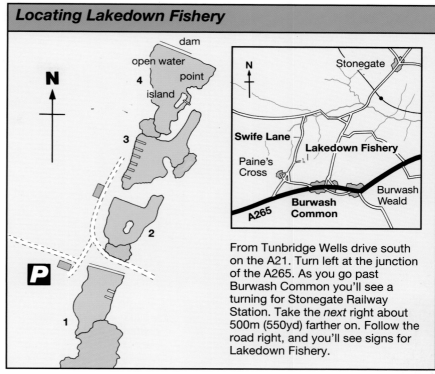

From Tunbridge Wells drive south on the A21. Turn left at the junction of the A265. As you go past Burwash Common you'll see a turning for Stonegate Railway Station. Take the *next* right about 500m (550yd) farther on. Follow the road right, and you'll see signs for Lakedown Fishery.

◄ *Fish around the margins of the island first, using the count-down method to explore all depths. Then from the clear end try an overhead cast to reach out into open water.*

means the trout won't be too far out." This is also useful to remember if other signs of fish are few and far between.

The points There are four main points on the lake, but the one north-east of the island appeals to Paul because he's caught here before under difficult conditions.

The water is deep close in. He points out

rainbow trout

Deep water off the point provides the trout with security. They make regular patrols and may come close to the bank.

Trout actively scour the bottom in search of damsel nymphs, bloodworm or coarse fish fry. Though reared artificially, the fish acclimatize quickly to their surroundings.

The clay bottom, mixed with rocks and patches of silt, supports a healthy crop of weeds. Even in winter the trout patrol the weeds in search of nymphs hiding among the decaying fronds.

Hatches of midges occur every day of the year, except perhaps in the very coldest weather. The flies usually hatch during the warmest part of the day – in the early afternoon.

three good fish-holding areas: the deep, weedy margins along the base of the point, the patrol routes of the channel directly out from the tip and the open expanse northeast of the point.

Weeds cover the bottom, and you can see the remains of tall brown reeds lining the margins. A casting platform is sited on the very tip of the point.

Paul begins fishing off the base of the point, standing well back from the water – about a rod's length away – just in case there are trout in the margins.

It's common for an angler to see the platform and immediately begin fishing on it without considering that trout may be only a rod's length out. The fish, becoming aware of his presence, move out to deeper water, decreasing his chances of catching.

Since nothing is showing on the surface, Paul works the area off the tip of the point. There's an underwater lip which extends a rod's length out. The depth then drops off steeply to reach a maximum of 3m (10ft) or so. The shelf usually gathers trout.

It's best to begin fishing along the margins and then work your way out towards open water. You may just connect with a hungry winter trout on patrol. (It may follow your fly all the way in because the water is deep, so don't just lift off at the end of the retrieve. Pause for a few seconds; then speed up before picking up the line to recast.)

It can't be stressed enough, says Paul: for any winter fishing, pick a mild day and don't waste time and money fishing under cold, windy conditions; and always look for fish showing on top.

▲ ◄ *Lake Four even has a mini waterfall (top). But because the water coming in is colder than the water present, trout such as this quality winter specimen (left) may avoid this area of the lake.*

▼ *Look into the water to determine the depth before fishing. The trout may not venture close to a shallow bank in winter. Long-range fishing then becomes essential.*

Fishery info

For more information about day tickets, contact Alan Bristow, Fishery Manager, Lakedown Fishery, Burwash Common, East Sussex (tel. 0435 883449).

Fishing for trout in deep lakes

Natural deep lakes abound in many areas of the British Isles – waters that are fished very little compared with modern stocked stillwaters. Bill Pennington gives you insights into food items and helps you to locate trout.

Finding fish in Britain's vast natural lakes is perhaps the most difficult task the angler faces. Water craft is essential if you are to cut out unproductive fishing in these wild waters.

Basic needs

A trout needs very few creature comforts to be content. Security, cool, well-oxygenated water and food are highest on the list. The volume of water and the extensive areas of deep water mean that oxygen starvation – common in our small, shallow stillwaters – isn't a big problem; security and cool, oxygenated water are readily available. Rock ledges near deep water offer areas of safety.

Follow the feeding

It would be easy to locate fish if they were evenly distributed throughout the lake. But this is very rarely the case: trout are localized. The major factors governing their whereabouts are food availability, weather and time of year.

During both the early and late season trout have only limited sources of available food. In summer there's plenty of insects and crustaceans for the fish to feed on – especially in the shallow areas of the lake. Here trout find shrimps, sedges, hoglice, mayfly and olive nymphs and many other aquatic food forms.

In late summer, terrestrial insects such as hawthorn flies, beetles, ants and daddy-long-legs fall or get blown on to the water, adding a bit of variety to their diet.

During the whole of late spring to early autumn, hatches of buzzers occur almost daily, especially in deep water.

Where do you find most of this food? With the exception of buzzers, the answer is simple – in water shallower than 6m (12ft). In fact, most insect activity occurs in water less than 1.8m (6ft) deep. You can find trout in shallow water most of the year. There are exceptions, however. During the early and late season (April and September) trout are in the warmer, deeper water. In mid summer, they retreat to the cool, dimly lit depths.

Most deep lakes are not blessed with extensive shallows, and consequently, the food availability is restricted to relatively small areas which can hold dense populations of fish.

▼ Deep lakes around the country support a healthy population of wild brown trout such as this immaculate three-pounder (1.4kg).

▲ Two anglers fish loch-style on a deep water in Scotland; the advantage of this method is that they cover new, unfished areas of the loch.

Approach shallow-water trout warily, making no sudden or clumsy movements, and keep false casting to a minimum.

In autumn trout are attracted by terrestrial insects such as hawthorn flies, beetles, ants and daddy-long-legs that fall or get blown on to the water.

On hot, bright summer days the fish move to the deeper areas - drop-offs – until darkness offers them cover.

A DEEP NATURAL LAKE IN SUMMER

The weather

The weather can affect food stocks and the trout's security. Trout won't feed when their security is threatened, and they are very loath to venture into clear, calm, bright shallow areas.

Cloudy days with a warm wind blowing are some of the best times to fish. Ripples – or better still waves – reduce light penetration, encouraging the fish to move into the shallows to feed.

During extremes of temperature – be they hot or cold – trout generally retreat to deep water. Extremely warm water is not normally a problem in deep lakes, but early and late in the season the water is cold, especially in the spring as the snow melts.

◀Anchoring over deep water seldom produces trout. Drift loch-style to find the fish. Don't wait for them to find you.

Some deep lakes to try

It's best to go to the nearest tackle shop in the region you intend to fish and get details of licences and day tickets.
● **Lake Windermere, Windermere, Cumbria** Free fishing with licence.
● **Tal-y-llyn Lake, Gwynedd, Wales** Enquiries tel 0654 77282.
● **Lake Ullswater, Cumbria** Free fishing with licence.
● **Lake Buttermere, Cumbria** Permits from The Gun Shop, Cockermouth, Cumbria.

● **Crummock Water, Cumbria** Day ticket from Mrs. Beard, Rannerdale Farm, Buttermere CAB 9UY.
● **Lake Coniston, Coniston, Cumbria** Ask at local tackle shops.
● **Ennerdale, near Whitehaven** Tickets from W. Hail Hardware Shop, 48 South St., Egremont.
● **Loch Tay, Tayside, Scotland** Ask at local tackle shops.
● **Lough Corrib, County Galway, Ireland** Trout fishing is free in the lough.

Shallow water around an island provides good prospects all season long.

Tip Line colour to the lake

Many believe that using green nylon in a clear or brown-tinged water may decrease your chances of deceiving a trout.

Likewise, using brown line in greenish water has a similar negative effect.

Match the water colour to your line colour. Failing that, carry a colourless (natural) nylon to meet any circumstances.

Hatching midges rise to the surface film where they hang for a moment before splitting their shucks and emerging as adults. Trout take advantage of the motionless pupae, picking them off by the hundreds.

A deep water inlet and underwater channel provide oxygenated water and hold early and late season fish.
The most productive times to fish for trout in summer are in the evening and throughout the night.

Trout become very lethargic and lack-lustre at this time. They are reluctant to expend energy for little in return, and they are also unlikely to feed avidly since the food is limited.

General assessments
So how do you make general assessments about all the variables that affect the trout and its environment? Reviewing tactics over the season provides some general guidelines.

Early season
The water is cold, and food is far from plentiful. The trout are recovering from the trauma of spawning; they're lethargic, trying to expend as little energy as possible to gather the available food.

Excellent locations to find fish are stream or river inlets with access to deep-water channels. Food is brought to the trout (and other fish) on the current and little energy is spent gathering what's available. Other areas to try are banks with narrow strips of shallow water next to deep-water shelves. Caddis larvae, shrimps, mayfly nymphs

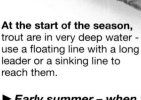

At the start of the season, trout are in very deep water - use a floating line with a long leader or a sinking line to reach them.

▶ *Early summer – when the water warms rapidly – is the best time to tempt hefty brownies such as this one from the upper layers of the lake or from the shallows off the bank.*

and hoglice are concentrated here.

April and early May

With the longer hours of daylight the water starts to warm. Trout gather where the food is concentrated, but they are far more active in the warmer water and are prepared to cover great distances in search of easy meals. Ideal areas are shallows, especially with weedbeds – which provide habitat for large numbers of nymphs – submerged islands and shallows around fully extended islands. All these areas should contain more fish if they border deep water or have rough, rocky areas.

The main food for trout at this time consists of fry, shrimps, hoglice, olive and mayfly nymphs (and chironomids when the trout resort to deep water under calm conditions). Hatching midges and daphnia are blown to and thus concentrated near the downwind bank.

In mid-summer

At this time there are long hours of sunlight and often calm conditions on the surface of the lake. The trout are fit and very active but reluctant to feed under bright, calm conditions. They are likely to concentrate their feeding during early and late times of the day over the shallows.

Main food items are nymphs and sedges (and chironomids when the trout are in deep water). This is one time in the season when fishing deep water within casting distance of the bank can pay off.

In September

As the water along the shallow areas cools, insect activity decreases, and trout once again move to their early season haunts – the deeper, warmer water – not so much for food quantity or availability but in preparation for running up feeder streams to spawn. Some good-sized fish can be taken at this time, but they should be returned to maintain the population for the future.

Bank fishing in the early season is an underrated method to connect with margin-patrolling trout. The angler in the distance is fishing from a slim, rocky point of land.

▲ *Though finding wild brownies such as these may seem daunting on large waters, it's not something to worry about during the season, for the trout usually come in to feed on aquatic insects in water less than 12ft (3.6m) deep. An angler fishing from the bank has a great chance of catching.*

CHAPTER THREE

RIVER TACTICS

Dry fly fishing

Casting a dry fly to a trout and seeing the fish take it or turn away at the last moment makes the heart of even the most seasoned angler beat faster. John Roberts takes a closer look.

Dry versus wet

Dry-fly fishing allows you to see the fly as it drifts downstream: unlike wet-fly fishing, you know if it's working as it should or not. Again, when it comes to bite detection, you can see the fly when the fish takes it and strike accordingly.

▼ *There are few things to match the excitement of watching your dry fly being engulfed by a brown trout on a clear chalk stream.*

Trout often feed at the surface of the water on newly hatched aquatic insects or female flies returning to lay their eggs. Terrestrial (land-based) flies and other insects are also important food items as summer progresses.

Matching the hatch

If you want to catch a feeding trout, your best chance is to offer it an imitation of the natural fly it is taking. By looking at the water or along the river bank you can discover what the trout are feeding on.

Size is an important feature. Few fish are duped by a fly too small or too large. Also take into consideration the shape and colour of the natural insect's body, legs and wings. Is the dry fly designed to copy a sedge fly or a dun (a newly hatched upwing fly), an egg-laying spinner or a terrestrial? Wings don't have to be included – often the blur of the hackle is a sufficient suggestion.

Rise forms

Trout feeding at the surface reveal clues about the insects they are consuming. The simple or plain rise is the commonest form. Trout taking duns, motionless adult sedges and most terrestrial insects produce regular concentric rings on the surface – sometimes with a tell-tale bubble.

When a trout moves quickly to grab a fly off the surface, it causes a splash, displacing a lot of water. This is the slashing rise, a signal which suggests the trout is taking fast-moving, hatching sedge pupae. If sedges aren't around, the trout may be feeding on large terrestrial insects. Fish a sedge pupa imitation in the surface film of the water. If that fails, try a large terrestrial.

The dimple, sip or kiss rise is difficult to detect on rippled or fast water. It's much easier to see on calm stretches. The trout moves unhurriedly to its prey – knowing the food can't escape – and sucks the insect in without breaking the surface of the water, producing very gentle ripples.

Spent spinners, stillborn flies or those trapped in the surface film are the likely

How a river trout takes an insect

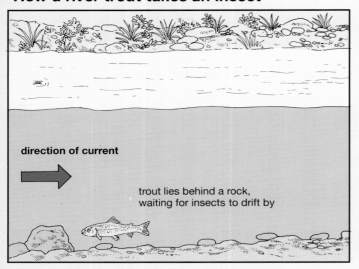

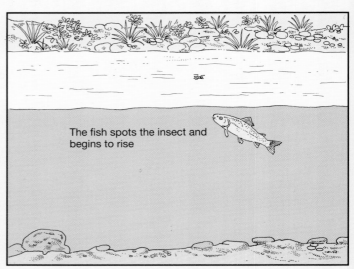

direction of current

trout lies behind a rock,
waiting for insects to drift by

The fish spots the insect and
begins to rise

Seeing a trout rise is a welcome sight. But many anglers
don't take into sufficient account *the depth of the water or
the speed of the current.*

The depth and speed of the river affect where the trout makes
its rise and where the angler sees the rise. In this position
the trout is about 90cm (3ft) from its lie.

Tip *Real illusion*

Though dry flies catch
trout even when the fish
aren't rising, you might
create the illusion that a
hatch is occurring by
casting to a lie several
times. This may stimulate
the fish to feed.

items the fish is going for here. A trout feeding in this way is usually stationed very close to the surface and feeding frequently. Because there is often plenty of food, trout do not move very far to feed. Present the fly in line with the trout.

▼ *A prime time to fish a dry fly is during an evening insect hatch. Offering an appropriate imitation to a wild brown trout is often successful – and great fun.*

Proper presentation

Selecting the right pattern is half the problem; the other half is presenting the fly correctly. Drag, the main concern for the dry-fly angler, occurs because the speed of the current varies across the surface of the river, and the line pulls or 'drags' the fly at an unusual speed. A fly which doesn't drift exactly where the current takes it looks unnatural, and trout refuse it. There are exceptions to this (mainly egg-laying

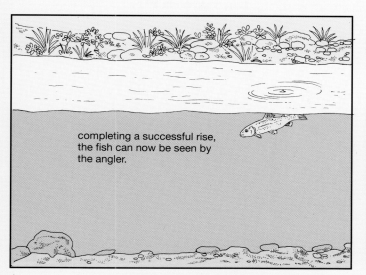

Trout have an angle of view of 97° irrespective of depth. The *size* of a trout's window increases as it swims deeper and decreases as it swims towards the surface.

completing a successful rise, the fish can now be seen by the angler.

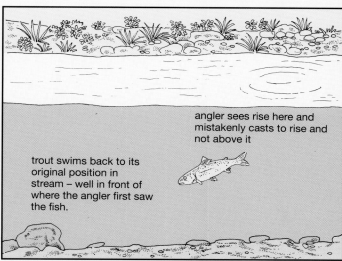

The trout is usually about 60-120cm (2-4ft) upstream of its rise, but remember you still need to cast about 90cm (3ft) in front of the lie, so the fish can see the fly coming.

angler sees rise here and mistakenly casts to rise and not above it

trout swims back to its original position in stream – well in front of where the angler first saw the fish.

sedges), but 95% of your presentations must be drag-free.

You can overcome drag by casting the line leader and fly on to water which has a *minimum* variation in current speed. You can also cast slack or excess line on to the water, so the current has to straighten it before drag can begin.

If you cast across the current, any faster water creates a downstream belly in the line and causes the fly to drag. You can avoid this by mending the line – flicking the line upstream so that the belly moves upstream of the fly (shown on page 90).

On smooth, unrippled surfaces mending line may alarm fish. A reach cast moves the line in the air on the forward cast so that it lands upstream of the fishing zone. The longer a fly is allowed to drift, the more likely it is to drag. Another answer is to fish with short drifts.

Presenting the fly downstream offers some advantages – the fly is the first thing the trout sees, and the leader and line are less visible. Fishing this way can be a very effective way of taking shy fish.

Fishing tips

If rising trout refuse the artificial fly, there are a number of things you can do. In moderate to slow water – where trout can take a long, hard look at the dry fly – use a pattern a size or two smaller than the one you tried first. You can also try a low-riding pattern which rests in the surface film. Copying an emerging or trapped fly in this way is often successful. In fast water where trout might

▶ **When you're fishing in ultra-clear water and trout are refusing to rise to your fly, use a fly a size or two smaller. If that doesn't work, try a bushy sedge pattern.**

Mending the line – across current

This technique is very effective if you're trying to avoid 'drag' – when the current grabs the line and pulls the fly at an unnatural speed.

If the line is straight or if the fly is starting to drag, you can create a belly in the line by flicking the rod upstream (left in this case) to allow the fly to drift freely in the current.

But mending the line on very calm parts of the river may spook the fish.

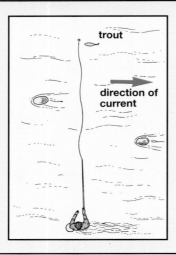

trout

direction of current

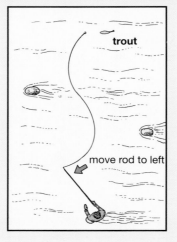

trout

move rod to left

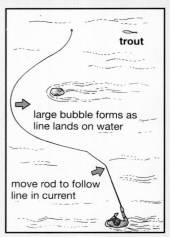

trout

large bubble forms as line lands on water

move rod to follow line in current

easily miss a fly, move up in size to make sure they see your imitation.

Another possibility is to offer them a food source such as a bushy sedge or a beetle pattern that might be more attractive. If that fails cast upstream and, as the fly drifts 30cm (1ft) or so in front of the trout, twitch it gently. This singles it out from motionless natural flies and gives it some life. Adding a bit of life to the fly is perhaps one of the most difficult characteristics to give to an artificial.

If trout aren't rising or if you can't find them, try searching the faster water with an attractor pattern such as a Wickham's Fancy. Or cast a terrestrial pattern in slow water so that it lands with a 'plop' that attracts the attention of lethargic fish. At dusk use a bushy sedge pattern. Fish it downstream, giving it an occasional twitch. Using a finer leader (which makes the line less visible) or softer nylon (which allows a freer drift) may also help. Fishing the dry fly often means continually changing your approach to tempt shy fish. The problems that the trout presents are part of its charm.

▼ *Probably the worst time to fish is mid-day in summer. Extreme stealth and patience are needed on small, slow-flowing rivers.*

Tip Skating flies

This is an effective technique when trout refuse to rise. Apply a floatant to an Elk Hair Caddis, and grease the leader and 1.2m (4ft) of the fly line.

Cast downstream or across. Lift the rod tip, skipping the fly across the surface to imitate a caddis fly trying to fly.

Nymph fishing

Since trout take most of their food below the surface of the water, nymph fishing is perhaps the deadliest type of fly-fishing. Charles Jardine explains both upstream and downstream 'nymphing'.

▲ *Fishing for trout on the Welsh Dee. The gap between two riffles is a perfect place to use a nymph along the bottom.*

Always strike

When upstream nymphing, if you see your line hesitate or twitch at all, strike immediately! Sometimes the nymph gets caught on rocks, debris or weeds, giving the impression that a fish has taken it. There is, in fact, no way of telling until you strike.

A remedy for a rocky, problematic bottom is to put on a lighter pattern which won't snag so easily.

Nymph fishing in its literal sense is angling with the imitations of immature insects such as mayflies, caddis flies, midges and others. But it also applies to other underwater creatures such as shrimps and corixas (lesser water boatmen). Even snails are labelled under the term 'nymph'.

Getting set up

Nymph fishing on rivers requires light fly line – AFTMA 4, 5 or 6 – to present the fly delicately without slapping the water. It doesn't matter what the taper or colour of the line is – as long as it floats. A rod with a fast action (middle-to-tip) and 8½-9½ft (2.6-2.9m) long is ideal.

Leaders should always be somewhat longer than the depth you are fishing. For example, deep runs and holes of 2.7m (9ft) require a 3.7-4.6m (12-15ft) leader. For general fishing conditions, though, a 2.7-3.7m (9-12ft) leader is best. To extend the life of a knotless tapered leader, add a tippet section to the end. You then have to replace only the tippet when it's used up, not the entire leader.

Since river fish usually don't grow as big as their reservoir cousins, consider the pliability of the line and the size of the fly when choosing the proper tippet breaking strain. Soft line allows the nymph to move freely and easily in the water, imitating a natural, free-swimming insect. Stiff or thick line hinders the nymph's movement and puts fish off. As a general guideline, hook sizes 18-20 require 1½-2lb (0.7-0.9kg) line. You may need 3-4lb (1.4-1.8kg) line for hook sizes 12-16. Heavily weighted patterns in sizes 6-10 require line up to 5-6lb (2.3-2.7kg).

The upstream approach

One of the most celebrated and effective methods is the upstream approach. There are two basic variations of this style of fishing, the dead drift and the induced take.

The dead drift is simply casting upstream of a trout (or a likely lie) and allowing the fly to run with the current towards the fish.

The induced take is similar to the dead drift, but just as the fly is about to reach the quarry, move the nymph either sideways or upwards by quickly lifting up the rod tip while pulling the fly line. This imitates a fleeing, panic-stricken insect and stimulates the trout to feed.

Water craft is vital when fishing upstream: you should have a good idea where the trout are, or where they are likely to be, so that you don't waste time fishing in inappropriate stretches of water such as shallow runs only about 15cm (6in) deep.

Another important yet often overlooked consideration is choosing a correctly weighted pattern which fishes at the trout's level. If a trout's lie is just off the bottom in very deep fast water, for example, you need a heavy nymph to get right down to the fish. The alternative is to cast far enough ahead of the lie so that the fly has extra time to sink to the required depth.

Whether you use the dead drift or the induced-take method of upstream nymphing, keep a low profile – kneel on the bank or cast from behind the cover of tall grass.

Another point which may help you catch wary trout in clear rivers is to change the angle of your cast. If you are casting to a trout directly upstream, your line lands above the feeding fish – this could spook the trout. But by casting upstream and across, you place the line and leader at a slight angle to the fish, helping to conceal the fly line.

In clear water – where you can see the

▲ *Though more common on stillwaters, dragonfly nymphs also thrive in the slow-moving rivers of southern England.*

Nymphs scurry along rocks and weeds and are fairly good swimmers.

Perfecting the roll cast

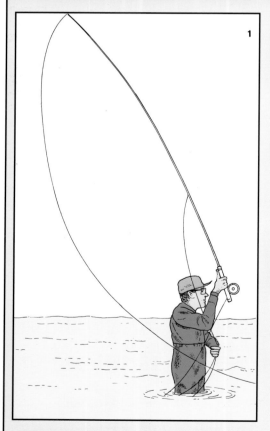

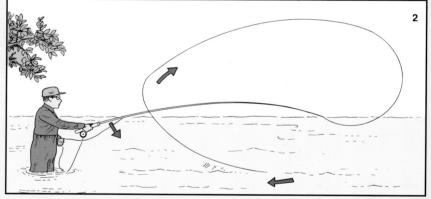

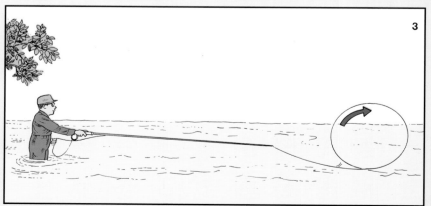

Use the roll cast when trees prevent an overhead cast. Raise the rod up until the line forms a belly behind the rod **(1)**.

Bring the rod down hard and fast – as if you're hitting a nail with a hammer. Your arm completes a 90° angle **(2)**.

As the rod is thrust downward, the line is picked up off the water and hurled towards the target in a circular form **(3)**.

▲ *The upstream approach is an effective method for fly-fishing small rivers such as this West Country water. This angler is using short drifts to work the nymph in front of and behind the boulders.*

fish – detecting the take isn't difficult. A trout or grayling's sudden movement upwards, downwards or to the side usually indicates that the fish has hit your nymph. A speedy but gentle lift of the rod sets the hook. Whatever the water conditions, if you don't see a fish but your leader stops or twitches in the current, strike! Your attitude should always be to strike first – ask questions later. Trout and grayling can sometimes spit out imitations as quickly as they take them.

When trout are surface-feeding the same principles of upstream nymphing apply – though there are distinct parallels with dry-fly fishing. G.E.M. Skues founded this style of angling in the early 1900s; later it came to be called 'emerger' or 'damp' fly-fishing. Follow the same principles as with the dead-

drift method, but use a pattern (such as a sedge pupa emerger) which hangs in the surface film, and cast closer to, but still upstream of, the rising trout or grayling. Takes are again visual. They look like an ordinary rise – if you see one anywhere near your fly, set the hook immediately.

The basic upstream nymph tactic is applicable throughout the season, and by varying the weight and style of your artificial you can accommodate everything from the surface-feeding brownie to the bottom-grubbing grayling.

Downstream nymphing

Another method of nymph fishing is the traditional 'down and across' technique. Drag on the nymph isn't too much of a disadvantage when fishing downstream. Cast across the stream and let the current sweep the nymph down. This is one of the easiest methods of fly-fishing because there isn't much casting involved.

By controlling the line flow, you're not limited to imitation solely by appearance – you can make a heavily weighted nymph, for example, 'swim' in a deep pool by gently twitching the fly upstream and then letting it move down again. This adds life to the nymph.

Water craft isn't as important when fishing downstream. An intimate knowledge of the river's deep pools and seething eddies isn't necessary because your nymph covers a wide fish-holding area, and you take a few steps downstream after working a stretch.

Unlike fishing upstream – when the current has control of the fly – 'nymphing' downstream allows you to dangle a tantalizing fly just above a sunken log, a boulder

The outlaws

On some rivers fishing the nymph upstream is banned while on others (chalk streams) fishing it downstream is illegal. Make sure you *check* the rules before you go.

Pattern points

Too many anglers take far too many nymphs with them. All you really need are a Stickfly, Pheasant Tail Nymph, Gold Ribbed Hare's Ear, Montana, Damsel and Dragonfly Nymphs, GE Nymph and various shrimp patterns.

When fishing with nymphs (upstream dead-drifting especially), ensure that the tippet section and fly descend rapidly through the surface film. Leader-sink agent should be applied after every 10 or so casts.

If the leader has any grease on it, it is more visible to the trout. Degreasing is crucial when fishing emergers in the surface film.

Some river and stillwater specials

▶*From left to right: the Stickfly (1) imitates a caddis fly nymph; the Montana (2) suggests a stonefly nymph; and the Dragonfly Nymph (3). Most imitations are tied on long shank hooks, sizes 6 to 16.*

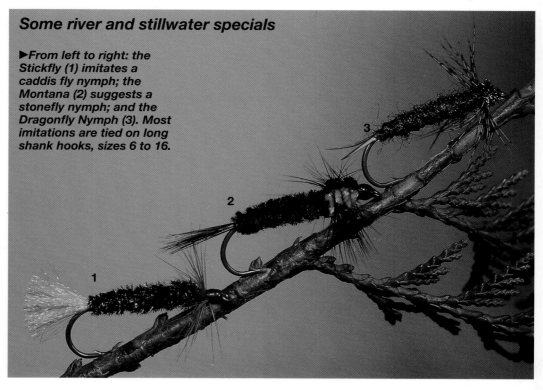

or a snag-strewn heap of branches: you can explore the river without worrying too much about losing your favourite fly.

There are certain disadvantages when fishing downstream, though. First of all, you can sometimes be visible to the trout. The importance of stealth cannot be over-stressed. Walk quietly to the bank; fish from the cover of vegetation; and wear drab clothing. This is especially important on calm stretches of shallow water. Fish with a lot of line out in such places.

A second disadvantage comes when you try to read takes. Generally, you can feel them more than you can see them. If you're not careful and controlled when setting the hook, you could easily pull the nymph *away* from the trout's mouth (since the fish usually points or faces towards you).

Hooking isn't usually a problem when you're fishing upstream because the trout is in front of you or at your side – striking pulls the hook *into* the fish's mouth.

Some say fishing the nymph is much more problematic than using the dry fly (especially when detecting takes). But this deadly style of fly-fishing isn't beyond the reach of anyone. Proficiency and confidence come with practice and patience.

◄ *Nymphs trundled slowly along the bottom often attract the attention of big grayling, such as this 2½lb (1.1kg) River Test resident.*

▼ *Major insect hatches occur at dawn and dusk. An 'emerger' (one fished in the surface film) is your best choice at this time.*

Side and reach casts

Even when you have to reach difficult lies, it's important in fly fishing to present the fly as delicately and precisely as possible.

The side and reach casts are just two of the many types of casts developed to overcome very difficult situations in river fly fishing.

The reach cast You see a big brown trout directly across from you in fast water. How are you going to present your dry fly without the line pulling the fly under right away? The solution is to try a reach cast, a slightly modified version of the overhead cast that puts an upstream belly in the line. It's used only when casting across the river.

When you fish with a dry fly, the upstream belly (slack line) allows the fly to drift drag free over the trout. And when you use a nymph or wet fly, the same upstream belly allows the flies to sink, rather than be swept across the current near the surface.

The side cast You're fishing on a small, deep river; its banks are lined with bushes and tall trees. The shade of the trees encourages trout to rise to hatching upwings (iron blues).

You can't use an overhead cast because the water is too deep to wade and the trees are in the way. The side cast allows you to work upstream yet avoid the troublesome tree branches.

Again, in many ways this cast is similar to an overhead cast except that it's done to one side. The important point to remember is that the rod must move smoothly back and forwards at a 90° angle and generally remain parallel to the water.

▲ *This angler uses the side cast from under the bough of a tree to present his fly to a Yorkshire grayling.*

Fly casting

Casting champions spend up to eight hours a day practising. Attach a piece of yarn to your leader and sharpen your skills in your back garden.

▼ *Learning alternative casts may help you catch more fish – such as this handsome brown trout.*

The reach cast (A)... and the side cast (B)

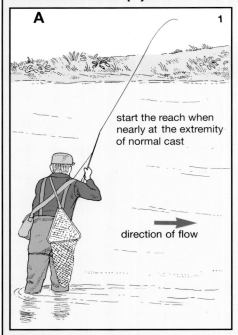

A 1

start the reach when nearly at the extremity of normal cast

direction of flow

2

sweep arm to side (upstream)

3

slack line stops the leader from dragging

1. Make an overhead cast. The line begins to unfurl forward, pulling excess line through the rod rings.

2. Move your rod left (or upstream) *as the fly line continues to shoot* smoothly through the rod rings.

3. When the fly is just upstream of the trout, stop the line. You now have a large upstream belly in the line.

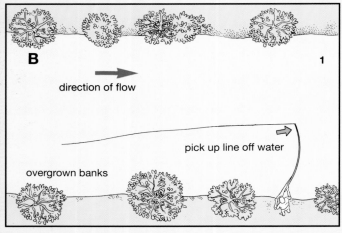

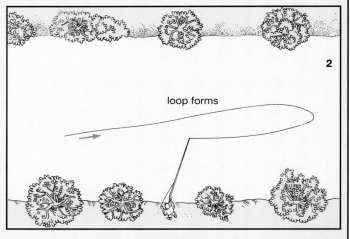

B 1

direction of flow

pick up line off water

overgrown banks

2

loop forms

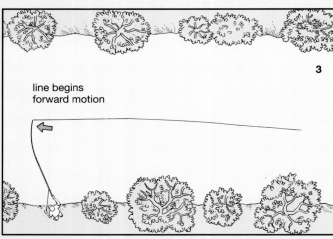

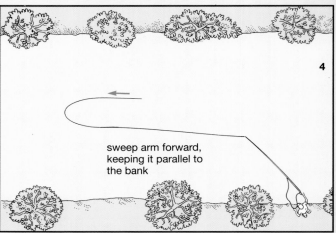

3

line begins forward motion

4

sweep arm forward, keeping it parallel to the bank

1. Face the direction in which you want to cast. Bring the rod back to 1pm. *Keep the rod parallel to the water during the cast.*

2 & 3. The line shoots back in a tight loop. When the line is nearly unrolled, bring the rod forward or towards the left.

4. Stop the rod at about 10am. The line shoots forward in a tight loop, and the fly swings around towards the target.

Mid-water nymph fishing

Knowing how and when to fish the mid-water zone in rivers will increase your catch rate. John Roberts explains the basics of mid-water nymphing and suggests two effective techniques for you to try.

▼ *Where there are weeds, trout sometimes position themselves in mid-water to take drifting nymphs. Weedless rivers see little trout activity in mid-water, except during a hatch.*

Weedy chalk streams such as this crystal clear carrier of the Itchen are perfect places to use the Sawyer Method.

The two main feeding zones in a trout stream are on the river bed and on or just below the surface of the water. The distances between the zones may vary from a few inches to several feet, depending on the depth of water.

In a weedless river the only time mid-water becomes a feeding zone is during a hatch when trout and grayling follow emerging flies as they head for the surface. When hatches aren't underway, the fish look for food along the bottom (and possibly on the surface for any terrestrials which may have fallen in or been blown on the water). The mid-water zone is barren.

But in weedy streams and rivers the mid-water zone often holds trout. The current in this zone carries nymphs and shrimps dislodged from the weeds. No insects live in mid-water except among the weeds. Trout learn that food can be found downstream of a clump of weeds and often adopt positions in mid-water while searching for food.

The two essential mid-water techniques, the Leisenring Lift and the Sawyer Method, involve moving the nymph. The fly's ascending motion induces the fish to take. Both were developed on weedy chalk or limestone-based rivers.

▼ *Caddis, shrimp and nymph patterns work exceptionally well whether you're casting to visible trout or just likely lies.*

From left to right, the flies are the following: Goldhead Caddis (size 14); Red Spot Shrimp (14); Grey Goose Nymph (16).

▲ *John Roberts fishes a nymph upstream on a weedy, Yorkshire river.*
On most rivers fishing upstream is the norm. Check it's allowed before fishing downstream.

The Leisenring Lift

American Jim Leisenring developed a technique of inducing a trout to take a nymph in mid-water a couple of decades before Sawyer devised his method. The technique, called the Leisenring Lift, was originally used on visible fish, but you can also try it in areas where you can't see the fish but expect trout and grayling to be.

The artificial nymph is fished to represent a natural moving to the surface. The Leisenring Lift is especially effective when a hatch is underway (but it can also work when there isn't much fly activity). A drifting nymph that suddenly rises towards the surface is likely to be devoured pretty quickly if a trout is watching nearby.

Locate a fish (or prospective fish-holding area), and move upstream of it (so you are fishing downstream). With a floating line cast slightly farther upstream to allow the fly to sink, taking into account current speed, depth and the sinking rate of the nymph. Keep the rod tip low.

You want the nymph to fish dead-drift at the same level as the trout, so line mending is usually essential to avoid drag. When the fly is 30-45cm (12-18in) in front of the trout, raise the rod tip (there should be no slack line at this point). This causes the nymph to lift – imitating a hatching caddis or nymph ascending to the surface – and swing to one side. You can either leave the nymph to rise to the surface smoothly and uniformly or stop the rod briefly at intervals to produce an uneven rise.

When you're fishing to unsighted fish, the takes are felt through the line or seen by watching the line move. To set the hook, keep lifting the rod upwards while pulling the line downwards with your other hand.

One variation when fishing blind is to drop the rod tip after completing a fruitless

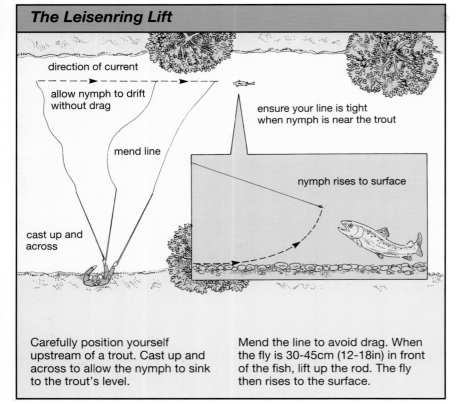

The Leisenring Lift

direction of current

allow nymph to drift without drag

mend line

ensure your line is tight when nymph is near the trout

nymph rises to surface

cast up and across

Carefully position yourself upstream of a trout. Cast up and across to allow the nymph to sink to the trout's level.

Mend the line to avoid drag. When the fly is 30-45cm (12-18in) in front of the fish, lift up the rod. The fly then rises to the surface.

► *Whether you stalk individual fish or try likely lies, the Sawyer Method and Leisenring Lift can help you to catch trout such as these three fine wild river browns.*

Two success stories

"I can attribute my biggest ever river brown trout of 3lb 9oz to the Leisenring Lift," says John. "In a clear chalk stream I stalked the big fish. It refused every pattern I threw at it. But I soon realized the movement of the fly was the key, not the pattern. Just as the fly began to lift, the trout lunged at it.

"When I fish with a bug for autumn grayling it is quite possible for the whole shoal to eye the fly with suspicion as it drifts through. The Sawyer Method solves the problem. The movement is the trigger for the fish to hit the fly."

lift, and allow the nymph to sink again. By lifting the rod again the procedure is repeated a little way downstream.

The Sawyer Method

Frank Sawyer, a riverkeeper on the Wiltshire Avon, developed a style of nymph fishing during the 1950s appropriate to waters where trout expect to find drifting food well below the surface.

One of Sawyer's requirements was to be able to see the fish and the nymph. Obviously for this to be possible you need clear water and must fish at fairly close range. Trout spotting on a clear, slow moving stream isn't too difficult.

But you don't have to limit yourself to clear water – you can also try the Sawyer Method when fishing for unseen trout or grayling. Just use it on parts of the river or stream where you expect fish to be.

To begin, set up with a floating line and a nymph such as a Pheasant Tail or Grey Goose. Single out a trout (or likely fish-holding area), and make sure you are downstream of the fish.

Cast up and across, allowing the nymph to drift without drag. When the fly is within inches of the trout, raise the rod tip slightly

The Sawyer Method or Induced Take

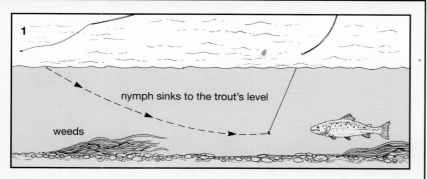

1

nymph sinks to the trout's level

weeds

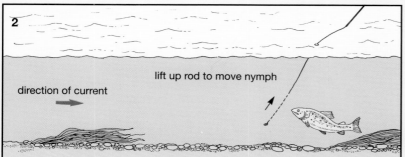

2

direction of current

lift up rod to move nymph

1. Find a fish or likely holding area. Take into account the speed of the current, the depth and the weight of the fly. Make a delicate cast upstream and across (slapping the water with the line spooks the fish).

2. When the fly is 3-15cm (1-6in) in front of the trout, lift the rod. This causes the fly to rise in the water (or sometimes to swing to the side). Strike gently when you see or feel the fish take the fly.

Tip *Fine enough to fool but strong enough to hold*

Light leaders (down to 2lb/0.9kg) are essential for success in ultra-clear water. But remember – don't lift up too eagerly when a trout takes. Strike gently to avoid break-offs – common when you're trying the Sawyer Method and Leisenring Lift.

Another thing to bear in mind is weed. Will your leader hold if the trout entangles itself in a weed bed? If the fish does manage to reach the haven of a clump of starwort, give it some slack line. The fish may just swim out again. If that fails and the water is shallow enough, carefully wade to the area and try to lead the trout into clear water.

▲ Nymph fishing using the Sawyer Method on the Kentish Stour. As long as you wade slowly, carefully and quietly, you can get close to trout when moving upstream to them.

▼ The fruits of your efforts can be fish such as this fine 1½lb (0.7kg) grayling. But practice and perseverance are the keys.

– this causes the nymph to rise about 15cm (6in). After the fish takes the nymph, strike gently before the trout spits the fly out. Stalking trout and grayling and watching for their reactions to your fly are exciting, to say the least.

The Sawyer Method requires a repertoire of skills to catch regularly: accurate casting, adroit line control and excellent eyesight to spot takes. You also need the reflexes to beat Jesse James to the draw – a trout can take in a fly then reject it in a flash.

If you can't see the fish you're casting to, the movement of the leader or fly line indicates a take. It may stop abruptly or twitch insignificantly. It may even dart forward as a trout inhales your fly.

The most important feature of the Sawyer Method is the nymph's rising movement just in front of the fish: this is what triggers the trout into taking.

Frank Sawyer developed a series of weighted nymphs for mid-water fishing. Prior to his innovations, most artificials were unweighted and fished just below the surface film. He devised slim nymphs such as the Pheasant Tail and Grey Goose Nymphs (which have now established a world-wide reputation) without hackles. The underbody of copper wire helped them to sink quickly.

Nymph patterns

It is essential that all artificials should be weighted – and don't spare the lead. They need to sink quickly to reach the required depth. In addition to the Pheasant Tail and Grey Goose Nymphs, any other natural imitations of shrimps, upwinged nymphs or emerging caddis work well. Although imitations should match a natural for size, shape and colour, it is the movement of the fly that is the key to success in these two techniques. Proficiency doesn't come overnight – the more you practice both methods, the more trout you catch.

Advanced nymphing

The bottom is probably the most overlooked and underfished part of a river. John Roberts explains four effective methods of reaching trout lying on the bottom.

Tip The lead game

Tie the bulk of your lead along the top (the outside) of the hookshank. That way the fly rides over the bottom with the hookpoint up, lessening the chances of getting snagged on rocks or debris.

▼ *In deep, fast water you want to get your fly to the bottom quickly and keep it there.*

Brooks' method or the downstream dead-drift is suitable here.

The river bed is a fishing zone that needs to be explored – especially when you consider the amount of time trout spend there and the vast store of food it contains. In sea and coarse fishing the bottom is the major target area – only in river fly fishing has it been overlooked.

During a hatch of flies or when other food is available at the surface, trout adopt positions in the upper layers of the river. In a weedy stream shrimps and nymphs often dislodge from the weeds and drift in mid-water. But nearly all the trout's subsurface food comes from the stream bed. For much of the trout season you can find trout lying on the river bed.

When there is a minimum of fly activity – as in early spring – trout stay deep. In the low water and bright sunlight of summer and early autumn, deep, cool water along with calm pockets close to the river bed in the well-oxygenated riffles are attractive lies for trout.

Depth is relative: in the riffles it may mean only 30cm (12in), but in the pools it's possible to fish in water 1.8m (6ft) deep or deeper, depending on the speed of the current. The main point is that no matter how deep the water, the trout are usually on the bottom – so you must present your fly there. One of the most influential fly fishers of all time, American Lee Wulff, said, "Since that's where the trout are most of the time, deep-drifting nymphs are probably the single most effective way of taking trout."

It is essential to use weight in the dressing of a nymph. The amount of lead depends on the depth to be fished, how much time the fly has to sink and the speed of flow of the river. Carry the same patterns in several different weights to experiment with. Additional weight – a split shot on the line above the nymph or a sinking braided leader – also gets your fly to the bottom and keeps it there. A floating line is standard for 95% of nymph fishing. But one technique – the live nymph – requires the use of a sinking (or fast-sinking) line.

The following are some of the best methods to tempt hard-to-reach river trout or grayling in deep water (up to 3.6m/12ft) with drag-free presentations.

Brooks' method

American Charles Brooks devised an excellent deep-nymph technique for high and very fast water using lead-core fly line. The method has been amended slightly with the introduction of fast-sinking braided leaders, which are just as effective and make it easier to modify your floating line.

Brooks opened up fast-water fishing areas which many anglers previously believed to be unfishable (because the nymph wouldn't fish along the bottom).

Though not many anglers fish in fast water, trout are there, hugging the bottom in calm pockets etched on the river bed. Since the fish have poor visibility and impaired hearing in fast, turbulent water, you can come near your quarry and use short casts to control the line much easier than in long-range fishing.

To begin, attach a fast-sinking braided leader (Roman Moser or Airflo) to a floating line. At the end of the braided section connect a 60-90cm (2-3ft) length of level nylon of about 5lb (2.3kg) b.s. Tie on a heavily weighted nymph.

Cast upstream and across. The heavy nymph and leader sink rapidly as they drift towards the effective fishing zone – the area opposite and just below you. Hold your rod high to keep as much line off the water as possible.

As the line drifts downstream, track your body around and lower the rod. Watch the end of the line for any sudden movements, indicating a take. At the end of the drift the current causes the leader and nymph to lift; this rising away from the stream bed often prompts a take from a fish. After fishing through an area a few times, move up or downstream or extend the cast across the current. Trout have to hit drifting food hard, so takes are usually very positive.

Note that some of the heaviest leaders

Well served – even in the dead of winter

"Brooks' variation," says John, "serves me well when fishing in winter for grayling. North Yorkshire rivers are often high during the winter, and for the most part big grayling stay right on the river bed in deep water.

"Even when there is snow on the ground and during the most unpleasant weather it is possible to catch fish by using this method."

Flies for deep nymphing

Make sure you have a range of patterns in various weights, including some real heavyweights. These are some of John Roberts' favourites for tempting big brown trout and grayling.

1. Stonefly Nymph
2. Leadhead
3. Gold Head Hare's Ear
4. Gold Head Killer Bug
5. Edwards' Shrimp
6. Caseless Caddis Larva

pull down the end of the fly line. Buoyant strike indicators are invaluable for detecting takes. With its fluorescent tip section, Cortland Nymph Line can also help you spot takes in fast water.

Fishing Brooks' variation on a fast-flowing river

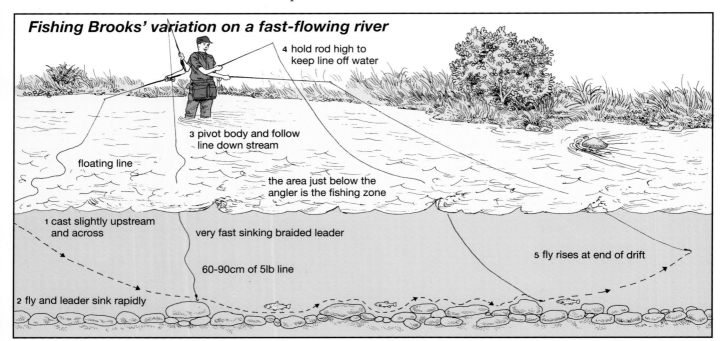

4 hold rod high to keep line off water

3 pivot body and follow line down stream

floating line

the area just below the angler is the fishing zone

1 cast slightly upstream and across

very fast sinking braided leader

60-90cm of 5lb line

5 fly rises at end of drift

2 fly and leader sink rapidly

When to fish a deep nymph

Fishing deep water for trout with a heavy nymph comes into its own in the early season – late March and early April – when the air and water temperatures are cold and the trout are down deep in slow water, expending as little energy as possible.

► *Rain-fed rivers often yield surprisingly big trout. This angler, fishing on the River Whiteadder (in The Borders Region), nets a brown of about 3lb (1.4kg).*

Downstream dead-drift

With this method the nymph fishes close to the bottom and drifts in a natural manner downstream of you. You can use the downstream dead-drift in fast-flowing stretches of water, pools, deep runs and other features, but keep the weight of the flies relative to the feature you are fishing. A fly which is too heavy catches on the bottom again and again.

As in all methods, a long rod allows better line control. With a weighted leader, if necessary, cast the nymph up and across. Follow the line downstream. To prevent drag from forming, mend where needed. When the fly is opposite you it's fishing along the bottom and continues to do so, as in Brooks' method.

But instead of allowing the line to swing around and lift the nymph up at the end of the drift, pay out line from the reel and shake it through the rod to create slack. This effectively increases the area downstream that the nymph fishes naturally along the bottom. If you pay out too much slack, you may lose control and miss takes. Paying out not enough may cause the line to tighten, lifting the nymph from the bottom. Again, watch the strike indicator or fly line for any sudden movement.

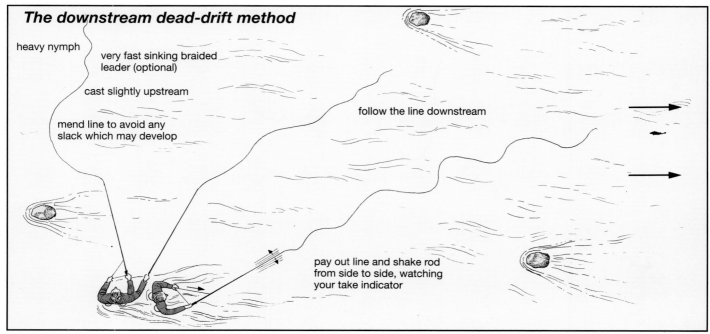

The downstream dead-drift method

heavy nymph

very fast sinking braided leader (optional)

cast slightly upstream

mend line to avoid any slack which may develop

follow the line downstream

pay out line and shake rod from side to side, watching your take indicator

The rolling or dragged nymph

Neil Patterson, fishing for fastidious River Kennet trout, invented the name of this technique, though it has been around a while. The rolling or dragged nymph is effective only on visible fish because it requires the angler to manipulate the fly delicately before it drifts past the fish.

From a position across and below the trout, cast upstream of the fish so that by the time the nymph sinks to the trout's depth, it is about 30cm (12in) upstream of the fish. As the fly drifts closer to the trout, draw it to one side. A dragged or rolled nymph moving away diagonally often induces reluctant trout to feed. Watch the fish carefully because it may be impossible to see the nymph. If the trout moves, strike.

Pinch a split shot 45cm (18in) above the nymph to make it sink faster if necessary.

The live nymph technique

This method uses either a fast-sinking line and a short leader or a floating line with a fast-sinking braided leader. Choose a heavily weighted nymph. For fast water attach a 5ft (1.5m) leader, but lengthen it to 12ft (3.6m) for slower water. The live nymph technique imitates crawling nymphs and caddis edging their way across or upstream.

Cast across and downstream. By the time the line and leader have swung around and are directly downstream of you, they should be on the bottom. Retrieve the nymph upstream. Vary the retrieve speed and rhythm until you are successful. As a general rule, a fast current requires slow pulls and a slow current fast pulls.

The rolling nymph

when fly is about 30cm upstream of the trout, it should have sunk to the bottom

drag or roll nymph to one side by lifting rod

visible fish

if fish moves, strike

The live nymph technique

cast down and across river

fast-sinking line

retrieve fly upstream, varying rate of retrieve

heavily weighted nymph

line and leader are lying on river bed

◄ ▼ *Large, stream-wise resident brown trout (left) spend a lot of time on the bottom. Fishing the pools (below) with a heavy nymph or even a lure is sometimes the only way of catching them.*

Chalk streams for trout

The vast weed growth on England's startlingly clear chalk streams creates perfect resting and feeding places for trout, says river fly fishing expert Charles Jardine.

Fishing for trout in summer on one of the rare, idyllic chalk streams of Southern England is something all too few anglers experience these days – the expense and difficulty of booking puts it out of the reach of most. But should the chance come your way, you'll find it pays to understand what makes chalk streams special.

▼ *A beautiful rainbow comes to the net from this clear, reed-fringed stream on a fine day in late summer – tempted by a dry fly.*

Streams to try

The problem with chalk streams is that there are not very many of them. Since they offer such magnificent fishing, owners charge heavily for fishing rights. They are also booked up months in advance. The fisheries listed here offer some day ticket fishing at a reasonable price.
● **Dever Springs Trout Fishery,** near Andover, Hants. (Tel 0264 72592.)
● **Rockbourne Trout Fishery,** Rockbourne, Fordingbridge, Hampshire SP6 1QG. (Tel 07253 603 or 0425 52479.)
● **Rooksbury Mill Trout Fishery,** Rooksbury Road, Andover, Hampshire. (Tel 0264 52921.)
● **Powder Mills Fishery** (part of Albury Estate Fisheries), Chilworth, near Guildford, Surrey. (Tel 0483 570419.)

Since all rivers and streams owe their existence to rain, you might expect them all to have a similar flow and appearance – but this is far from the case.

The streams that thread their way down mountains and hillsides and tumble through valleys – although fed to a certain extent from springs – rely almost entirely for their water on rainfall and snowfall. They trickle down or run in spate according to how little or how much water has fallen to swell the flow. Chalk streams are quite different. Their water comes mainly from springs fed by deep underground resources (aquafers) which collect and hold huge amounts of rainwater.

As a direct result the true chalk stream offers fish one of the richest, most stable of all freshwater habitats. The chalk stream is 'born' on the downlands of eastern and southern England. Rain works its way through the porous chalk, gathering calcium, phosphates and other nutrients, and comes to rest in aquafers deep below the surface. Eventually the water appears in springs at ground level, creating the infant chalk stream. It can take four months – or even longer – for the water to surface in a spring after falling as rain.

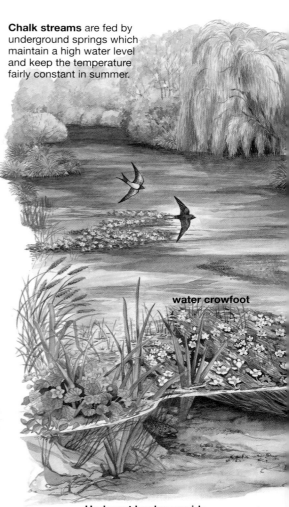

Chalk streams are fed by underground springs which maintain a high water level and keep the temperature fairly constant in summer.

water crowfoot

Undercut banks provide sheltered lies for trout and grayling.

Unique features

This process of delay creates a variety of special features. The temperature of the water is remarkably stable. Even in the warmest weather it is rare for a chalk stream to rise above 12°C (54°F) – or to fall lower than 9°C (48°F) in cold weather.

The ever-present system of springs, often along the river's entire length, provides a con-

▲ *Chalk streams are famous for their lush growth of weed which provides trout with excellent cover and also harbours a host of insects for food. Hollows in undercut banks are favourite lies for the fish.*

▶ *The extreme clarity of most chalk streams means it's essential to approach the water with extreme stealth and caution – this dry fly angler on the River Itchen has found a handy patch of tall plants to disguise his presence.*

SUMMER ON A SOUTHERN CHALK STREAM

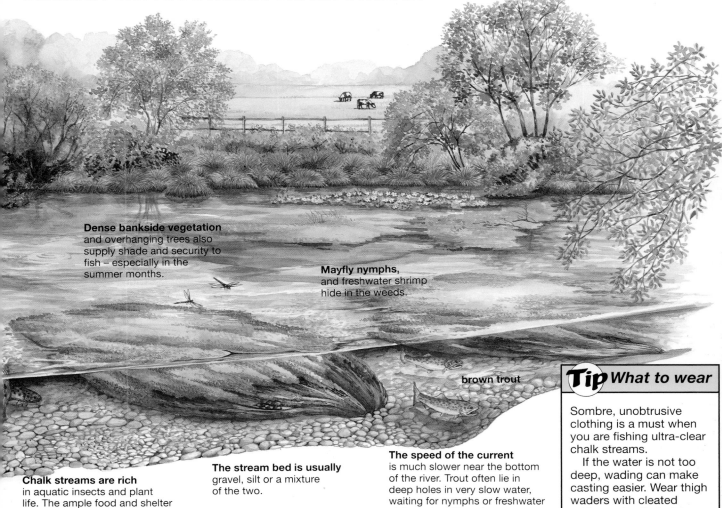

Dense bankside vegetation and overhanging trees also supply shade and security to fish – especially in the summer months.

Mayfly nymphs, and freshwater shrimp hide in the weeds.

brown trout

Chalk streams are rich in aquatic insects and plant life. The ample food and shelter often support large numbers of big river trout.

The stream bed is usually gravel, silt or a mixture of the two.

The speed of the current is much slower near the bottom of the river. Trout often lie in deep holes in very slow water, waiting for nymphs or freshwater shrimps to drift past.

> **Tip** **What to wear**
>
> Sombre, unobtrusive clothing is a must when you are fishing ultra-clear chalk streams.
>
> If the water is not too deep, wading can make casting easier. Wear thigh waders with cleated rubber soles that give a good grip on gravel, but bear in mind that wading isn't allowed everywhere.

sistent level of water and also a permanent saturation of vital calcium, nitrates and carbon dioxides. These, in turn, give rise to the startling clarity and purity of chalk streams.

Speed of flow is also fairly constant. A chalk stream is far less likely to flood or suffer the huge variation in flow of other rivers. Flow in a chalk stream is balanced, though swift – it runs at about 4mph (fast walking pace) along its length from source to mouth. Flow of water at the surface is much faster than it is deeper down.

Finding trout lies

These rich, stable conditions mean plant and animal life prospers. Anglers often think chalk streams are for game fish only – even now most of the larger rivers have salmon and sea trout runs, though they are more familiar as trout rivers. But the richness of chalk streams in fact encourages most running water fish – roach, dace, barbel, chub, pike and grayling can all reach specimen weights here.

Weed growth in chalk streams is heavy, rooted in the gravelly or pebbly bed. Look for trout sheltering among the thick swathes of

water crowfoot and banks of starwort that create excellent lies in the channels – perfect resting and feeding places for the fish.

Man-made hatch pools and weir pools, with their reverse flows and overhanging trees, are all-important fish-attracting features. The hatch pool pushes water through a small controlled opening, creating a mini weir pool. This makes for a fast central cur-

▼ *All's serene on the Itchen at Abbots Worthy near Winchester. Where weed growth is not too dense, spend some time studying the water for signs of fish.*

rent which divides and reverses to either side. Trout lie in this highly oxygenated area, waiting for food to come their way.

Overhanging trees on any water offer fish abundant security and shade. They are not so important in chalk streams, but they are still places the canny fly fisherman finds well worth investigating – lots of flies and grubs fall on the water from them and the fish appreciate the shade when the rest of the stream is in bright sunshine.

Undercut banks Trout favour holes and lies tucked under the banks and hollowed by erosion and water movement. The fish are often shielded by reeds, grasses and other plants that also harbour a variety of insects on which the fish feed. These are places you should explore, though because they are so close to the bank, you'll need to exercise extreme caution and stealth.

Follow the feeding The lush weed growth, which has to be cut at regular intervals on most streams to regulate flow and avoid localized flooding, harbours a vast array of aquatic insects. Most chalk streams have a healthy population of ephemerals (upwinged mayflies) and caddis (sedges), as well as small two-winged flies (diptera) such as midges and smuts. Every time you go down to the water to fish, check to see if the trout are feeding on one insect to the exclusion of others. When they are – imitation is the order of the day. Most fly fishing on chalk streams is concerned with the use of an imitation of an upwinged nymph (wet) or a dun (adult, dry), though a dry sedge, especially near nightfall in the

▲ *Retrieving line on the River Wylye in Wiltshire. The white flowers are water crowfoot. The weed growth on streams like this is often so dense that it has to be cut and cleared several times a year.*

◄ *A healthy brownie is returned to its home in the River Test. The gravelly river bottom here is typical of chalk streams. This angler is wearing polarizing glasses – vital for spotting fish.*

summer, can be deadly. You'll find that fishing upstream with a dry fly is the only permitted method on most chalk streams until August, when a nymph may be used.

Check the flow Although the variation of flow in a chalk stream is not as dramatic as it is in other types of river, different depths do affect the speed of the water. Some sections offer elongated shallows which the fish seem to favour during the evening. Slower, deeper sections often hold larger trout, but don't be deceived into choosing larger flies. Colonies of small diptera and other insects mean it's essential to use tiny flies (size 18-20) on fine tippets of 1½-2lb/0.7-0.9kg b.s.

Overall, however, a chalk stream averages a depth of 1.2-1.8m (4-6ft) and is fairly uniform along its length – making trout location fairly constant.

Chalk streams

These are some of the chalk streams of E. and S. England. The lower reaches of some do not have all the chalk stream features.
● **Berkshire** R. Lambourn; R. Kennet.
● **Buckinghamshire** R. Chess.
● **Dorset** R. Frome; R. Piddle; R. Stour.
● **Hampshire** R. Avon; R. Itchen; R. Test.
● **Hertfordshire** R. Lea (above Chingford).
● **Humberside** Foston Beck and Driffield Beck (tributaries of R. Hull).
● **Wiltshire** R. Wylye.

Baitfishing for trout

Fly fishing is not the only way you can catch trout. Baitfishing for the wild brown trout in Scottish and Welsh waters is a highly successful, exciting technique.

The rivers and lakes of Scotland and Wales are full of all sorts of fish but the brown trout is by far the most popular. Trout fishing is there for the taking at very little cost. In many places all you need do is get the permission of the riparian owners – this is important since it is their land you're treading on. Go on – ask.

Choice of bait

Take plenty of bait with you and look after it carefully so it doesn't spoil. One way to be safe is to order extra bait from a tackle shop near where you are fishing.

Worms Several species of worm attract trout. You can dig lobworms from your own garden, and find brandlings and redworms in dung heaps and compost heaps.

Keep the worms in a clean jar or plastic box with some fresh moss. Lobworms take about a week to toughen up while brandlings take two to three days.

Maggots Buy large white, red, bronze or yellow maggots and keep them dry and plump by putting them into either fresh sawdust, maize meal or a little bran. Store them in the fridge or a cold, dark place until you are ready to use them. Don't overcrowd them and they won't let you down when you fish with them.

Minnows and bullheads These little fishes provide some of the best sport when baitfishing. You can catch them in a jar or minnow trap by laying the trap, baited with bread, in a small stream with the mouth facing the direction of the current. The minnows swim in but can't get out again. Put them in a bucket of clean water, and use an aerator pump to keep them healthy.

Naturals Stonefly nymphs and caddis larvae, crayfish, grasshoppers, leeches, slugs, docken grubs and so on are all worth a try.

▼ *You can freeline, floatfish or leger a juicy lobworm for trout – match your method to the water and you should pick up some lovely specimens.*

▲ *Baitfishing for trout in spring on a small fast-flowing river. Check that baitfishing is allowed BEFORE you start fishing.*

Go barbless

When you're baitfishing, you'll find the trout often take the hook very deeply – so if you plan to release the fish at once, use barbless hooks and strike as quickly as you can.

Not everyone succeeds with them, but some anglers swear by them.

The tackle you need

Tackle for this technique is much like that used in coarse fishing.

Hooks Use a single hook – say a size 12 – for worms, maggots and naturals and for lip-hooking a minnow. Or, to increase your chances of keeping a fish on the hook, choose a double hook – sizes 14 and 16 are usually successful, especially for holding on to a large specimen.

Another useful set-up is the Pennell – two hooks tied in tandem. It's good for hooking on minnows and naturals, giving them a bit more support when casting. An exten-

sion of the Pennell is the Stewart – a three-hook set-up useful when the fish are nipping the tails off the worms. This little outfit soon puts a stop to that.

Floats You need a selection of floats – perhaps a couple of each of the following kinds: stick floats, small grayling floats and a few small bubble floats. You also need split shot and a few small ¼-½ oz pear or ball weights. Take some swivels and anti-kink vanes.

Rods and reels The ideal rod is small – no more than 7-11ft (2-3.4m) long – and light but strong enough to cope with a big fish.

Using a bullhead deadbait

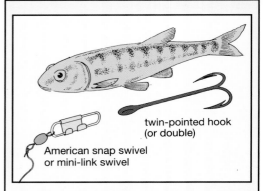

twin-pointed hook (or double)

American snap swivel or mini-link swivel

1. If you use a double or twin-pointed hook it can help a lot to increase your overall hooking potential.

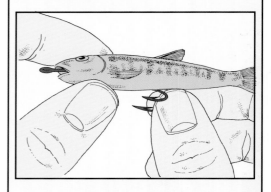

2. For a secure hold, pass the shank of the hook through the opening near the bullhead's anal fin.

3. Make sure the hook shank comes out at the baitfish's mouth. Attach with an American snap swivel.

Livebait and deadbait rigs

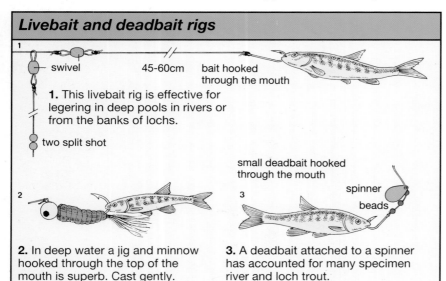

swivel   45-60cm   bait hooked through the mouth

1. This livebait rig is effective for legering in deep pools in rivers or from the banks of lochs.

two split shot

small deadbait hooked through the mouth

spinner

beads

2. In deep water a jig and minnow hooked through the top of the mouth is superb. Cast gently.

3. A deadbait attached to a spinner has accounted for many specimen river and loch trout.

Hooking a caddis larva

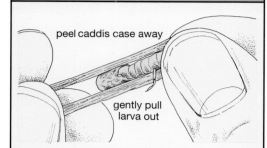

peel caddis case away

gently pull larva out

Carefully peel or break away small parts of the case until you can grasp the larva. Pull it out slowly, making sure you don't break it in two (it's very fragile).

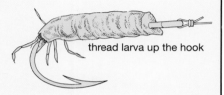

thread larva up the hook

An alternative to breaking up the caddis case is to push the soft larva out very gently using a small paintbrush.

Thread the larva carefully up the hook, tail first, or (somewhat easier) you can hook it through the tail end.

▲ *Trout absolutely love all kinds and colours of maggots. Take along red, bronze or yellow ones as well as large whites.*

▼ *Keep worms for several days to toughen them up. You'll benefit when you put them on the hook. There's nothing worse than trying to hook up a limp, foul-smelling worm.*

On the day you go fishing put a little sand in the bottom of your jar. This gives you a much better grip on the slippery bait.

You can use a spinning reel for loch fishing and a centrepin for river work, or a spinning reel for both. You don't need more than 6lb monofilament – but don't use less than 3lb line.

Landing net A small landing net is useful. One with a long handle is a good idea, especially for river work.

Using baits for trout

As in coarse fishing, there are various different ways to fish natural baits. Here are just a few of the more important ones.

Freelining One of the easiest methods of using naturals is freelining – fishing without a float or weight. It can be deadly in rivers when trout are lying in water less than 1m (3ft) deep. Freelining isn't suitable when the fish are in deep, fast flowing water – in runs or glides – because the bait fishes near the surface, but if the fish move up in the water and begin taking hatching insects, it can work well. The method succeeds perfectly well in a deep, still pool.

To begin freelining, simply hook a worm, for example, to a size 12 hook (a good general size for river browns), cast across the current and allow the bait to swing round. Or, drop the bait in and let the current take it. Feather the line smoothly to avoid large

Tip Don't knock the docken

All the live baits mentioned have a fair rate of success, but one that's especially potent is the docken grub – the larva of the ghost moth – that lives among the roots of dock. Dig around the base of a dock – or docken – plant (the one that soothes nettle stings). Once you've found a few of the brownish, large grubs, off you go – fill your bag with fish!

Docken grubs are better on rivers than lochs – and even the wily sea trout will take one occasionally.

bellies of slack line. Freelining upstream makes bite detection difficult, but keeping a tight line by picking up the slack helps.

Takes are more often felt than seen, especially in fast water, though in slow-moving stretches you may see the fish hit the bait.

Freelining in lochs is often successful when the fish are feeding near the surface.

Float fishing on rivers allows you to present the bait at a precise depth over long distances. For example, a 20m (22yd) fast glide (about 1m/3ft deep) may have trout lying hard along the stony bottom. By setting the float just short of depth and spacing the shot close to the hook, your bait fishes just off the bottom, minimizing your chances of getting snagged. The float also serves as an excellent bite indicator.

Jig and minnow/leech combo Casting a spinner, plug or jig is an effective technique in itself – the movement serves to attract trout. Adding a deadbait, worm or leech to a jig gives it smell as well as movement and makes it even more lifelike. Use jigs in lochs and deep sections of rivers by bouncing them off the bottom in quick lifts.

Legering A seldom-used technique for trout, legering exploits the fish's excellent sense of smell. You can leger in lochs, tarns and even rivers.

Their defences down, larger trout become active at night. A juicy lobworm or small livebait legered hard along the bottom of a deep, swirling pool can draw many fish, especially the large ones. Success doesn't depend on your approach alongside the bank (as with freelining), your casting or the weather conditions. Legering has built-in stealth in that, after casting into a likely pool, you wait for the fish to come to you – instead of your going to the fish. The trout comes to you unwary, its belly empty, and seldom turns down your offering.

▲ *Playing a trout on coarse tackle. Scotland is a far cry from trout fisheries down south. There is plenty of room, fresh air – and solitude.*

◄ *A fine catch of loch brown trout – caught on legered baits. Legering is a good method at dusk when the fish are hungriest.*

Tip **Timely tips**

● Do remember to dress for the weather in Scotland – it can be pretty chilly and wet even in the height of summer.
● If you come to Scotland in summer, don't forget the insect repellant.

Fishing North Country wet flies

Yorkshireman, expert fly-tyer and river angler, Oliver Edwards explains two methods of fishing North Country sparsely dressed wet flies. Both upstream and downstream presentations are equally effective for catching rising trout.

What do you need and what river features do you look for to begin North Country fly fishing? Oliver Edwards makes a few suggestions about equipment and how best to present your flies.

Tools for the technician

Rods have traditionally erred on the long side (over 10½ft/3.2m) for this style of fishing. But one of 8½-9½ft (2.6-2.9m) long, with what might be classed as a middle action, is ideal – especially if you intend to fish the dry fly and nymph as well. (In fact, to fish with North Country wets all the time – deadly as they sometimes are – would be unwise.) Avoid stiff, poker-like rods.

Match this with a light, single-action reel that has a smooth click ratchet and a well-ventilated drum which can hold a floating DT 5 or 6 and 30m (33yd) of Dacron or 10lb (4.5kg) nylon mono for the backing.

Double tapered lines are recommended rather than weight forward ones. In North Country fly fishing much of your casting is 'picking off and laying down' – long shoots play only a minor role. It's true that you can pick off and lay down a fixed length of weight forward fly line, but its front-heavy profile can result in a clumsy presentation in the hands of a beginner. There is nothing worse than seeing a delivery hit the water like a sack of spuds. The trout don't appreciate it either!

The leader

By tradition the North Country style is fishing with a team of three flies, often called a leash – consisting of a point, a middle and a top dropper.

The make-up of the leader is quite straightforward. For good balance the distance between the three flies should be 36-42in (90-105cm). Measure a length of 2.6lb (1.2kg) mono. Using a double surgeon's knot (two-turn water knot) for connecting the sections of line, knot together an identical second length of the same b.s., leaving a 4in (10cm) tag beyond the knot for the middle dropper. This second length of 2.6lb (1.2kg) mono is connected to an 18in (45cm) length of 3.2lb (1.5kg) mono, again leaving a 4in (10cm) tag beyond the knot for the top

▼ *A River Nidd (Yorkshire) brown trout that fell for a North Country wet fly.*
Because of the heavily tree-lined river banks, you'll need to wade in and fish with short drifts.

dropper. Finally, the other end of this 3.2lb (1.5kg) line is knotted to the fine end of a 3-4ft (0.9-1.2m) steep tapered knotless leader, one that tapers from 12lb to 4lb (5-1.8kg) at the point.

To make the leader manageable and also easy to change, glue the thick end of the steep tapered leader inside one of the modern braided mini-connectors, the type with the small, neat purpose-made loop. Also glue the end of fly line as a permanent feature to a looped mini-connector.

To avoid tangles when casting the three-fly leader, slow down your action slightly, and strive to produce a more open loop with a pause at the end of each back cast. Avoid false casting whenever possible.

Where to start

Ideally, look for a riffle which is moving at a moderate pace – walking speed – and which has a regular popply surface and a depth of 45-60cm (18-24in). The bottom should be an equal mixture of rocks, stones and pebbles. Avoid stretches peppered with boulders, for they throw up standing waves and bubbly 'line drowners' on their downstream side. Such areas are tricky to fish.

Why fish a riffle anyway? First of all, such water is very well oxygenated and is usually home to thousands of aquatic insects. Secondly, it offers good cover for fish. Broken, rippled water makes it difficult for natural predators to detect trout lying on the stream bed. These two reasons alone

ensure that most riffles are usually well stocked with trout and grayling. At certain times of the year – summer in particular – riffles may hold 70% of the river's total fish population.

From the wet-fly fisherman's point of view, the riffle is perfect: the broken surface which hides the trout so effectively also gives the fish an unclear view of the angler. So fishing at short range is practical. Furthermore the rippled surface helps disguise the fakes you are presenting as food. North Country wets generally fish in the upper layers, the very place where surface disturbance and distortion are greatest.

The presentations

Many fly fishermen, when discussing or writing about the North Country style, insist that it must be practised upstream. This is rubbish! They have read too many old books.

Every square yard of river is different, so the fly fisherman must vary his approach and angle of attack. The experienced angler assesses the situation constantly as he starts each new cast. He makes these decisions unconsciously and appears as fluid as the stream he fishes on.

A riffle with a popply surface and a depth of 45-50cm (18-20in) is excellent for fishing the upstream method – especially on a warm day in late May with a hatch of olives just underway. Farther downstream, the water probably gushes through a rocky gulley, pours into a deep angular pool and then runs out through a broad glassy flat. There

▲ *The team of flies is in front of the angler, so he raises the rod to be in direct contact with the flies – and to keep as much of the line off the water as he possibly can.*

are many fish-holding pockets throughout the stretch, yet some areas can be devoid of fish while tenanted at other times of the season. How can anyone who's familiar with Britain's northern rivers seriously suggest that you fish North Country wets correctly only when working upstream? It's nonsense.

However, there's fishing downstream and fishing downstream! Standing stork-like, casting downstream at a 45° angle and then allowing your team of flies to swing back towards the bank in an arc – the popular concept of downstream wet-fly fishing – is definitely out.

To understand fully what the North Country angler is trying to achieve, you must start with the fish and imagine what it expects to see as it gently fins the current. Most food items which the fish see can be classed as small, very small or tiny. The

◄ *Fishing North Country wets early in the morning resulted in this fine brace of wild brown trout from the River Nidd.*

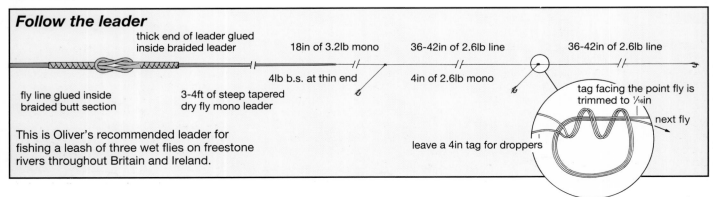

Follow the leader

thick end of leader glued inside braided leader

18in of 3.2lb mono

36-42in of 2.6lb line

36-42in of 2.6lb line

fly line glued inside braided butt section

4lb b.s. at thin end

4in of 2.6lb mono

tag facing the point fly is trimmed to 1⁄16in

3-4ft of steep tapered dry fly mono leader

next fly

This is Oliver's recommended leader for fishing a leash of three wet flies on freestone rivers throughout Britain and Ireland.

leave a 4in tag for droppers

Method one: 'the escalator'

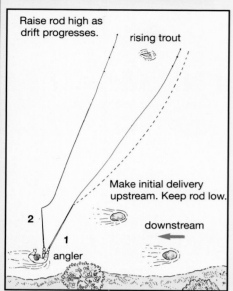

Raise rod high as drift progresses.

rising trout

Make initial delivery upstream. Keep rod low.

downstream

2

1

angler

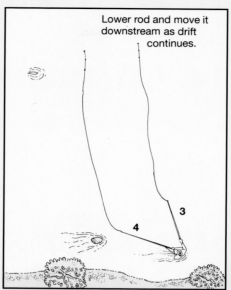

Lower rod and move it downstream as drift continues.

3

4

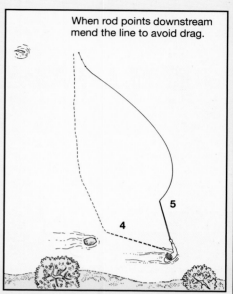

When rod points downstream mend the line to avoid drag.

5

4

The head of a riffle stretches below you for 40m (44yd). Begin by degreasing the leader. Then work out 9-10m (10-11yd) of line, and make your delivery at an upstream angle. Finish the cast with your rod low and parallel to the surface of the water. Mend a small loop upstream **(1)**.

As the line and flies drift downstream, begin raising the rod **(2)** while tracking the rod around with your hand towards your left.

There is no room here for sloppy fishing with lots of uncontrolled slack line. As the flies drift downstream of the position where you are standing **(3)**, begin to lower the rod. When your team of flies is a rod length below your stance, the rod is well lowered. If you allow the flies to continue to drift **(4)**, they will be dragged by the current, putting the trout off.

To avoid this, mend a loop of line upstream with a crisp, well-executed rotating wrist flick.

The mend **(5)** has bought you more dead drift because your rod hand has moved back upstream, with the rod held high again. As the flies continue drifting downstream, again track around with your rod, lowering it as they drift away. The rod passes across your body.

Throughout the drift, be aware of any rogue downstream bellies forming. Mend them immediately. Before the flies begin to drag again, move downstream and recast upstream.

Method two: reach and lean

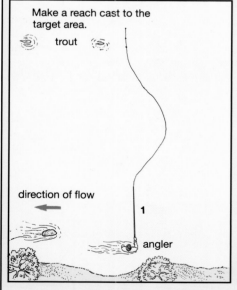

Make a reach cast to the target area.

trout

direction of flow

1

angler

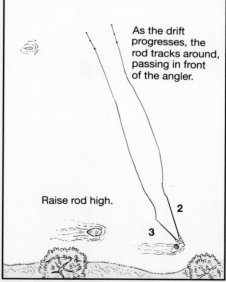

As the drift progresses, the rod tracks around, passing in front of the angler.

Raise rod high.

2

3

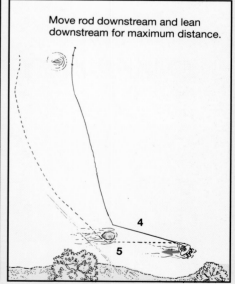

Move rod downstream and lean downstream for maximum distance.

4

5

Trout are rising along the far bank. Stand slightly upstream of the first group of fish. Work out enough line to reach the target zone; then strip off more line (about 1.8-2.1m/6-7ft). The left hand holds the line. The excess hangs down on the surface. Now make your delivery to the target with a reach cast (See Fishing round-up, 18, Game). The flies should land 1m (3ft) upstream of the first fish **(1)**.

As your team of flies drifts towards the first fish **(2 & 3)**, track the rod around your body (as with the escalator method shown above). Keep pace with the flies by raising or lowering the rod as the drift demands. If troublesome bellies form during the drift, carefully mend them out.

Again, takes are often visible, but if there's movement of the line, lift the rod positively, but not too hard.

You can gain some extra drifting time by leaning downstream **(4)**, hence the name 'reach and lean.' The drift is fished out when your rod is pointing downstream **(5)**. At that point, take a step or two downstream and repeat the process.

Both styles of fishing are slightly more difficult – but still possible – for a right-handed person when the river is flowing the other way from that shown here.

nymphs, duns and spinners of various insect orders, as well as myriad diminutive terrestrial creatures which fall from overhanging trees, are trapped either on, in or just below the water surface. As spring bursts forth into the summer, this 'soup' of goodies increases daily and is carried along as if on an endless conveyor belt.

These insects cannot make headway against a strong current. Instead, they have to go with it. At the most, they may make a little progress sideways as they are swept downstream. Even nymphs classed as darter/swimmers are carried downstream as they rise to the surface to emerge.

So upstream or downstream, the trick is to imitate the behaviour of the insects. Strive wherever it is possible to fish the team of flies *dead drift with the current and without drag*.

(See page 115 for detailed instructions on upstream and downstream fishing tactics.)

Ten North Country flies to cover the season

"My selection of flies will not be to everyone's liking. My choice comprises most of the patterns used by myself and friends in the Yorkshire Dales. They are effective wherever you find brisk rivers and streams."

1. Waterhen Bloa (hook sizes 14-16) First choice when large dark olives are hatching.

2. Winter Brown (12-14) Excellent when the medium-sized early brown stonefly and February Reds are hatching.

3. Greenwell's (winged or hackled in 14-16) Useful when the medium olives are on the water.

4. Spring Black (16-20) Despite the name it's more of a summer and autumn fly for imitating small black terrestrials, such as black gnats.

5. Partridge and Orange (14-16) This is my "if you could only have one..." fly. You can take trout on it throughout the season.

6. Brown Owl (14-16) Excellent during low-water, summer conditions. It's useful for hot evenings when small sedges are about.

7. Snipe and Purple (16-20) An old favourite – especially useful when the iron blues are hatching.

8. Starling Bloa (16-20) I cannot find a better pattern for pale wateries in autumn.

9. Dark Needle (14-16) Use during a needle fly hatch.

10. Aphid (18-28) Lethal when the leaves start falling in autumn.

Trout fishing in highland streams

Jon Beer dons his Welly-Waders and dark glasses and takes to the hills in pursuit of upland brownies. He describes the good sport you can have on high – if you are prepared for it.

The uplands of the British Isles are veined with a network of small stony streams that tumble down steep slopes to the softer lowlands where they join together to become the great trout and salmon rivers of the north and west.

Many of the fat fish of the lowlands were hatched in these headstreams where spawning conditions are usually better than in the food-rich silty waters lower down. But many fish stay put in their upland nursery waters, supplying each of these unregarded highland becks, burns, gills – call them what you will – with a resident population of brilliantly speckled wild brown trout.

Flexible fishing

The key to fishing a highland stream is improvisation. Because the hardness and formation of the underlying rock determines the character of a stream, the current

▶ You may have to walk some distance over hilly country to find good spots like this to fish. So do yourself a favour and travel as light as possible. One idea is to carry everything you need on a belt.

Don't forget to include an ultra-light packaway jacket, essential for a long day in the highlands.

on a beck changes from yard to yard, twisting between rocks, cascading in waterfalls into small, deep pools, trickling over gravel or spilling over smooth bedrock.

This is the fascination of fishing in high country. No two becks are alike: each pool must be assessed anew, each cast improvised. You cannot 'go through the motions' on a highland stream.

▼ River Taf Fechan in the Brecon Beacons. The water rushes down in two white wands and splashes into a deep pool which looks like a good spot for a trout. The disturbance created on the surface helps to hide the angler and the line from any keen-eyed fish.

A bottleneck in a pool concentrates the food without creating turbulence, making it a good place to look for trout.

Deep water under a waterfall at the head of a pool is certain to hold trout.

A HIGHLAND STREAM

The richest aquatic larders are in slower pools where pockets of pebbles, gravel and mud have gathered.

Much of the trout's food in small streams falls on to the surface.

The best and biggest trout are usually found in the deepest and most secure lies.

Smaller fish tend to be pushed into less productive shallow water.

Most of the food arrives at the head of the pool first - that's why the biggest trout often wait there.

Pool potential

Brown trout are territorial. A large fish will chase a lesser rival from a good lie – a spot that provides maximum food and security with minimum effort. If you want to catch good fish the trick is to identify the best lies.

Depth On a small upland beck look for depth which provides fish with vital security and shade. By lying deep a trout can survey a wide surface area for anything drifting by or falling on to the surface – and on windswept highlands much of the trout's food arrives that way.

There is another reason why depth is a key feature for good trout. On a highland stream, variations in width and depth and hence speed of water, can be enormous. Long stretches of a steep beck can be scoured to smooth bedrock or large stones where aquatic larvae and nymphs find it hard to cling on and survive.

The richest aquatic larders on these streams are where pockets of pebbles, gravel and detritus have gathered in the slower pools. All this is not lost on the larger trout which elbow lesser fish into the swifter sections.

Observation Never try to spot trout in an upland pool before fishing it. The trout see you long before you see them – and fish in these small waters are easily scared. Search instead for deep pockets and unsuspected holes from as far away and as low down as possible. Try to predict where the deepest parts of the pool are from the way the rocks are tilted across or down the course of the stream. If the pool is deepest at the head where a small waterfall tumbles into it, there is certain to be a trout lurking – possibly a good trout that has lain hidden and unsuspected below the fragmented surface for some time.

▶ *Berry-laden rowan trees (mountain ash) overhanging a lovely stretch of river – its upper reaches are full of highland trout.*

▲ *Instead of trying to spot individual trout, look for deep pockets that might hold good fish. Polarized sunglasses often help.*

Beck and crawl

Approaching the trout is another problem. A typical upland beck is steep and often lies in a steep-sided gully. If you approach a pool from the side you tower over the water, sending any fish bolting for cover. Approaching from upstream again you are considerably higher than the pool and obvious to the trout which lie facing upstream. The best approach on a steep highland beck is from downstream. By standing in the pool below, you can keep low and out of sight of fish in the upper pool.

From this point you can study the pool. Look first for any possible lies close to you. It's very annoying to see a good fish shoot upstream from an unseen lie nearby – not only do you lose that fish but you may well spook another one higher up as well.

Constrictions If the pool is long, look for a narrow neck halfway down. This is a favourite lie, providing a concentration of food and no turbulence for the trout to cope with. The likeliest lie, though, is at the head of the pool if there is depth. This is where much of the food arrives. It also has the

advantage of the most surface disturbance to hide the line and angler from the fish.

Current Look to see how the current affects your line. Accelerating water pulls the bait or fly quickly through the slower water at the head of the pool. Water decelerating down the pool concertinas the line – it's easy to lose touch with the bait or fly this way.

Wind is ever-present on exposed uplands. As always you must improvise – shift your position and adapt your cast to suit each pool.

Wellied wally

It helps to have waders. You may feel a bit of a buffoon wearing waders to stand in a 25cm (10in) deep beck, but you'll feel even dafter stepping into an unseen 60cm (2ft) cleft wearing only wellingtons. Whatever type of footwear you choose, it should have felt or rubber-and-ministud soles, since smooth rock and summer algae can be slippier than winter ice. The best solution is Welly-Waders – studded wellingtons with a lightweight, roll-down wader top.

Fishing a highland beck is a mobile game and you can cover several miles in a day over quite hilly terrain. Your tackle should therefore be as light and as compact as possible. A succesful angler identifies the most likely spots, fishes them carefully and moves on – a couple of casts on each pool and then a climb up to the next or a walk past an unpromising stretch.

Seasonal bonus

Exposed uplands can be cool, but this is sometimes advantageous. When the more noble rivers of the lowlands are hot and dead in the heat of a summer's day, there is

▲ *Glen Einich, Rothiemurchus in the Scottish Highlands. This stretch has relatively easy access to the water.*
Upland streams often have steep banks, so be prepared for some climbing and try not to frighten fish by approaching from an exposed position on a high bank.

Tip Co-ordinated trout

Use an Ordnance Survey map to spot possible highland venues. Look for a highland area where a river, marked by a wide blue line, becomes a thin blue line. Find the nearest town and check the local angling societies or tackle shops for details.

still sport to be had on the highland becks. Again, these small stony rivers of the hills are often still fishable when the lowland rivers are in brown flood. And if you are fishing towards the end of summer there is always the chance of a fat lowland fish making its way into the high waters to spawn. If you can't step across a stream in comfort, then it probably has trout. All you have to do is catch them.

Head for the headwaters

You can find enjoyable fishing on small highland streams in all the regions of Wales in south-west England, in the hills of northern England and throughout Scotland. You get a splendid day's sport for very little cost – fishing for wild trout with no other angler for miles around.

The headwaters of many rivers offer this kind of fishing. The upper reaches of the Wear, Tees and Tyne, Neath and Taff, tributaries of the Wye and Tweed, East and West Dart and the high stretches of Yorkshire rivers are just a few examples to try.

These higher reaches are often controlled by local angling associations (sometimes private) so pick your river and contact them for details.

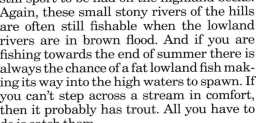

◀ *A brace of early season brown trout taken on the dry fly from the River Usk in Wales.*
Always check open seasons in areas you plan to visit for highland stream fishing.

Tactics for river trout

When you have tried all of the techniques in your arsenal and you still fail to catch stream-wise fish, it's definitely time to try something radically different, says top river angler Cyril Lennox-Brown.

If you're willing to experiment, a whole range of fly fishing tactics (and their many combinations) await to help you tempt more trout from rivers. Here are four unusual tactics to get you started.

Skating a sedge

The many species of sedges may hatch at any time during the day and night throughout the trout season. Artificials such as Moser's Balloon Sedge and Troth's Elk Hair Caddis make excellent search patterns when hatches are sparse, and feeding trout even more so.

Not all sedges take flight immediately they emerge from their nymphal skin. Some flap their wings and hop on the surface film for a long way (mostly up and across the current) in their attempts to fly. Undoubtedly this sustained, concentrated activity can send fish into a feeding frenzy.

After rising to the surface and hatching, large cinnamon sedges shoot towards the shore on top of the water, creating a V-shaped wake on the surface.

▲ *An angler drifts a fly across the current in the startlingly clear water of the River Eden in Cumbria.*

For difficult trout in low, clear and slow-flowing water such as this, try using a minute nymph or North Country wet with a mini strike indicator.

▶ *Wise old Scottish browns such as this may have seen and rejected myriad flies. Catching them may require a different, unorthodox approach.*

Skating an artificial imitates a sedge trying to take off after emerging from the nymphal skin. It also copies a mature female skittering across the surface while depositing eggs.

By just fishing the traditional upstream dead-drift, you dramatically reduce your chances of catching a sedge-feeding fish – especially one crashing in the margins and leaping out of the water to catch its fast-moving prey! Successful dry fly fishing with sedges involves presenting the fly the way the fish expect to see it. Sometimes that means dead-drifting, but most of the time skating is the key to success – whether there's a hatch on or not.

There's more than one way to skate a sedge, and more than one direction for that matter – downstream, across and even upstream.

With a floating line, a buoyant sedge and a well greased 2.7m (9ft) long leader, cast across and down, for example, while keeping the rod up at about a 45° angle to the water. At erratic intervals quickly strip in anywhere between 15-60cm (6-24in) of line at a time. You may also want to try wiggling the rod to accentuate the movement of the artificial fly.

The fly swings downstream while you're retrieving, hopping and skating across the surface to imitate the natural. If the fly dives under the water, try greasing the leader to keep everything afloat.

To fish this method upstream is a little more difficult – you've got to keep the line tight as the fly drifts downstream because there's no drag to keep tension on the line

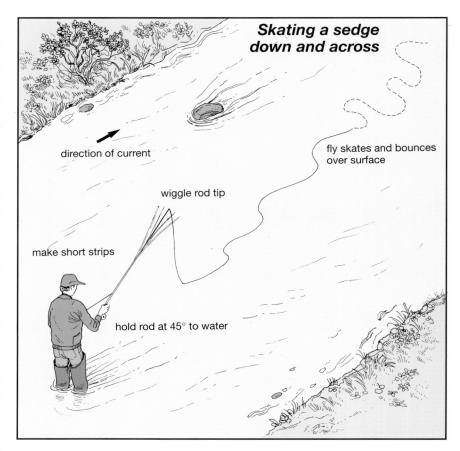

Skating a sedge down and across

direction of current

fly skates and bounces over surface

wiggle rod tip

make short strips

hold rod at 45° to water

and to help move the fly.

Some anglers fish directly downstream. After casting, keep the rod tip 10° below the vertical then make 30-60cm (1-2ft) strips combined with quick wiggles of the rod. It is best to experiment to discover what is most effective for you.

▼ *Skating a sedge during hatchless periods often beguiles a trout or two.*
  Here an angler fishing upstream skates an Elk Hair Caddis on the River Avon in Wiltshire.

▲ **If you're fishing up and across and a trout rises downstream of you, why not use the downstream release to cover it immediately, as this angler is doing? Otherwise, if you're wading in mid-river, you must walk to the bank, move downstream and then cast, putting the fish down in the process.**

Remember, it doesn't just work for fish holding near the bank.

Downstream release

A trout near a grassy, undercut bank rises sporadically to terrestrials blown in by a downstream wind. The wind is a nasty factor to contend with if you want to fish upstream. What's more, you have to face a fly-starved bush just waiting to strand your best efforts at the vice.

Such scenarios are typical on some days when river fly fishing. But by fishing downstream, you can overcome the wind and any obstacles, if the need arises.

Stand well upstream of the fish to keep out of sight. Your aim is to position the fly about 0.9-1.2m (3-4ft) upstream of and in line with the trout.

Cast across and just downstream of the quarry. As the fly swings in the current the tricky part is to bring in line very quickly while raising the rod tip.

When you drop the rod tip, the fly should float without drag right over the fish. If you pay out line from your initial position instead of casting, it's difficult to maintain and control a drag-free drift all the way to the fish.

Flat-water risers

Summer is the time of prolific insect activity. But with such an abundance of food available, trout can be exceedingly choosy about their meals – particularly in slow, clear water. They have a long time to scrutinize their quarry.

It's not unusual to cover rising trout with a suitable dry fly and have it rejected again and again. At these times you can quickly empty the contents of your box, losing your confidence as you do so.

One trick which may just help you catch more fastidious, slow-water trout is to fish minute nymphs or spider patterns in sizes 18-22 just under the surface film. Sawyer's Pheasant Tail and Grey Goose Nymphs as well as the Partridge and Orange, Snipe and Purple and Waterhen and Starling Bloa are all excellent flies for ultra-selective trout.

Fishing a small nymph or North Country wet up or downstream just under the surface isn't new. But using a mini strike indicator positioned a few inches away from the fly is. With a very long, low diameter leader

The downstream release

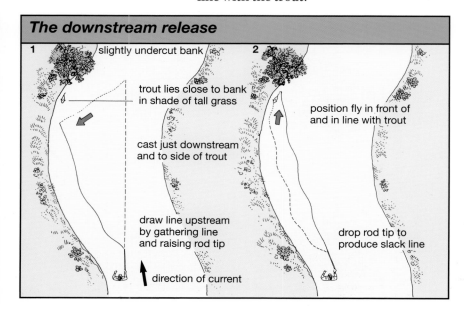

1. slightly undercut bank

trout lies close to bank in shade of tall grass

cast just downstream and to side of trout

draw line upstream by gathering line and raising rod tip

↑ direction of current

2. position fly in front of and in line with trout

drop rod tip to produce slack line

(up to 3.65m/12ft) use a mini strike indicator anywhere from 5-15cm (2-6in) away from the small fly.

To form a mini strike indicator from a flat foam square, cut off a narrow strip (2mm or so). Peel off the protective backing; then *roll* it on the leader near the fly. Fish your small nymph and mini strike indicator dead-drift – either up, across or downstream.

At this time of year the fish may take in and reject your pattern before you can set the hook. A strike indicator registers even the meekest, most half-hearted of takes, allowing you to set the hook. Any hesitation at all should be met with a firm strike.

There shouldn't be the problem of false takes with the indicator positioned so close to the fly unless it is very weedy. If you use a full-sized strike indicator, you might spook the trout.

Fishing a lure

Bullheads (miller's thumbs) form a large part of the trout's diet. Trout take bullheads and small coarse fish when they are available, yet few British anglers fish with imitations of the small fish in rivers. Imitative lures such as Whitlock's Sculpin (bullhead) often catch the bigger river trout, and not many lean, plain Janes.

There are a number of ways to fish a lure. One is simply to fish it dead-drift with the current in a deep pool or fast-moving run, as you would a nymph.

Use a floating line and strike indicator. To begin, cast up and across with a heavily leaded lure, adding slack line to allow the

---

Hitch-hiking gnat

size 10 Elk Hair Caddis

size 24 Griffith's Gnat

30-60cm length of fine monofilament

If you are fly fishing with a tiny dry fly (size 20 or smaller), you can easily lose track of it in flowing water – especially if the surface isn't completely smooth. This means detecting takes is all the more difficult, if not altogether impossible.

To solve the problem tie the small fly to a larger one. Here a size 24 Griffith's Gnat is tied to the bend of a size 10 Elk Hair Caddis. If a trout rises just behind the bigger sight fly, the small fly is probably the target. But you can sometimes even get takes on the bigger fly.

---

fly to sink to the bottom. You want the lure to fish directly along the bottom, and not in mid water. Carefully watch the strike indicator as the fly drifts downstream. Mend line when necessary to avoid drag. Takes aren't subtle – when the strike indicator is yanked under savagely, lift up firmly.

For slow-moving glides and areas of shallow water try fishing a heavily leaded lure down and across. Make 30-60cm (1-2ft) strips as the fly swings downstream. Drag in this instance isn't excessive and doesn't matter too much because the water is slow-moving and fairly shallow.

▼ *Fishing a bullhead imitation across and down in a deep pool such as this may just provoke a savage response from a big brown.*
If trout aren't showing on top (no hatches), give this method a try.

Fishing for grayling

Understanding the grayling's feeding habits is essential.

The grayling is a beautiful fish, so sensitive to pollution that you'll find it only in clean, clear rivers. The season is the same as that for coarse fish, but fly fishing for them is best from late July or August – when the fish have recovered from spawning – through to early spring.

► *Four dry flies to try for grayling. From left to right: Terry's Terror, Treacle Parkin, Grayling Witch and Red Tag. Many anglers find that grayling are particularly attracted to the colour red.*

▼ *In warm weather grayling are found close to the banks of fast streams, and in glides of good depth. In the winter they move into deeper, warmer water.*

Basic equipment

You need the same equipment, and similar artificial flies, as for river trout fishing. An 8½-9ft (2.6-2.8m) rod, with a 4-5 weight floating double taper line, is suitable in most situations – Yorkshire Dales rivers, Welsh Dee or chalk streams.

The leader, whether for a single dry fly or for nymphs or wet flies, should end in nothing heavier than 3lb (1.3kg) b.s.

Top and bottom feeding

Grayling fishing techniques are much the same as those used for brown trout in rivers – and the fish live in the same habitat and eat the same food. Grayling are both bottom feeders and surface feeders, rising to the surface to take gnats and other insects.

Grayling waters

A few waters are open to the general angler: parts of the **River Ribble**; the **Avon** near Salisbury; the **Welsh Dee** at Bala and Corwen; the **Derbyshire Wye** from the Peacock Hotel at Rowsley; and parts of the **Yorkshire** and the **Derbyshire Derwent**.

But because of damage from pollution and water abstraction, many waters are highly preserved and can be fished only with special permission.

The Red Tag

Perhaps one of the best known grayling patterns, the Red Tag is at least 140 years old. It can be fished wet or dry. Terry's Terror and Treacle Parkin are variations.
Hooks: Sizes 14-18
Thread: Brown
Tag (tail): Scarlet or bright red wool
Body: Peacock herl
Hackle: Natural red cock or hen

Tip Other baits

Flies are not the only food grayling go for. Bait fishing with maggots, small red worms or brandlings is effective in autumn and early spring. They also take bread and natural baits such as caddis larvae and grasshoppers.

▼ *A lovely autumn-caught grayling. This fish often uses its long sail-like dorsal fin to create resistance against the current as the angler plays it in.*

Unlike trout, they don't adopt a position in mid water. After a rise the grayling returns at once to the bottom.

Grayling are shoaling fish and all go on the feed simultaneously – when you've found one, you are likely to find more. Shoaling persists throughout the year, the fish gathering in more compact groups the colder it is. All this means your approach to grayling fishing should be different from that for the territorial brown trout.

Choose your flies

In most cases, your aim should be to match the hatch, just as in trout fishing, using artificials to imitate olives, pale wateries and gnats. Fish for grayling at the depth at which they are feeding. If you see a shoal steadily picking off small dark olives at the surface, for instance, try a size 14 dry Blue Dun – it's an old pattern, but the fish go for it. In general grayling prefer flies in sizes 16 to 20 or even 22.

Surface fishing Often the rise of a grayling occurs in the form of tiny sipping rings. The mistake is to think that they are taking a fly from the surface. Countless anglers have suffered frustration as their dry flies have been ignored. The fact is that the fish are taking pupae trapped just under the surface film.

This is where tiny size 18 (or smaller) dark artificial flies are necessary, fished just under the surface, and where the Red Tag – another very old pattern – comes into its own. The nearer the surface it is used, the smaller it must be.

In the north, the spider type of wet fly is much used for sub-surface fishing. Patterns such as Snipe and Purple, Water Hen Bloa and Partridge and Orange are all effective on size 14 hooks.

River bed fishing For grayling feeding on the river bed, a size 14 or 12 leaded shrimp may be necessary. A whole series of flies, such as Sawyer's Grayling Bug and William Rufus, are weighted with copper wire for quick and deep penetration of the stream. In winter, when the shoals may be tightly packed in a deep pool, a heavy nymph or bug – such as the Killer Bug – which sinks right down to the level of the fish may be your best bet.

Fly fishing for salmon

Fly fishing is probably the most challenging way of fishing for Atlantic salmon. Veteran salmon angler Arthur Oglesby recommends equipment and tactics which should increase your chances of catching the fish.

Though Atlantic salmon don't feed when returning from the sea to spawn in fresh water, you can still catch them with lures, plugs, natural baits or flies. No one knows for certain why they take – but take flies they do! Perhaps the salmon have some memory of feeding which triggers a response to strike. They may also hit lures or flies out of sheer aggression or to defend their lies from intruders.

To fly fish effectively for salmon, you need to switch tactics as the seasons change. There are two overall approaches – the big fly fished deep for early and late-season salmon and the small fly presented near the surface for late spring, summer and early autumn fish.

But it's important not to be too dogmatic about your approach. Though anglers fishing during the early season catch mostly on large sunk flies, you might also tempt

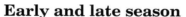

▶ *An angler fly fishes on the River Helmsdale in northern Scotland during the early season (March).*

At this time of year, use a fast sinking line to present the fly deep. But keep moving from pool to pool to find fresh-run fish.

salmon with a small sparsely dressed fly. Remember, if one particular tactic isn't working, experiment to find one that will.

Early and late season

The water is generally cold and sometimes high during the early and late season. The salmon are reluctant to move too far, so you need to use a heavy brass tube fly and a sinking line to drop the fly to the fish's level.

▼ *The reward of finally catching a salmon on a fly far outweighs the price you sometimes have to pay in terms of hard work and long hours.*

Here a delighted angler cradles a cracking 8lb (3.6kg) salmon, caught in late April.

Equipment Anglers plump for a double-handed fly rod between 13-18ft (4-5.5m) long for most of the salmon fly fishing in Britain. You can control the line easier with a double-handed rod than with a shorter rod. And better line control means better presentation.

Also, you can cast farther and more effectively with a double-handed rod – especially if the area behind you is obstructed with foliage – punching out the line quite a way with a Spey or Double Spey cast. But with a short single-handed rod, this is far more difficult – you just don't have the leverage or the power.

Most anglers plump for a 15ft (4.5m) double-handed carbon-fibre fly rod rated for a 10-weight line. Combine this with a weight-forward fast sinking line (such as a Wet Cel II) and a 6ft (1.8m) leader of 15-20lb (7-9kg) breaking strain, and you're nearly ready to begin.

Water craft During the early and late season the salmon hold in sheltered lies where they don't have to expend too much energy contending against the current. The slow, deep pools are prime areas when the water is at its normal level.

Finding salmon when the water is cold and high is fairly straightforward: the fish concentrate near the banks, away from the main channel in the middle of the river.

Fishing in the early and late season To begin fishing for salmon, cast directly

▼ *An angler fly fishes for salmon with a single-handed rod in low-water conditions in early autumn. Notice that he has plenty of room for his backcasts.*

A general guide to salmon lies

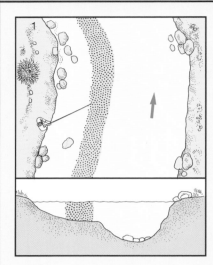

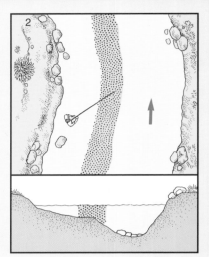

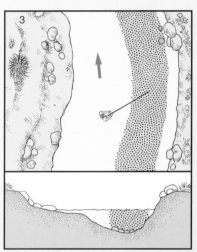

1. When the water is high, the salmon may lie close to the bank – sometimes no more than a rod's length away. The current isn't as fast close as it is in the middle of the river.

2. You may need to wade when the river is just above its normal level. The salmon can be spread out, but most lie in the indicated strip.

3. Under normal and low-water conditions (usually in the summer) you can often find the salmon in the deep pools, but it's also worth trying the runs and riffles.

across the river or slightly downstream and across, then let the fly swing around gently in the current. Ideally, you want the fly to drift 1-2ft (45-60cm) above the river bed.

Perhaps the biggest mistake beginners make is to allow the fly to swing around too quickly. Always try to fish the fly as *slowly* as possible. This can't be overstressed, especially when the water temperature is below 10°C (50°F) and fish are reluctant to move around. In fact, a good principle to remember is that the colder the water is, the slower you must present the fly.

It's always better to cover a lot of water quickly in the early season, taking a step or two after each cast, than to plod about the pool or run slowly and aimlessly. This is especially true when there are fresh fish in the pools, and they are still in the process of moving upstream – however slowly.

Fresh-run salmon take flies more readily than resident fish, which have been in the river longer and tend to be more reluctant to strike.

Sometimes casting a long way is helpful,

Down-and-across fly fishing for salmon

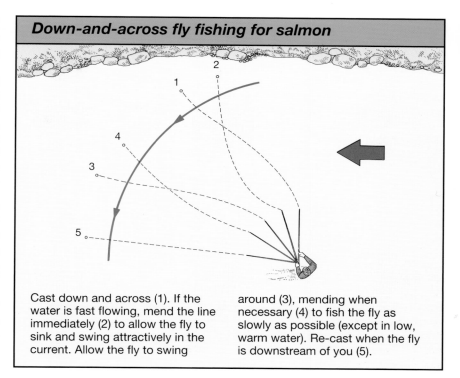

Cast down and across (1). If the water is fast flowing, mend the line immediately (2) to allow the fly to sink and swing attractively in the current. Allow the fly to swing around (3), mending when necessary (4) to fish the fly as slowly as possible (except in low, warm water). Re-cast when the fly is downstream of you (5).

but it's much better to know roughly where fish are lying and how best to cover them. It makes sense to hire a ghillie, if you can afford one. He will take you to the most prolific sections of a river. Without local advice, you have to look for deep water and simply learn from experience.

Warm-water fly fishing

Fishing for salmon in late spring and early autumn can be fabulous, depending on the river and the number of fresh-run fish coming through. Your prospects in summer aren't usually that good because most of the fish are residents and the water levels often plummet, but you can get away with using

A rough guide to water temperatures and fly sizes

Water temperature	Fly size
0-7°C (32-45°F)	The larger the fly the better. Use tube flies 2-3in long.
7-12°C (45-54°F)	Try using tube flies 1-2in long, or size 4-6 doubles or trebles.
12-15°C (54-59°F)	Small flies work best in warm water. Try fishing with singles or doubles in sizes 6-12. Trout flies may also catch.

Five of the best

Many beginning salmon anglers carry boxes and boxes of flies to the riverbank. You don't need dozens of patterns – just a range of large and small ones for the different times of the year. Here are some of Arthur Oglesby's favourites (from left to right): Willie Gunn, Oglebug, Stoat's Tail, Munro Killer and Blue Charm.

▶ *An early autumn salmon comes to the net on a Scottish river. The angler used a single-handed rod, floating line and small fly to tempt the fish from the low, clear water.*

lighter gear at this time of year – in some cases your trout rod will do!

Equipment As soon as the water warms above 10°C (50°F) and provided the air is warmer than the water, you can put aside your sunk line tackle and resort to an intermediate or full floating line. The floater is easier to control than a sinking line because you can mend it. Mending prevents the line from dragging in the current and allows the fly to sink to the proper depth.

Sometimes in the very low water of summer you may want to use your trout fly rod (rated for 7-8 weight lines), a floating line and leader of 6-8lb (2.7-3.6kg) breaking strain. Under such conditions it pays to use very small flies (sizes 10-12). Many anglers have taken salmon on trout flies such as Muddlers, Goldhead nymphs and traditional wet flies.

Finding salmon Under low-water conditions throughout the summer, search deep water below stretches of fast water. But you can also find fish in runs and even riffles. Fast water appeals to salmon because its oxygen content is high.

Fishing approaches Though the water may now be lower and warmer than during the early or late season, your tactics for fly presentation are basically the same as before. Obviously, the fly fishes much closer to the surface when you use a floating line, but again swing it over the salmon (or probable lie) as slowly as possible.

Long casts are often necessary on large rivers – where the salmon might be spread out over a large stretch of water. But again line control is more important.

Under low-water conditions you can temporarily abandon fishing your fly slowly. In fact, a fly cast upstream and retrieved sometimes provokes a salmon into taking.

▲ *Local knowledge is as precious as gold. Here, a ghillie recommends a fly for normal conditions in the early season.*

◀ *Salmon freshly run from the sea are silvery white and in top condition. This double-figure beauty was taken on a large fly, fished slow and deep with a fast-sinking line.*

Winter baitfishing for grayling

Baitfishing for grayling is usually reserved for the winter when fly hatches are sparse and the river is high, clearing and possibly coloured. A tempting trail of maggots rarely fails to catch a brace or two of fine grayling.

Before you begin, check that baitfishing is allowed. On most freestone rivers this isn't usually a problem since you can find stretches open to non-fly methods.

What you need to begin

When you are baitfishing for grayling, it's best to use coarse fishing equipment.

Rod, reel, line Your rod should be long – 12-13ft (3.6-3.9m) – so you can keep as much line off the water as possible and control the tackle when trotting. Most anglers prefer using a fixed-spool reel loaded with 3lb (1.4kg) mono, but if you want direct contact with the fish it is worth mastering the centrepin reel, which is a much more sensitive instrument for this style of fishing.

Effective baits It's no secret that maggots (white, red or bronze) work wonders. But perhaps the simplest and cheapest bait of all is the worm. A small, 4cm (1½in) long worm is ideal. Hook it just below the head. (Whatever you do, don't prevent the worm from wiggling by threading it up the hook.) Grayling may also take cheese, sweetcorn and casters.

Techniques to try

In the colder months the fish move to the slower-moving sections of the river – the deep pools.

Position yourself at the head of a pool. If maggots are allowed, take one to two pints. Begin by loosefeeding a dozen or so every cast at the head of the pool. Use a trotting rig set slightly over depth (see *Trotting rig* on page 132).

With one or two maggots nicked on a size 16 or 18 hook, cast in at the top of the pool. As the float and bait drift downstream, track around with them. Takes, when they come, are positive. Simply lift the rod smartly to set the hook.

Legering with a small blockend feeder is reserved for the coldest days of the year, when the fish are extremely lethargic. Use a 10-11ft (3-3.4m) quivertip rod.

◄ *The simple worm often proves irresistible to hungry winter grayling.*

▼ *The Derbyshire Derwent in the dead of winter. Grayling respond to both bait and fly fishing, and you can do both here.*

Slow drift

For deep, seething channels and smooth-flowing glides trotting tactics are again the order of the day. Avoid freelining worms in winter, for the grayling are lying along the bottom and reluctant to chase – which means that anything presented above them is usually ignored. Exploiting the river bed is the best way of tempting winter grayling, so sometimes you may just want to inch your bait along by holding back.

Obviously, when holding back you should fish downstream. Instead of allowing the float and bait to drift naturally with the current, give line gradually so that the bait bumps along the bottom. Space the shot evenly down the line for covering slow-moving stretches. For faster water, bulk the shot two-thirds of the way down the line between float and hook and watch your float carefully for takes.

Holding back

If you've drifted your bait and float through a pool a few times with no response, you may want to try holding back – that is, gradually pay out line so that the bait inches downstream along the bottom (right). The fish may not want to chase the bait at all on really cold days and this technique can score well.

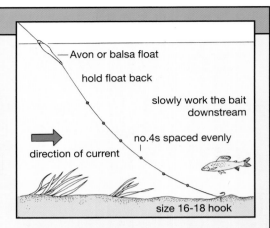

— Avon or balsa float

hold float back

slowly work the bait downstream

no.4s spaced evenly

→ direction of current

size 16-18 hook

▼ *The natural drag of a centrepin reel allows you to trot the bait at half the flow of the river – this is essential even for fishing on slow-moving chalk streams.*

Trotting rig

— Avon or balsa float

— 3AAA bulk shot

no.4 dropper shot

15-30cm hooklength

size 16-18 hook

This is a good trotting rig for fishing in pools and runs. Vary the hooksize according to the bait you intend to use.

Tip Slow pool – stay still

A common mistake when grayling fishing in winter – or in autumn for that matter – is to fish in fast, shallow water. Though you may have caught many fish in riffles during the warm summer months, they won't be there come winter.

Grayling are very sensitive to temperature. Unlike brown trout which tend to be territorial, grayling are nomadic, moving up and down a river in search of ideal lies as the seasons change.

Find one likely pool and concentrate your efforts there. If after 20 minutes, for example, you don't get anything, move on to the next pool.

Spinning, shrimping and worming for salmon

For many, catching salmon on the fly is a sacred art. But it isn't the only skilful and sporting way, argues bait and lure specialist Andy Nicholson.

There is a growing army of salmon anglers thirsting to extend their knowledge and improve salmon-catching skills with bait and lure techniques. It's beginning to dawn on salmon hunters that these methods can be as skilful, and in some cases more demanding than, the fly.

But fly fishing is a traditional and proven salmon method, so why bother trying anything else? First of all, not every angler wants to fish the fly all the time. You might enjoy bait and lure fishing for a change.

Secondly, there are many salmon rivers throughout the UK that quite simply are not conducive to fly fishing. For instance, rivers with slow moving currents, or small rivers with overhanging trees, may have excellent runs of salmon, but they call for a different approach and new skills to fish them properly.

Tackle for baits and lures

As far as basic tackle goes, Andy Nicholson prefers an 11½ft (3.5m) rod which lets him flick light baits out long distances. It should have a sensitive tip for bite detection and a fast taper for quick pick-up and striking purposes, and then plenty of power in the rod for playing a big fish. With such a long rod you can control the bait correctly.

You don't need a particularly specialized reel. Go for a good quality ball-bearing fixed-spool reel with a large line capacity and a first class drag system.

Worm fishing

Worming is a versatile method suitable for flooded, coloured rivers, and low water conditions. Lobworms and brandlings are best. Tackle shops sell both, or you can find brandlings in compost heaps, and lobs on lawns at night after it has rained.

It is very important to keep the bait moving when worming and to explore as much water as you can. Read the water and fish all the likely lies behind boulders, in the necks of pools and in deep runs where the

▲ *A River Shannon salmon taken on a Flying Condom. Always make sure a fish is well beaten before attempting to net or beach it. Many a salmon is lost at the net through rushing when it still has plenty of life in it.*

current is fast. When you are fishing water with virtually no movement, cast your bait in the most likely spot, leave it a while and then twitch it in a few inches at a time.

There are several effective ways of rigging up for worming.

The standard worming rig is the simplest way to fish worm baits along the bottom of a swim. Feed the main line through a

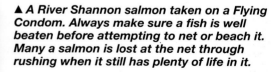

◀ *A wormer explores a high and coloured River Dee at Bangor in Wales. He uses enough weight to keep the worms moving along just off the bottom.*

Worm presentation and bouncing bullets

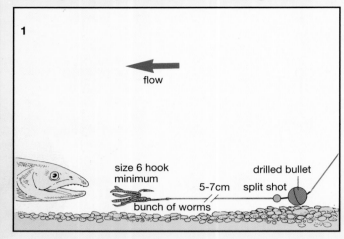

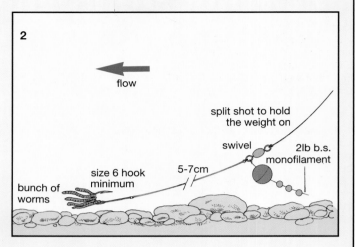

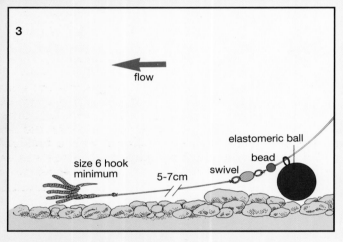

1. Standard worming rig Don't put any shot above the bullet so a taking fish can pull line through the bullet with little resistance. Be careful in choosing the size of bullet – you have to consider carefully the strength of current flowing – too light a bullet moves too fast in the flow. It's a matter of practice and experience. Use sturdy hooks for salmon.

2. Snagless rig Here the weak line snaps if the bullet snags. Some anglers use a loop of twisted lead wire to replace the bullet on the link. The thin wire is less likely to get snagged.

3. Bouncing Betty The beauty of Bouncing Betty is that it travels over the boulders and rocks – actually bouncing its way along, much the same way a rubber ball does. It's a great way to avoid snagging and creates a very steady rhythmic drift down the stream.

Worm welcome

Pay attention to bait restrictions. Find out what methods are allowed before you start wielding a prawn or a bunch of worms. It's handy to have a number of techniques at your fingertips but always fish within the law and the rules of the fishery.

drilled bullet and tie it directly to the hook. Secure the bullet with a split shot some 75-90cm (2½-3ft) above the hook.

Choice of line strength is important. When fishing a big flooded river use 15lb (6.8kg) b.s. or more, stepping down in diameter as the river drops away and clears. Only consider going below 8lb (3.6kg) when the river is very low and the fish are timid and difficult to tempt.

Worming rig with added trace Instead of a split shot on your standard rig, attach a swivel so you can tie a finer trace through to the hook. This saves you having to change the main line if you want to go finer.

Snagless rigs For snaggy bottoms try this rig. Tie the main line to a swivel and attach the trace line as before. Then tie a small piece of thin line (about 2lb/0.9kg b.s.) to the bottom loop of the swivel and secure the desired weight on the weak line with split shot. When it gets stuck the fine line breaks and you lose only the weight.

The Bouncing Betty is Andy Nicholson's favourite. It's a round elastomeric ball (a heavy sort of rubber) with a swivel attached. Fix it above the swivel and trace and it bounces its way along over boulders and obstacles.

Takes when worming are usually a series of short sharp jerks. If you hold the line by the reel with a finger you can feel what's going on through the rod tip. Sometimes bites are timid and it is worth waiting a little while for the salmon to take the worms. Then set the hook with a firm strike.

Shellfish tactics

Salmon have a surprising fondness for boiled shrimps and prawns. They are definitely worth a try, especially when the fly is out of the question. You need a keen sense of touch for this method. Get your supply of shrimps in various colours from any good

Spinning procedure

far bank

systematically cover a wide area

flow

Cast to the far bank and fish the spinner back towards you in a series of arcs. Control the speed of retrieve and use the current to keep the bait off the bottom – covering a large area and exploring features.

- - - - cast

——— retrieve

angler

Key to top lures

The lures on the right are all proven salmon catchers.
1. **Flying Condom** Saucy bait with powerful rippling action.
2. **Copper Mepps** Subtle flutterer fished slowly.
3. **ABU Droppen** Heavy body is handy for fast water.
4. **Flying Bucktail** A hint of the fly about this one.
5. **Blair Spoon** Formidable wobbler often fished high in the water.
6. **Devon Minnow** Comes in many colours and left or right spin option.
7. **Toby Spoon** Successful in gold and silver.

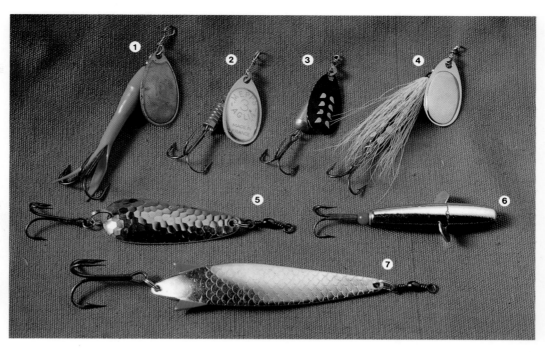

Tip Pick pockets

It is very important to be mobile and not burdened down with too much tackle. This leaves you free to explore all the water available to you. Wear a waterproof jacket with plenty of pockets to carry all your tackle bits.

game fishing tackle shop. Ruby reds, pink and purple are top choices.

Mounting There are a number of mounting possibilities but the basic idea is as follows. Hold the shrimp or prawn on its back and insert a shrimping pin (threaded on the line) above the paddles on the tail. Section

by section, feed the pin into the shrimp to straighten it. Next position one or two trebles (tied to the end of your line) to the shrimp's undercarriage between the feelers. Secure the shrimp with a half-hitch around the tail and pin. If using a prawn you may need to bind it with copper wire to

Seafood preparations

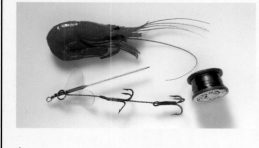

◄ *Ruby red prawn and mount with two trebles and spinning vane, with copper wire to bind the prawn.*

▶ *Mounted purple shrimp and yellow prawn. Note the position of the spinning vane and the copper wire binding the prawn in place.*

1. Shrimping pin and treble ready for mounting.
2. The shrimp is straightened out with the pin and the treble is placed among the feelers.

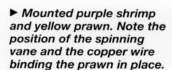

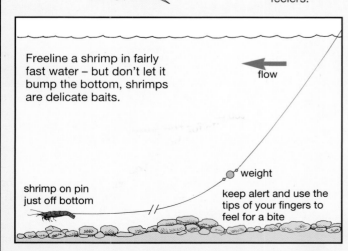

Freeline a shrimp in fairly fast water – but don't let it bump the bottom, shrimps are delicate baits.

shrimp on pin just off bottom

keep alert and use the tips of your fingers to feel for a bite

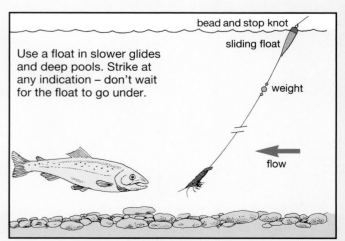

Use a float in slower glides and deep pools. Strike at any indication – don't wait for the float to go under.

bead and stop knot
sliding float
weight
flow

help keep it all intact and straight.

Freelining Use this method in fairly fast currents. The rig is like the worming set-up but with a shot above the weight as well as below. Mount the bait with a shrimping pin and a treble. Fish the shrimp in the current but don't let it touch the bottom – it's very delicate and soon falls apart. Cast across the pool and allow it to swing round in the current towards the near bank, then retrieve it slowly. Only one game fish will take a shrimp and that is the salmon. So, you must react to the merest tweak or pluck on the line with a fast strike – a salmon can eject the bait in a trice.

Float fishing When confronted with slower glides and deep pools the floatfished shrimp is a must. Use a sliding balsa float weighted with shot to make it cock. Tie a stop knot above the float to set the depth – usually 30cm (1ft) or so above the bottom. Ease the float down the current to the waiting fish. Strike at any hint of a bobbing float or if the float pauses along its glide. Don't wait for the float to go under – you will be too late.

Shrimp spinning Mount a shrimp with a spinning vane and fish it like a spinner. You can buy mounts with pins, trebles and vanes from the shops. You should include a swivel on the line somewhere above the mount – and any weight required.

Spinning winners

Spinning for salmon is a skilful method which enables you to cover a great deal of water relatively quickly. It's most effective when there is some colour in the water.

Fished almost like the fly in an arc formation, the secret is to use the current, allowing the lure to flutter enticingly in the stream. Retrieve as slowly as you can, giving the fish as much chance as possible to see the lure.

Whatever tactics you use, when a fish takes, strike firmly, and when you hook one hold the rod up high, making full use of the bend in the rod. Never try to stop a fish on its first run – usually its most powerful. Set the clutch according to the breaking strain of the line. Never backwind but allow the line to run off the clutch. Fresh salmon have soft mouths and if you're too rough you can easily pull the hook out. If the fish jumps, lower the rod tip to avoid breaking off.

▲ *Vermicelli whiskers – a writhing gobful of worms snapped up with gusto by a ten-pounder (4.5kg). Store your worms in damp moss with a sprinkling of sand to toughen them up for use.*

▼ *Prawn fishing for salmon at Galway Weir, Ireland. When float fishing a prawn it's often a good trick to hold the float back and allow the shrimp to rise tantalizingly in the water.*

Probing rivers for salmon

Stan Headley, Orkney game angler and writer, advises a mixture of method and flexibility in his canny approach to salmon fishing.

▲ *Sandy footprints set against a mountainous backdrop in Laggan, Scotland – evidence of salmon angling activity on a stretch of the River Spey.*

◀ *You don't need to head for the wilderness to catch decent salmon. The River Corrib is a splendid salmon water which flows through the city of Galway.*

Luxury lies

Locating the likeliest salmon lies is half the battle.

Try to identify areas where fish can rest with the minimum effort and the maximum comfort and security.

If you apply this rule, with reference to water height and temperature, you won't go far wrong.

Brigadoon! – the only place you'll find a 'typical' Scottish salmon river. Pity it doesn't exist – except as a mythical land in the Lerner and Loewe musical.

In reality you never get a typical salmon river. They are too varied in character to fit a rigid formula. Some are fast, rocky torrents, others are extremely slow and canal-like – and there is every variation in between.

Nevertheless there is a sort of overall skeletal pattern to salmon rivers – many have a series of pools, with fast water at the head, a steady flow in the middle and slacker water towards the tail.

This neat formula is correct as far as it goes, but it is too simple a pattern to be useful when applying water craft skills to spot all the likely salmon lies in a river. In practice boulders, rocks, islands, deep holes and various other features complicate the picture a great deal.

You must consider each variable feature along a stretch of river in order to get a complete picture of the water. This helps you to fine-tune your tactics and focus your efforts in the places most likely to furnish you with a salmon.

A sharp bend in the river creates a stretch of deep, slow-moving water close to the bank. The depth offers salmon security while the slow current helps the fish conserve precious energy.

Big boulders divert the current and salmon are attracted to the area of slow water behind them.

Salmon often pause before continuing their strenuous journey upstream.

When the water temperature is below 10°C (50°F), salmon prefer to stay in slow to medium-flowing water.

READING A SALMON RIVER

Tip Vital variables

By reading a stretch of salmon river you're aiming to optimize your chances of catching fish. It pays to be adaptable and observant and it's useful to have a checklist of essential considerations.
● **Height** of water
● **Shape** of riverbed
● **Speed** of flow
● **Temperature** of air/water
● **Time** of day
● **Quantity** and mood of fish
   The shape of the riverbed is relatively stable but the other features can change from day to day.

Short stay or settled in

Salmon return to the rivers of their birth throughout the year, but the main runs occur in spring, summer and autumn. Some rivers have all three runs, a very few may have only one run, but most have at least two distinct runs of fish.

As the fish make their way up-river, they stop from time to time to rest, to wait until river conditions are right, or for other reasons known only to salmon. Some of the stops may be for a few minutes only, while other stays may last for weeks.

Running fish A fish that stops for short periods is classed as a running fish. You'd be hard pushed to catch one when it's actually travelling, but it is eminently catchable during its rest stops.

Resident fish A fish that stops in one place for a long period of time is classed as a resident and is a very difficult proposition.

In a nutshell What you need to do to fish a

salmon river successfully is read the water, locate the 'taking lies' and present a lure in an acceptable fashion to a receptive tenant. It's no use wasting valuable fishing time in unproductive water.

Turbulent twaddle

There is a popular misconception that salmon are always found in 'white water' – that is, the very fast, turbulent areas at the heads of pools. It is rarely true. Salmon don't feed when they're in the river, so they depend on the limited amount of nutrition already locked in their tissues. This means they have to conserve energy.

Therefore the fish have a tendency to inhabit water where there is adequate flow to allow their streamlined shape to hold position in the river with the minimum expenditure of energy.

As far as the salmon is concerned, suitability of water speed is directly related to

The **full force** of the river's current is too strong for salmon to lie in. They rest in hollows just off the bottom where the current is much slower than at the surface.

▶ *Salmon prefer to keep out of very strong spring currents. It makes sense therefore, at this time of year, to concentrate your efforts in the steady flow, paying only passing attention to the heads and tails of pools.*

A gently shelving bank of shingle and sand has shallow water close in. Shallow lies so close to shore don't offer salmon comfort – the water may be either too hot in summer or too cold in winter.

Water warmer than 10°C (50°F) tempts salmon to rest in lies with fast water over their heads.

▼ *Salmon depend on their stored energy reserves to get upstream without refuelling. Fish may need a lift to ascend a waterfall.*
At Buckfastleigh in Devon they get a leg up the River Dart with a salmon ladder.

its temperature. When the water is cold (below 10°C/50°F), fish prefer medium to slow flowing water. When it is warm (above 10°C/50°F) fish will hold in fast and sometimes white water.

Spring torrents
In the spring, rivers are usually full and often overflowing. Even if there has been no rain, melted snow may add many inches to the water level. Spring salmon tend to move slowly and steadily upstream because the low water temperatures at this time of year dampen more vigorous behaviour. They are prone to frequent pauses in their migration – and resting fish are usually taking fish.

Since they dislike vigorous activity, spring salmon avoid the strongest currents. So it makes sense to look for spring fish in the steady flow of the pools, in deepish water, and where rocks or other obstructions give respite from the full force of the current.

Features of the riverbed which slacken

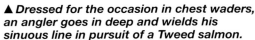
▲ Dressed for the occasion in chest waders, an angler goes in deep and wields his sinuous line in pursuit of a Tweed salmon.

▶ A proud angler displays a skyward gazing Irish salmon – reward for adapting to the changing features and conditions of a river.

the current and allow comfortable resting areas are hard to spot in swollen rivers. Often the only indication of their existence is disturbance on the water surface. Turbulence in otherwise steadily flowing water, and smooth water in a turbulent flow, indicate likely holding spots or lies for spring and autumn fish.

Summer stealth
In summer as the river shrinks, identifying salmon lies becomes easier. Rocks, holes, gullies and glides offering security and rest to fish are seen at a glance.

But the shallow water can also give you problems. If you can see clearly what's going on in the water you can bet the fish also have a fine view out. A clumsy approach to the riverbank warns every fish in the pool of danger. Water temperatures fluctuate wildly in low water conditions – so even the freshest fish are reluctant to take.

Summer fish tend to lie in the deep cool water during the heat of the day, but move into well-oxygenated streamier water during the cool of the night. Fast water in and out of pools in the late evening or early morning provides the best chance of a fish when the water is low and warm. But in a summer spate forget the nocturnal regime, and spend every possible daylight hour beside the water. As long as an adequate flow of fresh water is coming down the river the chances of fine sport are high.

Past the sell-by date
In autumn, the most difficult task is often distinguishing between stale, unwanted salmon, and fresh fish new off the tide. There's no easy answer, but if you concentrate your efforts over water which attracts running fish, you won't go far wrong.

Temperature is the important factor in autumn. If the water is warm, expect fish to use summer lies. If it's cold, fish generally use lies in the steadier flows.

◀ Surface disturbance indicating a likely lie shows some way downstream of the obstruction causing it, particularly in deep water.

Sea trout in fast-flowing freestone rivers

In the middle of a hot summer, when ordinary trout fishing during the day is next to impossible, try fishing for sea trout at night. Bill Pennington explains what types of river features you should be aware of.

Attempting to describe one particular river as being a typical sea trout water is virtually impossible. The fish run any river system with clean water and enough gravelly headwaters for spawning.

At one time sea trout ran most of the rivers in the British Isles. Now, however, the runs are more often associated with west coast rivers, although some on the east coast – such as the Scottish Dee, Spey and Tweed – have prodigious numbers.

The River Lyn in Devon, the Glaslyn in Wales, the Kent in Cumbria and the Echaig in Scotland are sea trout rivers which could serve as suitable models. There are many more, but in character they are all very sim-ilar: boulder-strewn rivers that die away to near trickles in summer but, following substantial rains, become transformed into raging torrents.

When and where?

The peak runs of sea trout occur in June, July and August, so if you are planning a week's fishing holiday, mid July is your best

▼ *Though sea trout fishing is usually done at night, you can still tempt them from the deep pools during the late afternoon and evening. Here an angler plays a medium-sized sea trout from a deep pool on the River Spey near Grantown, Scotland.*

Sea trout rivers

Bill Pennington recommends the following rivers for sea trout.
● **River Coquet, Northumberland** Ticket information from tackle shops in Warkworth, Northumberland.
● **River Dart, Devon** Tickets and information from Wheeler Sports, 44 Fore Street, Totnes, Devon.
● **River Glaslyn, Gwynedd, Wales** Tickets and information from the Angling and Gun Centre, Madon Street, Porthmadog, Gwynedd (tel 0766 512464).
● **River Kent, Cumbria** Information available from Kendal tackle shops.
● **River Lyn, Devon** Ask at tackle shops in Lynmouth, Barnstaple or Minehead.
● **River Nith, Scotland** Tickets available from W. & W. Forsyth, Solicitors, 100 High Street, Sanquhar, Dumfries and Galloway.
● **River Spey, Scotland** Contact Strathspey A.A., 61 High Street, Grantown, Scotland.

Up the rivers

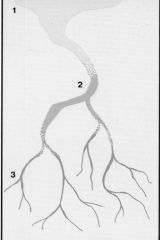

1. Sea trout enter the lower stretches of river any time between late April and June.
2. In July and August they move to the middle parts.
3. In September and October they are in the upper reaches and headwaters – ready for spawning.

▶ *Generally speaking, most of the sea trout move to the shallow stretches after dusk has fallen and can be taken on flies fished fast and close to the surface.*

Tip **The gear**

A 10-11ft (3-3.4m) rod which is rated for AFTM 6/7 line is the best choice. Take a floating and sinking fly line and plenty of nylon (6-10lb/2.7-4.5 kg) for making tippets.

Sea trout flies are legion. Limit yourself to Butcher, Dunkeld, Mallard and Claret and Invicta in sizes 6 to 10. Also take along a few tandem lures.

If you're going spinning, take some spinners and spoons in various colours.

all-round choice.

Water height is of paramount importance to the upstream movement of fish on most rivers. Until the first significant floods of late May and early June, there is no considerable influx of sea trout into the river systems.

Sea trout don't spread themselves evenly throughout rivers from the onset of these spates. Drought years concentrate fish in the lower beats and estuary until late in the season. Some river systems – in particular the big rivers – have genuine early and late runs of sea trout. The River Tweed system is a good example.

Once in the rivers, sea trout show a marked preference for pools with sluggish, deep water. They stay here during the day, especially if this section is blessed with a tree canopy. The fish love shaded pools where they can lie with some security from prying eyes.

A typical pool has a fast-water run at the throat, leading into a deep, tree-covered central part which in turn runs off into a

riffles

medium-paced glide

At dusk sea trout begin to be more active. Tell-tale signs are splashing and leaping.

deep pool

A SEA TROUT RIVER AT TWILIGHT

Deep, sluggish pools, shaded by trees and bushes, are prime lies for sea trout during the day.

long shallow tail.

During the daylight hours most fish are concentrated in deep water. But as night approaches they tend to move up into faster water at the throat of the pool and also drop back into the pool's tail.

The trout won't move all together: the deep water always holds fish. The best lies in the pool are usually tenanted by the better-quality specimens which may not actually leave the pool at all during the night.

As the night progresses, sea trout again swim to deep water and then have a tendency to stay put until first light when, once again for a short period, they move into the fast water at the throat and tail of the pool.

For anyone new to a section of river, there is no substitute for daylight reconnaissance to locate fish – provided the water clarity allows for it. Take careful note of the positions of sea trout, so you know where to fish your fly or spinner during the night.

Some truly wild rivers have deep, slightly coloured water and steep, tree-lined banks which don't make reconnaissance easy. But

there is no need to despair: sea trout are very obliging in betraying their presence. As darkness falls, you can often hear them jumping and splashing repeatedly in the gathering gloom. Again, mark well the position of the leaping sounds, and concentrate your angling efforts there.

The faster, shallower stretches of river contain many sea trout at night. Darkness gives the fish confidence to venture out from the safety of the pools - though some fish remain in the pools all night.

▲ *Incredibly powerful, a fresh-run sea trout surges downstream on the River Lune in Cumbria.*

Usually, the longer a sea trout is in fresh water, the harder it is to catch.

riffles

fast water

Gravelly headwaters and clean water are needed for sea trout to spawn.

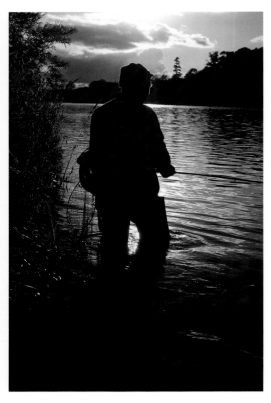

◄ *Fishing in complete darkness offers you the best chance of success, for sea trout are very wary and easily spooked.*

Tip The approach: a brief

1. It's dangerous wading in fast rivers at night.
2. Wait until it's dark before you begin fishing a pool. Leave the tail of the pool for a further hour before fishing there.
3. Always be conscious of your flies and the water speed. Keep the flies moving through the water during the first few hours of night fishing.
4. When sunk-line fishing in deep pools, work your flies as slowly as possible, and be alert for gentle takes.

is clearly defined by the fish themselves. Suddenly, as if a switch were thrown, the pools become lifeless – though the occasional fish may splash in the darkness.

Sea trout are loath to respond to a surface fly, and the angler must now revert to a deeply sunk lure up to 7.5cm (3in) long. fish it very slowly on a sunk line, and stick to the deep-water sections of the pool or to specific lies that you have noted previously.

The third phase doesn't last long – from the first signs of dawn into proper daylight. Sea trout activity during this period is generally confined to the faster water at the throat of a pool when the fish once again respond to the same tactics as in phase one.

Whenever you fish, be careful when wading into a fast-flowing river at night. Always carry a reliable torch and a sturdy wading stick with a rope handle.

▼ *A fresh-run sea trout from the River Conway in North Wales.*
  One of the best times to fish for sea trout is just after a summer spate when the water has dropped and cleared, and a new stock has moved up the river.

Why fish at night?

Before deciding on a strategy to catch sea trout, you must accept one strange fact: the fish don't feed while in fresh water. So how do you go about catching a non-feeding fish, you may well ask? If it is not feeding why does it take any form of lure? This is a puzzling question. But as the sea trout can't tell us themselves, we'll have to accept that they do and be thankful.

Sea trout are very shy, flighty and wary creatures. Although they can be caught during daylight, they are much more responsive to lures at night. They feed heavily at sea at dawn and dusk and continue to be active at these times. But this memory dims with time in freshwater. They become progressively more and more difficult to catch the longer they're in the river.

Your best time to take fish, therefore, is directly after a summer spate when the water has dropped and cleared and when the stocks have been replenished from fresh-run fish. At this time they can be very obliging and easily caught. But three weeks later they can be totally different propositions and very difficult indeed.

Times for fishing

There are three distinct phases to sea trout behaviour from dusk to early morning.
The first phase is from dusk to three hours later when sea trout are very active. They rove, splash about in the pools and are responsive to a fly fished quite fast and close to the surface.
The second phase runs from three or so hours after dusk until the first signs of dawn appear in the eastern sky. This period

CHAPTER FOUR

KNOW
YOUR FISH

Rainbow trout

This invader from the USA has all but ousted the brown trout in Britain as a sporting species – despite the fact that it rarely spawns here.

Distribution

Rainbow trout have been stocked in hundreds of waters in Britain because they can tolerate higher temperatures than brown trout and are usually hard-fighting fish.

Divided record

● The British brown and rainbow trout records have been split into cultivated and natural records. However, there are problems classifying natural rainbow trout, so only the cultivated record is undisputed.

● The cultivated record is 30lb 1oz (13.64kg), taken by P. Carlton at Dever Springs in July 1993.

● The specimen size for rainbows varies according to the water. In some, fish are stocked at over the record weight. Usually 5lb (2.3kg) is a specimen, but at some waters only 10lb (4.5kg) is worth a mention.

Like all members of the salmon family, the rainbow trout looks particularly well designed. Its slim, streamlined body is perfectly suited to a predatory life in fast flowing rivers and streams. The back is grey-green, the sides silvery and the belly white. Rainbows usually have a purplish stripe (rather like a petrol spill on a wet pavement) along their sides and it is this which gives them their name.

Follow the feeding

Rainbow trout eat almost anything in or on the water, at any depth – from nymphs and molluscs on the bottom, to insects falling on the surface – just like brown trout. Rainbows behave most like their cousins in running water, waiting in the eddies behind boulders for food to be swept down to them.

Like brownies, they become more predatory as they get older. At only a couple of pounds in weight, they attack shoals of minnows and sticklebacks, and by the time they reach double figures, they are eating any fish smaller than themselves. In still waters they stick together, often swimming at great speeds and feeding right on the surface – quite a sight. They also feed like mackerel, rounding up prey fish in the shallows and then attacking them.

In Britain most rainbow trout are raised

Vital statistics

Scientific name: *Oncorhynchus mykiss* (previously *Salmo gairdneri*)
Maximum weight: (Britain) perhaps 40lb (18.1kg)
Average weight: 3lb (1.4kg)
Maximum length: 40in (102cm)
Life-span: (in the wild) 8-10 years (stocked fishery) 5 years

The rainbow is the only trout found in Europe with spots on its tail fin.

The adipose (fatty) fin is a characteristic of the salmon family and the whitefish.

Adults have an iridescent pinky purple band running along the lateral line.

The small spots are black and cover the whole body except the belly and the pectoral and ventral fins. Unlike the brown trout, there are no red spots on a rainbow.

The mouth is large and filled with many small teeth.

20cm (8in) roach

45cm (18in) rainbow

in farms, so their diet consists entirely of trout pellets. Some anglers have reputedly made huge catches of young fish on flies tied to resemble these pellets (though these tales may be exaggerated).

Life in a cold climate

In the wild, rainbow trout spawn in redds (shallow pits) dug in gravel by the female – rather like salmon do. The eggs hatch out in two to three months, depending on temperature, and the immature fish have a yolk sac to keep them going for the first few weeks of life. At this stage they are known as alevins and they spend their time in the gravel where they hatched.

When the yolk sac is used up, the fry feed on plankton and quickly gain weight – they can double their weight in three weeks. Farmed rainbows are raised from eggs and milt (the males' sperm) stripped from adults, and end up either on a fishmonger's slab or in a fishery when they weigh anything from 1-20lb (0.4-9.1kg).

Rainbows have been introduced to Britain from the USA and are therefore used to slightly higher water temperatures and drier summers. Because of this, they begin to spawn in early spring – the time when the

Manufactured fish

If spawning does not take place, the fish retain the eggs or milt. Sometimes it is absorbed but more often it kills the fish. Recently, fish have been genetically 'engineered' to be unable to spawn and to have no spawning instinct. These 'triploid' fish can grow larger during spawning time and produce no eggs or milt, so the deaths caused by this are reduced.

levels of their native rivers are high enough. This may explain the rapid growth rate of rainbows – the parrs (fry) must be large enough to survive a winter after only about five months. European trout spawn in autumn, the eggs hatching after the winter. This gives the young all of the spring and summer to feed up for winter.

Whatever the exact reason, rainbows rarely breed in the wild in Britain. They are widely stocked because they are easy to farm, and their tolerance of higher temperatures helps them survive in small ponds which previously held only coarse fish. However, they spawn in few of these waters and the populations are actually self-sustaining in only one or two, including Blagdon Reservoir in Somerset and the River Wye in Derbyshire.

◄ *Some trout, if caught a few hours after stocking, are so confused they don't struggle. Big rainbows like this, from rich waters like the Aveley Lakes in Essex, grow on after release and fight hard to avoid capture.*

Top ten rainbow trout waters

- **Loch Awe, Argyll** Escaped rainbows have grown huge.
- **Lindholme Trout Fishery, Yorkshire** Good for healthy trout.
- **Esthwaite Water, Lancs.** A 200-acre natural lake and one of the few trout waters in the region.
- **Toft Newton, Lincolnshire** A concrete bowl but a popular fishery.
- **River Wye, Derbyshire** A self-sustaining fishery.
- **Blithfield Reservoir, Staffordshire** Many fish grow on to 10lb (4.5kg).
- **Rutland Water, Leics.** Over 1000 acres of water producing healthy fish.
- **Grafham Water, Cambs.** Another big reservoir with many good quality trout.
- **Weirwood Reservoir, Sussex** A 'put and take' reservoir with some nice overwintered fish.
- **Avington, Hampshire** A water with many big fish.

TRACKING DOWN RAINBOW TROUT

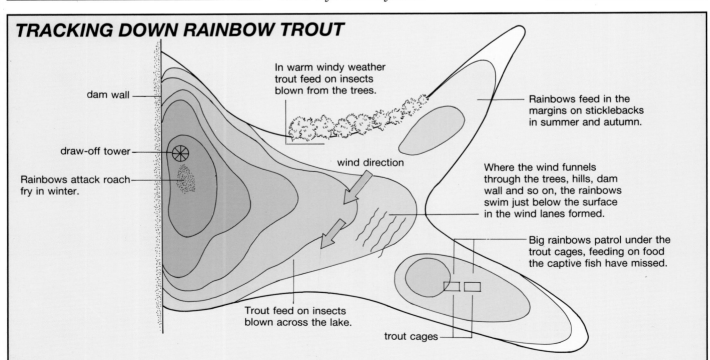

dam wall

draw-off tower

Rainbows attack roach fry in winter.

In warm windy weather trout feed on insects blown from the trees.

wind direction

Trout feed on insects blown across the lake.

trout cages

Rainbows feed in the margins on sticklebacks in summer and autumn.

Where the wind funnels through the trees, hills, dam wall and so on, the rainbows swim just below the surface in the wind lanes formed.

Big rainbows patrol under the trout cages, feeding on food the captive fish have missed.

Brown trout

The graceful brown trout only survives in cool, unpolluted water. Unlike the rainbow trout, it is native to Britain, making its home in well-oxygenated streams, rivers and lakes fed by springs or melted snow.

Record brownies

● The British record is held by J. Gardner for a 20lb 3oz (9.16kg) fish caught from Dever Springs Trout Fishery in 1991.
● The Irish record for a lake fish has stood since 1894 when W.Meares caught a fish weighing 26lb 2oz (11.85kg) from Lough Ennell, Westmeath.

F ew fish are more variable in colour than the brown trout (or brownie). Some are silver with several small black spots, others are almost black with a few large red spots. The colour depends on habitat, but most are golden brown with large dark brown spots on the sides, back and dorsal fins and a few large red spots here and there.

Like the other members of the salmon family, the brown trout has a small, rayless adipose fin between the rayed dorsal and tail fins. Its mouth is full of numerous small teeth, and its upper jaw-bone extends well past the rear of the eye.

Unlike the rainbow trout, the brownie can only thrive in cool, highly-oxygenated water. It is usually found in the upper reaches of rivers and chalk streams, and in some large lakes and lochs where the water is unpolluted. The species, native to Britain, is abundant all over the British Isles but this is largely the result of artificial stocking for the benefit of anglers.

Distribution

Because of artificial stocking, brown trout are found throughout Britain and Ireland. There is no area of the country where you would not be within 25 miles of brownies.

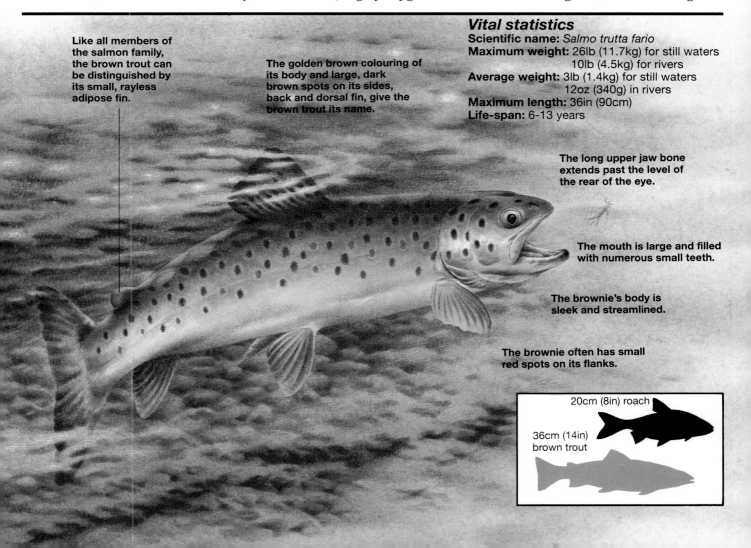

Like all members of the salmon family, the brown trout can be distinguished by its small, rayless adipose fin.

The golden brown colouring of its body and large, dark brown spots on its sides, back and dorsal fin, give the brown trout its name.

Vital statistics
Scientific name: *Salmo trutta fario*
Maximum weight: 26lb (11.7kg) for still waters
10lb (4.5kg) for rivers
Average weight: 3lb (1.4kg) for still waters
12oz (340g) in rivers
Maximum length: 36in (90cm)
Life-span: 6-13 years

The long upper jaw bone extends past the level of the rear of the eye.

The mouth is large and filled with numerous small teeth.

The brownie's body is sleek and streamlined.

The brownie often has small red spots on its flanks.

20cm (8in) roach

36cm (14in) brown trout

Going solo

The brown trout leads a solitary life-style. For most of the year it adopts a single, deep lie that gives shelter from predators, easy access to food and comfort out of the main force of the current. Generally, the brownie is a non-migratory fish and, once it has found a good lie, may never move far except in a drought, a spate or to spawn.

Many brown trout are farm-reared and released into a fishery when they have reached a takeable size; such fish are usually much larger than the average wild trout.

Fast-food lane

Living alongside a conveyor-belt of food carried by the main flow of the river, the brown trout doesn't usually have to venture far to feed. It has good vision and is one of the few members of the salmon family to feed at night.

Stillwater trout have to be more active in their search for food – they cruise the margins and bed of the lake during the day, and move to the surface at night to feed on insects. The brownie is a predatory fish, and even eats its own young if plentiful.

Matching the insects the fish are taking is an important part of the skill of fly fishing. Early in the season (April-May) the brownie tends to feed in deep water on nymphs, shrimps and caddis larvae. As the water temperature rises and insects become more active, the fish moves to the surface to feed on upwinged flies, sedges and midges. Anglers should try to ensure that the artificial nymphs and dry flies they use look and move as much like the natural insect as possible since brown trout are wary of any unnatural-looking flies.

Life-cycle

The brown trout needs shallow, fairly fast-

▲ *The colouring and size of brown trout vary greatly throughout the British Isles. However, most are golden brown with large dark spots – like this stunning specimen.*

flowing water for spawning. Those living in lakes and lochs move into the feeder streams in the early autumn to spawn. Spawning occurs between November and January – the female digs two or three hollows (redds) into the gravel bed with her tail, in which she lays her eggs. At the same time the male fertilizes the eggs, and the female then covers the nest with gravel. Eggs not buried properly are quickly eaten by other predators.

Within a few weeks the eggs hatch, and the larvae (known as alevins) feed first on their egg sacs and then on small water creatures until they are about five months old. Since growth is dependent on food supply, size is variable, but after a few years most wild brown trout reach a length of 20-38cm (8-15in).

Looking for brownie points

Recommended rivers for brown trout, and where you can buy tickets to fish.
● **River Tyne** The Fly Box, Corbridge, Northumberland.
● **River Wear** Post Office, Eastgate, Tyne & Wear.
● **River Wharfe** Chatsworth Estate Office, Bolton Abbey, North Yorkshire.
● **River Rye** Nunnington Estate Office, N.Yorks.
● **River Colne** The Bull Hotel, Fairford, Glos.
● **River Taw** Fox & Hounds Hotel, Eggesford, N.Devon.
● **River Severn** Post Office, Caersws, Powys.
● **Salford Trout Lake** Rectory Farm, Salford, Chipping Norton, Oxon.

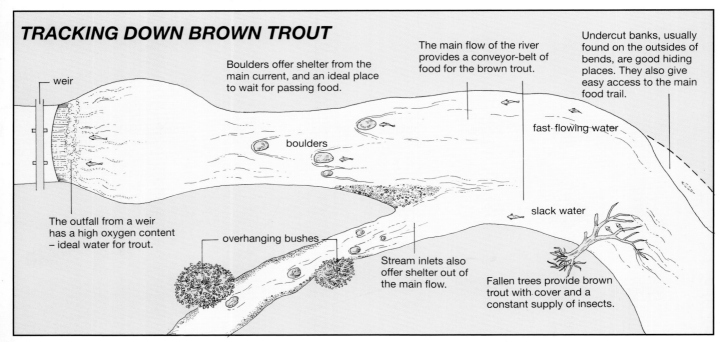

TRACKING DOWN BROWN TROUT

Boulders offer shelter from the main current, and an ideal place to wait for passing food.

The main flow of the river provides a conveyor-belt of food for the brown trout.

Undercut banks, usually found on the outsides of bends, are good hiding places. They also give easy access to the main food trail.

weir

fast-flowing water

boulders

slack water

The outfall from a weir has a high oxygen content – ideal water for trout.

overhanging bushes

Stream inlets also offer shelter out of the main flow.

Fallen trees provide brown trout with cover and a constant supply of insects.

Salmon

There is no doubt that the salmon is the best known fish in the world. While there are larger, stronger, more colourful fish, there is no other species that combines all these features so strongly as the salmon.

It seems extraordinary that a fish should travel thousands of miles across the Atlantic only to travel back again a year or two later to reach its exact place of birth to spawn. Although the salmon's homecoming marks the climax of an incredible journey and often ends in death, the spawning ground is where and how it all begins....

Most Atlantic salmon spawn between November and January because they need cold, well-oxygenated, fast-flowing water in which to breed. You can easily identify salmon that are ready to spawn – the hen (female) is dark grey with black spots and a bulging belly. The male is brick-red with elongated jaws, the lower of which hooks

Distribution

The salmon is most common in the rivers and coastal waters of Scotland, Ireland and Wales, though even here stocks are much smaller than they once were. English salmon are now fairly scarce.

upwards and is known as a kype.

Dig, dig, dig
The hen digs a shallow nest – called a redd – in gravel. She alternately flexes and straightens her body, flicking her tail to dis-

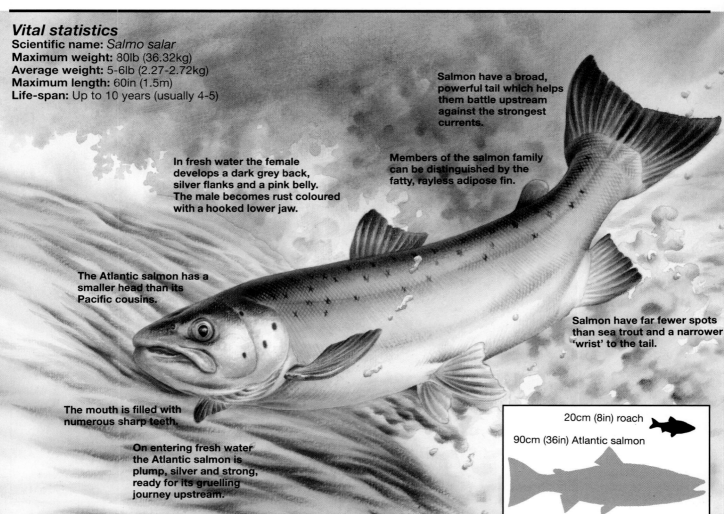

Vital statistics
Scientific name: *Salmo salar*
Maximum weight: 80lb (36.32kg)
Average weight: 5-6lb (2.27-2.72kg)
Maximum length: 60in (1.5m)
Life-span: Up to 10 years (usually 4-5)

Salmon have a broad, powerful tail which helps them battle upstream against the strongest currents.

In fresh water the female develops a dark grey back, silver flanks and a pink belly. The male becomes rust coloured with a hooked lower jaw.

Members of the salmon family can be distinguished by the fatty, rayless adipose fin.

The Atlantic salmon has a smaller head than its Pacific cousins.

Salmon have far fewer spots than sea trout and a narrower 'wrist' to the tail.

The mouth is filled with numerous sharp teeth.

On entering fresh water the Atlantic salmon is plump, silver and strong, ready for its gruelling journey upstream.

20cm (8in) roach

90cm (36in) Atlantic salmon

▲ *Before the male is ready to spawn its lower jaw becomes elongated and deeply curved (when it is called a kype); its scales turn a brick red colour.*

▶ *The dusky 'thumbprints' are just beginning to develop on this young parr. Many are eaten by predators at this stage, or die from starvation.*

lodge small stones, silt and plants. She tests the depth of the redd by pressing down with her anal fin and when it is 15-30cm (6-12in) deep, the male, who has been in constant attendance, swims alongside. They shed their eggs and milt simultaneously into the redd. (Oddly enough a large number of male parr – salmon under two years old – are sexually mature and nip in front of the adult male to fertilize the eggs themselves).

The female then covers the nest with gravel in the same way she prepared the redd. The eggs hatch in April-May, and the young transparent fish, known as alevins, shelter in the gravel and live off their yolk sac for the first few weeks.

First things first

Once the yolk sac has been absorbed, the infant salmon's first problem is that of finding food. As young fry they eat mainly insects – larval stoneflies and caddis flies in particular. Those that do find enough food to see out the cold spring and resist the attacks of predators, such as adult brown trout and herons, still have plenty of pitfalls to overcome.

The young fish remains in the upper reaches of the river. It slowly develops a row of dark grey 'thumbprints' along its flanks, with a red spot between each. At this stage it is known as a parr, and looks very similar to a brown trout of the same age. After two years, occasionally longer, physical changes begin to take place – salt-excreting cells form and the scales begin to turn silver.

Seaward ho!

When the young fish is fully silver and about 20cm (8in) long it is known as a smolt. As soon as the water begins to warm up the smolt begins its long descent downstream towards the sea. It is not until it reaches the

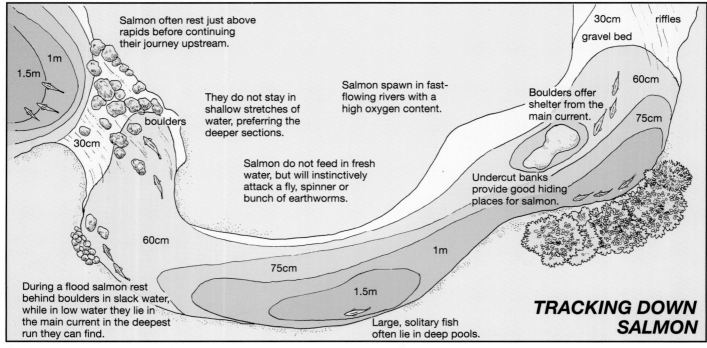

Salmon often rest just above rapids before continuing their journey upstream.

1m

1.5m

boulders

30cm

They do not stay in shallow stretches of water, preferring the deeper sections.

Salmon spawn in fast-flowing rivers with a high oxygen content.

Salmon do not feed in fresh water, but will instinctively attack a fly, spinner or bunch of earthworms.

30cm   riffles

gravel bed

Boulders offer shelter from the main current.

60cm

75cm

Undercut banks provide good hiding places for salmon.

60cm

75cm

1m

1.5m

During a flood salmon rest behind boulders in slack water, while in low water they lie in the main current in the deepest run they can find.

Large, solitary fish often lie in deep pools.

TRACKING DOWN SALMON

On the farm

Because of the sporting and food value of the salmon, many rivers are now stocked with the offspring of salmon hatcheries. In recent years salmon farming has become a boom industry in the sea lochs of Scotland and on Irish coasts.

Of interest to anglers are the salmon from fisheries that are being introduced into lakes and reservoirs. Although such fish will never breed, they offer anglers a chance to catch fish in areas that are otherwise starved of salmon.

▼ *Salmon leaping a waterfall on the River Lled in Wales. Such jumps are exhausting and the fish must rest for a long time before continuing their journey upstream.*

mouth of the river that the riches of the sea are exploited. Here it feasts on shrimps, whitebait, sandeels and small members of the cod family.

Some salmon stay in coastal waters, but others migrate – a few to the Norwegian coast – but most move to the west coast of Greenland. In the sea they face further threats from seals, gulls and predatory fish such as cod and conger eels.

The time spent in the sea fattens them up in preparation for the arduous journey upriver to spawn. At first they grow rapidly. The salmon's weight can increase by as much as 20 times in less than a year. Some return to spawn after only one year at sea and are known as grilse; others stay for another two or more years, reaching up to 40lb (18kg), before returning.

The long trek

The journey downstream as a smolt may have been exhausting – but the long haul back is even more gruelling. How the salmon finds its way from ocean to coast is an extraordinary feat of navigation. The fish finds its way back to its exact birthplace mainly by using its acute sense of smell.

Having survived the pollution and nets in

Taking it in stages

1 alevin

yolk sac

2 parr

8-10 'thumbprints' on the flanks

3 smolt

silvery coat

1. Alevin is the name for a newly hatched, transparent fish. For the first few weeks of life it lives buried in the gravel, feeding off its yolk sac.
2. From the age of six months to two years the immature salmon remains in the upper reaches of rivers and is known as a **parr**.
3. Once the young fish has turned silver and begins to swim downstream towards the sea it is called a **smolt**.

Family ties

Although the Atlantic salmon is the only salmonid common in Britain and Ireland, stray humpbacks turn up in northern rivers and can be identified by their spotted tail and dorsal fin. Relatives include the Pacific, chum and humpback salmon, native to Alaska, Canada and Russia, and the Danubian salmon, only found in eastern Europe.

▼ *This salmon was taken on a spinner. However, fly-fishing is the most popular method for catching this king of fish.*

the estuaries, the salmon stops feeding – it has stored up enough fat to sustain it for over a year. Swimming against the flow, the fish moves upstream in a series of runs – a task made easier when the water is warm and the river level high.

Fish are jumpin'

When it cannot overcome obstacles, such as weirs and waterfalls, by swimming, the salmon jumps over them. It can leap as high as 3.5m (12ft) as long as it starts from deep enough water, but it can only jump during the daytime since it judges where the top of the obstacle is by aiming for the light above it. This is how the salmon gets its name – the Romans called it *Salmo*, from the Latin verb *salire*, to leap.

Beginning and end

By November many have arrived at their birthplace, and from then until mid-January mating takes place. At the end of it the fish, now known as kelts, are weak and emaciated. Most males, and some females, die, either from exhaustion or from a fungal disease known as saprolegnia. Those that don't perish rest in deep holes through the winter or drift towards the sea, ready to repeat the cycle again.

Both sides of the 'pond'

The Atlantic salmon is found on both the North American and European Atlantic coastlines and migrates into the rivers of both continents to spawn. At one time its natural range in Europe extended from the most northerly rivers of Spain and Portugal to Norway and the River Pechora in Russia. However, today many of the rivers which formerly contained salmon no longer do so.

Nowadays there are few salmon south of the coast of Brittany – most of the stocks once found in France, Germany, Holland and Poland are either extinct or so small that they are endangered. English salmon are now also scarce and there are fewer in Scottish, Welsh and Irish waters than there once were. Only the rivers of Norway and Iceland contain appreciable numbers.

What's happened?

There are several reasons for the widespread destruction of salmon stocks. Weirs and dams on major rivers impede migration upstream; pollution, particularly in estuaries, has also diminished numbers.

In recent years the activities of the marine fishing industry have affected the food of the salmon at sea with fewer herring, sandeels and shrimps available. The angler is the least of its worries.

Where to fish

Salmon do not feed in fresh water. However, for some time after returning from the sea they retain the reflex to bite at anything that attracts them. The fact that they don't need nourishment is what makes them so frustratingly difficult to catch!

Unfortunately, most of the salmon fishing in Britain is very costly. Here are a few places out of a handful where you can find decent sport.
● The District Council Leisure and Recreation Department, 2 High Street, Perth, Scotland offers 20 day-permits on the North Inch throughout the season.
● Strathspey Angling Association has a weekly ticket for the River Spey for anglers staying in Grantown-on-Spey. For more information, contact G. Mortimer, 61 High Street, Grantown, Scotland.
● Monmouth DC has day-ticket fishing on the River Usk, Abergavenny, Gwent. Contact PM Tackle, 12 Monk Street, Abergavenny.

Char

Few anglers have ever seen a char, but those who have appreciate it as one of our rarest and most beautiful species.

Char records

- **For years** the record was about 2-3lb (0.9-1.4kg); then in 1986 it jumped to 4lb 13oz (2.26kg). Since then much larger char have come from salmon farming lochs. The record skipped to 5lb 7oz (2.46kg), 5lb 10oz (2.55kg), then 6lb 1oz (2.74kg).
- **The current record** is an 8lb (3.63kg) fish caught in 1992 by F. Nicolson from Loch Arcaig, Scotland.
- **Now rumour** has it that a 9lb 12oz (4.42kg) fish has been taken. A double-figure char seems to be just around the corner!

One of Britain's most mysterious fish, the char lives so deep and in such remote lakes that few people know it exists. Originally a sea fish that spawned in fresh water, it was stranded in lakes created as the ice caps retreated 10,000 years ago.

It has the adipose fin that distinguishes members of the salmon family and, like the trout, thrives in clean, cold water.

The female is generally greenish or a dusky violet-blue, sometimes shifting towards a sheen of lighter pearl. The male, especially in the breeding season, develops a sensational orange or crimson belly that sets off ventral fins edged in white. Both sexes are lavishly spotted with white.

These are the typical colours of mature fish. The char lives in the deep glacial lakes of Scotland, Ireland, Wales and the Lake District. Over thousands of years isolated groups have developed their own colours, markings, shapes and even habits.

Distribution

The char can be found in most of the deeper lochs in Scotland, especially in the north-west, and in some of the lakes in the Lake District (eg. Windermere) it also occurs in some Irish loughs and in two Welsh lakes.

Seasonal movements

Char vary their habits quite dramatically according to the season.

From mid winter to early summer most fish lie deep down in the loch in vast shoals, thousands strong. In the darkness

Vital statistics

Scientific name: *Salvelinus alpinus*
Maximum weight: In Britain 10lb (4.5kg)
Average weight: In Britain 2lb (0.9kg)
Maximum length: In Britain 60cm (2ft)
Life-span: Up to 10 years

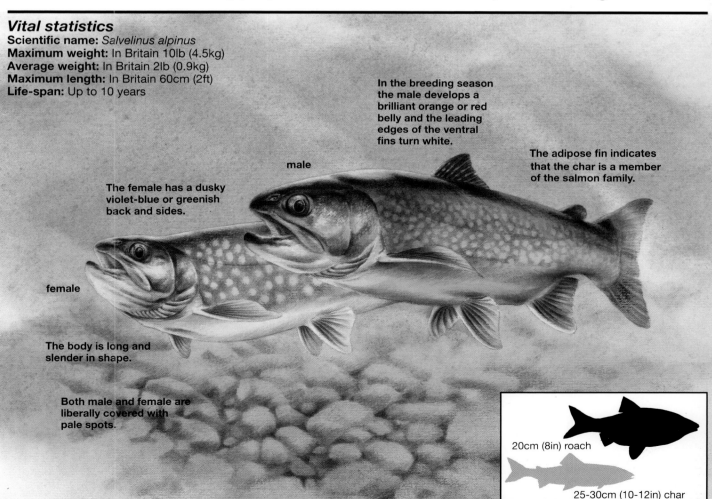

In the breeding season the male develops a brilliant orange or red belly and the leading edges of the ventral fins turn white.

The adipose fin indicates that the char is a member of the salmon family.

male

The female has a dusky violet-blue or greenish back and sides.

female

The body is long and slender in shape.

Both male and female are liberally covered with pale spots.

20cm (8in) roach

25-30cm (10-12in) char

hundreds of feet beneath the surface they drift with the currents, feeding on molluscs and small crustaceans.

In the summer, as temperatures rise, the char spend more time in the upper layers, feeding on insects and very small fish. In the evenings they may rise to surface flies or venture into shallow bays to investigate weed beds. Shoals break up and groups of fish 20 to 50 strong strike off together.

In the autumn mature char start migrating to their spawning beds, sited in the faster waters of any large stream entering or leaving the loch. They favour shallow, rocky ground, running the fast water from dusk through the night, then drifting back at dawn to the safety of the loch.

The brightly coloured males gather in the fast water where the larger, drabber females spray their eggs into depressions (redds) between the rocks and stones. It is a violently agitated courtship in which many fish break the surface of the stream.

Not all the char spawn at once. The process continues throughout September and October, with some fish appearing on the redds as late as February.

Growth is slow

Small char are heavily preyed on by eels and brown trout and grow slowly in most lochs, often only reaching 15-20cm (6-8in) at two to four years old. In many poor lochs the largest adult fish may be only 25cm (10in) long and weigh less than a pound (0.45kg). But growth rates do vary a great

▲ *Hours of despair for the angler are followed by hectic bursts of action when half a dozen char can be landed in minutes.*

deal. In richer lochs, especially those with salmon farms, char have access to food pellets and pack on weight. In such places 2lb (0.9kg) char are not uncommon.

Char aren't easy to locate; you can see them occasionally in the half light of the short summer night, dimpling for gnats or small surface flies but most of their lives are spent deep down in dark, cold water where you need a fish finder to track them.

▼ *Shoals move slowly all the time, often close to the bank and along a particular depth contour in search of food.*

Where to fish

● Shoals of char exist in most large, deep lochs in Scotland, especially above the Great Glen to the north-west.
● Famous populations exist in **Lochs Arkaig** and **Lochy** near Fort William, **Lochs Garry** and **Quoich** near Inverness, **Loch Ness** near Inverness, **Windermere** in the Lake District and **Lough Mask** in Co. Mayo, Republic of Ireland.

Grayling

John Roberts, Yorkshire grayling expert, examines the 'lady of the stream', a fish which continues to gain popularity and respect from both coarse and game anglers.

Record grayling

● The record has been broken many times during the 1980s. In August 1983, for example, I. White caught a 3lb 10oz (1.64kg) grayling from the River Allen in Dorset.
● That record was broken in 1988 by a 4lb (1.8kg) fish which was caught from a still water off the River Frome.
● Sean Lanigan holds the current record. On 8 January 1989 he caught a 4lb 3oz (1.899kg) grayling from the River Frome, near Trowbridge in Dorset.

Grayling appear to be an enigma for anglers to classify. They possess an adipose fin, a characteristic of the salmon family, but they spawn at the same time as coarse fish, and the grayling season corresponds to the coarse fishing season. Most anglers, however, agree that they are game fish.

Distinctively beautiful, grayling have silvery sides which are dappled with irregular dark spots and mixed with a riot of purple, green and copper hues. A noticeable feature is the huge sail-like dorsal fin, mottled with black and red bars, which is raised at times of stress. A grayling hooked downstream uses this fin to battle against the angler, often in a gyrating or figure of eight motion; the erect fin increases its resistance in the current as the angler draws the fish upstream.

Distribution

Grayling are found in many clean streams and rivers throughout England and northern Wales. Populations aren't as high in Scotland, and they're not found in Ireland.

Clean, clear waters

Of all the native British fish, grayling are the most sensitive to pollution, disappearing long before trout or chub. Less than half a dozen lakes hold grayling. They thrive in chalk and limestone streams but

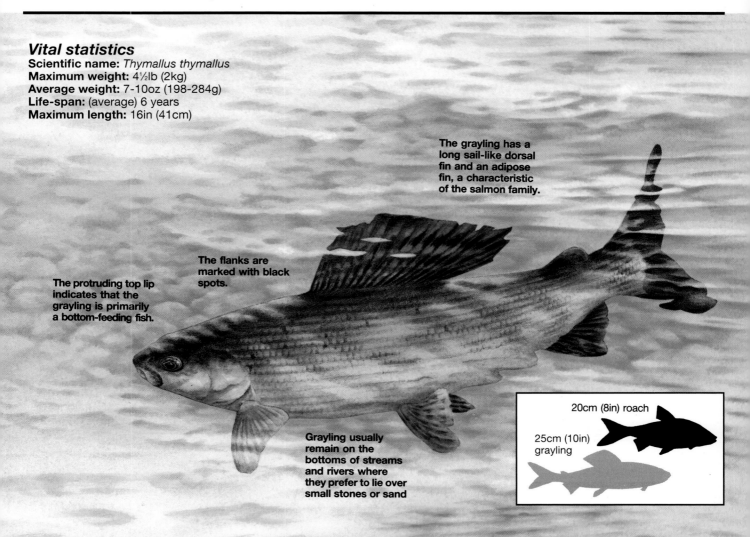

Vital statistics
Scientific name: *Thymallus thymallus*
Maximum weight: 4½lb (2kg)
Average weight: 7-10oz (198-284g)
Life-span: (average) 6 years
Maximum length: 16in (41cm)

The grayling has a long sail-like dorsal fin and an adipose fin, a characteristic of the salmon family.

The flanks are marked with black spots.

The protruding top lip indicates that the grayling is primarily a bottom-feeding fish.

Grayling usually remain on the bottoms of streams and rivers where they prefer to lie over small stones or sand

20cm (8in) roach

25cm (10in) grayling

are also found in neutral waters like the Tay and Tweed and their tributaries. Most of the time you can find them over gravel, small stones, weeds or sand. They do not seem to like lying over silty, muddy bottoms.

Grayling are sensitive to temperature change, and for this reason their favoured sheltering places vary within rivers and streams as the seasons change. In summer they prefer fast, well-oxygenated water and live near the heads of pools and in riffles where they actively seek insects caught in the fast current. In early autumn they move into moderately paced runs of even depth. In winter when the frosts come, grayling form shoals and move to deeper water such as pools.

Holding positions close to the river bed, they are rarely found above mid-water and almost never remain stationary near the surface for long periods of time.

Top and bottom feeders

Grayling are well equipped for feeding off the bottom because their top lip extends beyond their lower. Nymphs, caddis larvae, shrimps, midges and small crustaceans are some of their main food items. It is also thought that grayling eat trout

▲ *This specimen grayling was taken from a small southern chalk stream. Many grayling are needlessly killed by owners of trout fisheries, some of whom claim the fish are a nuisance and 'bad for business'.*

eggs. Fly fishermen can represent many of their food items with dry or wet flies, and anglers using maggots or brandlings are also successful. The most important thing to remember is to present the bait at the correct level where the fish are. Grayling rise from lower levels to feed on natural and artificial flies. Whether they take the fly or miss it, they usually return to the bottom.

Development

Grayling usually spawn between March and May. Females dig small pits (called redds) in gravel or sand and then lay their eggs. Several males may fertilize the eggs of a single female. About a month later the eggs hatch. The yolk sacs of the larvae don't last long, so the fry begin feeding on plankton at once.

When the fry are a year old, they are about 4-5in (10-13cm) long and tend to form shoals. After about three years they begin to spawn.

Grayling venues

Though many rivers and streams across Britain are privately run, John Roberts recommends these day-ticket waters.
● **River Wharfe,** The Red Lion, Burnsall, N. Yorks. Many excellent sized fish caught here.
● **River Ure,** The Rose & Crown, Bainbridge, N. Yorks.
● **River Nidd,** Stebbings Gift Shop, Pately Bridge, N. Yorkshire.

● **River Dee,** Brwyn Arms Hotel, Glyndyrfdwy, Corwen, Clwyd, Wales.
● **River Earn,** Morven Hotel, Auchterarder, Scotland.
● **River Tanat,** Horseshoe Inn, Llanyblodwel, Shropshire.
● **River Severn,** Caresws Angling Club, Llanidloes, Powys.
● **River Wye** (Derbyshire) Haddon Hall Fishery, Rowlsey. Book in advance. Tel (0629) 636255.

TRACKING DOWN GRAYLING

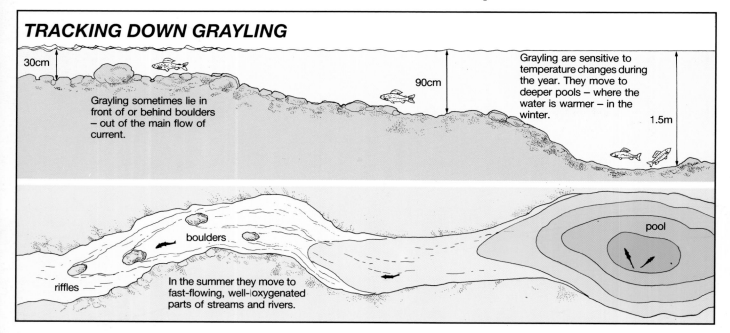

30cm

Grayling sometimes lie in front of or behind boulders – out of the main flow of current.

90cm

Grayling are sensitive to temperature changes during the year. They move to deeper pools – where the water is warmer – in the winter.

1.5m

boulders

pool

riffles

In the summer they move to fast-flowing, well-oxygenated parts of streams and rivers.

Sea trout

Is it a brown trout? A salmon? Or a totally separate species? In fact, the sea trout is a migratory brownie, but its silver colouring and life-style is more akin to that of the salmon.

Distribution

Sea trout are found in rivers with access to the sea on the west coast of the British Isles, the east coast of Scotland and south to North Yorkshire and along England's south coast. They are found along the same areas in the sea, as well as the North Sea.

Record sea trout

● The British record is held by S. Burgoyne for a 22lb 8oz (10.205kg) fish caught from River Leven, Scotland in 1989.
● The Irish record is for a 16lb 6oz (7.42kg) fish caught by T. McManus from the Shima River, Co. Down in 1983.

One of the great arguments among fish scientists over the past 150 years has been the relationship between the various kinds of trout in Europe. From a situation where up to a dozen types of trout were recognized in Britain, the pendulum swung to the opinion that there was only one species which varied considerably in response to local environmental conditions.

Echoes of this argument can still be heard: it has recently been claimed that Lough Melvin in County Sligo, Republic of Ireland contains three species of trout distinct from the trout in the rest of the British Isles!

As any angler who fishes for wild trout can confirm, the fish are remarkably different in appearance depending on whether they come from a Scottish loch, a Devonshire moorland stream or the west coast of Ireland.

The sea trout is not a separate species, but a migratory form of brown trout. As such it can be confused with both the brown trout and the salmon, having the body shape of the former and the colouring of the latter.

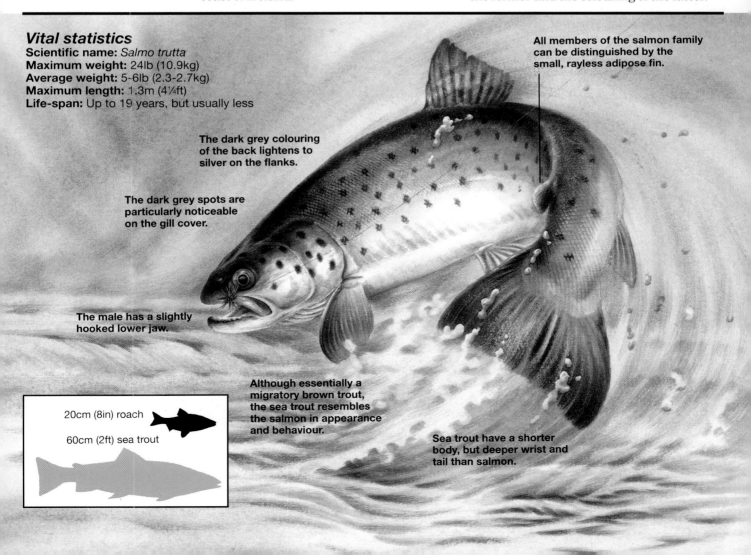

Vital statistics
Scientific name: *Salmo trutta*
Maximum weight: 24lb (10.9kg)
Average weight: 5-6lb (2.3-2.7kg)
Maximum length: 1.3m (4¼ft)
Life-span: Up to 19 years, but usually less

All members of the salmon family can be distinguished by the small, rayless adipose fin.

The dark grey colouring of the back lightens to silver on the flanks.

The dark grey spots are particularly noticeable on the gill cover.

The male has a slightly hooked lower jaw.

Although essentially a migratory brown trout, the sea trout resembles the salmon in appearance and behaviour.

Sea trout have a shorter body, but deeper wrist and tail than salmon.

20cm (8in) roach

60cm (2ft) sea trout

Hatching takes place after six to eight weeks, but the young trout stay buried in the gravel for a further month or so before emerging and starting to feed.

At this stage they are indistinguishable from young brown trout, but a year or two later they drop downriver towards the estuary, where they become silvery smolts. Why they do this – when ordinary brown trout stay where they are – is a mystery.

Seaward bound

Some of these young fish stay in the vicinity of the estuary and return upriver after only a few months – they are known locally as whitling, finnock, herling or slob trout – but very few of them spawn. Most, however, swim out to sea to feed on shellfish and other creatures for at least a year. Sea trout do not make the same long journey to the high seas as salmon, but stay in the coastal waters in search of rich feeding grounds. For example, the large numbers of sea trout off Norfolk have mostly come from Yorkshire and other north-east coast rivers to feed on the schools of sprats and sandeels.

Bloodhounds of the sea

Like salmon, sea trout are strongly imprinted with the scent of the river in which they were born, and most return to their home stream to spawn. However, the number of wanderers is greater with sea trout than with salmon. This accounts for the occasional appearance of sea trout in rivers in which it does not breed – the Thames and Medway for example.

Migratory species have suffered greatly from pollution in the lower reaches of rivers and from the construction of dams, weirs and locks. Recently populations of sea trout seem to have declined in areas where they were at one time extensive – a worrying development.

Hotspots for sea trout

From June onwards estuaries and the lower reaches of rivers are the best spots to catch sea trout as they make their run upriver.
- **Rivers Ailort and Wick,** Highlands, Scotland.
- **River Clwyd,** Wales.
- **River Costelloe,** Co. Galway, Rep. of Ireland.
- **River Esk,** Yorkshire.
- **River Fowey,** Cornwall.
- **River Newport,** Co. Mayo, Republic of Ireland.
- **River Ouse,** Sussex.
- **Rivers South Esk and Tay** Tayside, Scotland.
- **River Taf,** Dyfed, Wales.
- **River Tavy,** Devon.

▲ *Most fishing for sea trout is done at night, since this is when they are most active. They are extremely resilient fish and put up a very hard fight when hooked.*

The sea trout has a thick wrist to the tail fin and the long upper jaw bone of the brown trout, contrasting with the slender wrist and shorter jaw bone of the salmon. Brilliantly silver in colour, the sea trout has more black spots than the salmon, particularly on its cheek and gill covers.

First dig your hole

Having entered fresh water during the summer, sea trout spawn between October and January – the eggs are laid in fine gravel well upstream. The spawning redd is dug by the female who bores into the surface and then dislodges the small stones with powerful sweeps of her tail. In contrast to salmon, which usually die after spawning, sea trout spawn year after year.

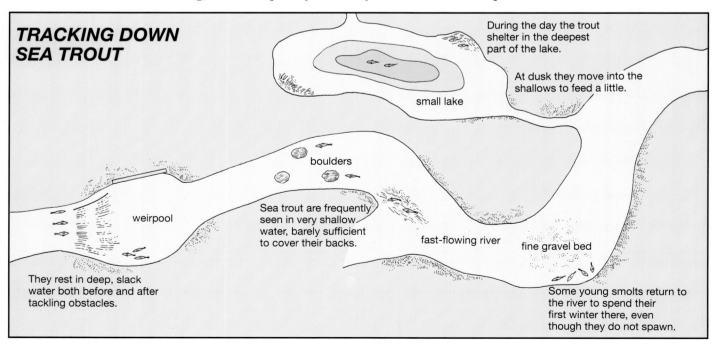

TRACKING DOWN SEA TROUT

During the day the trout shelter in the deepest part of the lake.

At dusk they move into the shallows to feed a little.

small lake

boulders

weirpool

Sea trout are frequently seen in very shallow water, barely sufficient to cover their backs.

fast-flowing river

fine gravel bed

They rest in deep, slack water both before and after tackling obstacles.

Some young smolts return to the river to spend their first winter there, even though they do not spawn.

Whitefish

Three species of whitefish – the vendace, powan and pollan – live isolated in the lakes of north-west Britain, stranded survivors from the Ice Age.

Distribution

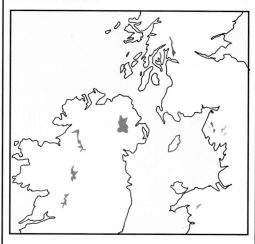

KEY

1. ● Powan   2. ● Schelly
3. ● Gwyniad   4. ● Vendace
5. ● Pollan

1. Powan Loch Eck, Loch Lomond, Scotland.
2. Schelly Haweswater, Ullswater and the Red Tarn in the Lake District.
3. Gwyniad Llyn Tegid (Lake Bala), Wales.
4. Vendace Derwentwater and Bassenthwaite in the Lake District.
5. Pollan L. Neagh, Dearg, Ree, Erne, Ireland.

Whitefish records

The British Record Fish Committee will not accept any record claim for whitefish because they now have protected status.
● Before this ruling, the only British whitefish record was a schelly of 2lb 1oz 9dm (0.950kg), caught in 1986 from Haweswater by S. M. Barrie.

Whitefish are related to the trout and salmon and possess the adipose fin typical of game fish. A small fleshy fin with no rays, it is sited between the dorsal and the tail fins. Whitefish differ from their salmonid relatives in possessing large scales (a lot fewer than either trout or salmon), and in having virtually toothless jaws and a small mouth. They are pale in colour, the back being greeny-blue and the sides and belly silvery to white. It is this absence of dark colour that gives them their name – whitefish.

What's in a name?

Three species of whitefish live in the British Isles, all in lakes in the north-west. However, over the years there has been

---

Vital statistics

VENDACE
Scientific name: *Coregonus albula*
Maximum weight: 8oz (226g)
Average length: 20cm (8in)
Life-span: 5 years

Vendace are slightly deeper bodied and smaller than the other species of whitefish.

POLLAN
Scientific name: *Coregonus autumnalis*
Maximum weight: 2½lb (1.2kg)
Average length: 30cm (12in)
Life-span: 10-15 years

Vendace have protruding, curved lower jaws.

POWAN, SCHELLY or GWYNIAD
Scientific name: *Coregonus lavaretus*
Maximum weight: Just over 2lb (0.9kg)
Average length: 30-36cm (12-14in)
Life-span: 10 years

The tail is deeply forked.

The small fleshy adipose fin between the dorsal and tail fin is characteristic of the salmon family.

Powan have fairly large mouths.

All whitefish are pale and silvery in colour with large scales, rather like grayling.

Large eyes are useful for feeding at depth in deep mountain lakes.

20cm (8in) roach
20cm (8in) vendace
30cm (12in) powan/pollan

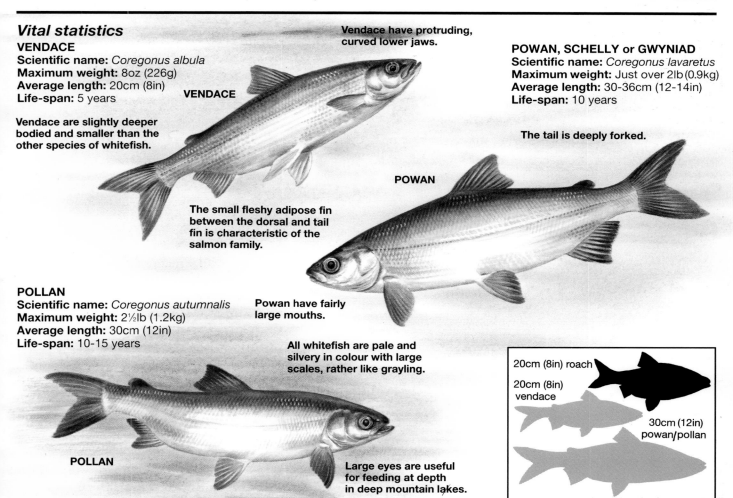

enormous confusion about their identity and, indeed, about how many species there were in our islands.

The problem was caused partly by their isolation – they are found in widely separated lakes, and each population had acquired a separate common name – and partly because over centuries of isolation each population had evolved to possess slightly different features. This led scientists to give a distinct scientific name to each species or sub-species they thought they had recognized.

Since whitefish are also found across the whole of Europe, northern Asia and North America, many in lakes similar to those in Britain, the number of populations bearing scientific names was immense.

However, modern studies have now produced a situation where only three species are recognized in Britain. All three are also found in Europe or North America.

The first species is *Coregonus lavaretus*: it lives in Loch Eck and Loch Lomond in Scotland, where it is known as the powan; in Haweswater, Ullswater and the Red Tarn in the English Lake District, where it is called the schelly; and in Llyn Tegid (Lake Bala) in Wales, where it goes by the name of the gwyniad.

Another, somewhat smaller, species – the vendace *(Coregonus albula)* – lives in Derwentwater and Bassenthwaite in the Lake District. It was formerly found in Castle and Mill Lochs at Lochmaben in Dumfriesshire but is now believed to be extinct there.

The third species, *Coregonus autumnalis,* known as the pollan, lives in Ireland in Loughs Neagh, Dearg, Ree and Erne. In many ways this is the odd one out since its nearest relatives seem to live in western

North America; the other two species are found in many lakes in northern Europe and the Alps.

How did they get here?

The whitefish are believed to have lived in the immense 'ice lakes' that covered large areas of Europe at the end of the Ice Ages, but they may also have lived in the low salinity seas surrounding the partly frozen land mass, migrating into rivers every year to spawn. Over thousands of years these 'ice lakes' disappeared as the glaciers melted, causing the land to rise as the weight of ice was removed.

The result seems to have been that populations of several kinds of whitefish (probably very closely related) became stranded in geographically restricted areas and eventually land-locked in the lakes in which we know them today. Ten to fifteen thousand years of isolation have caused tiny changes in each population in response to slight differences in environments.

Feeding and breeding

The whitefish in Britain feed mainly on minute crustaceans, particularly daphnia (water fleas) and copepods, but as they grow larger they eat insect larvae and even bottom-living molluscs as well. In winter, when planktonic crustaceans are scarce, they tend to feed near the lake bed on a variety of insect larvae.

They spawn in early winter, laying their eggs on gravelly lake beds, usually in moderate depths. The orange eggs take up to 10 weeks to hatch. The fry then feed on their yolk sacs for a few weeks, ensuring the young fish begin to swim in early spring – a time when the smallest planktonic creatures are readily available.

▲ *This gwyniad, from Lake Bala in Wales, is a typical whitefish with its adipose fin, silvery body and large scales. Fishing for this and other whitefish is now prohibited.*

Protection factor

In Britain the whitefish are a protected species and it is an offence to attempt to catch them; if you catch one by accident, return it unharmed to the water immediately. This protection is as much a response to the limited number of populations we have as to any rarity in the lakes in which they live.

However, two out of the four populations of vendace are believed extinct – which shows how vulnerable isolated lakes can be. Of the factors which contributed to the extinction of the vendace in the Lochmaben area, one was related to the introduction of roach and bream by anglers – these fish being successful competitors with the vendace. The more recent introduction of ruffe into Loch Lomond may have serious consequences for the powan in that lake.

CHAPTER FIVE

FLIES, LURES AND SPINNERS

Selecting flies for stillwater trout

Understanding what a trout is feeding on can help the boat and bank angler catch more fish. Taff Price looks at some insects which are major food items for stillwater trout, and he also recommends how and when to fish imitations.

Too many game anglers dismiss the study of insects as being too complicated and not that important when fly fishing. This is simply not true.

Six stillwater giants
The following are some of the most important groups of insects and crustaceans for trout.

Midges Because of their sheer numbers, midges (chironomids) are one of the most important insect groups for stillwater trout. Like most other insects, a midge has four stages of growth: egg, larva, pupa_and adult. The colours of the immature insects range from black to olive, brown, orange, green and red.

The fly fisherman is concerned mainly with only two stages of this insect – the larva and the pupa, both of which can move around. An adult imitation is only important when mated females return to lay their eggs on the surface of the water.

Midge larvae, known as bloodworms, can grow up to 19mm (¾in) long. They live in the silt at the bottom of lakes. To fish a bloodworm imitation, slowly retrieve it directly along the bottom.

Midge pupae or 'buzzers' grow by moulting their outer skin. In the pupal stage they can be found at all depths of water.

▼ *Mid-season tactics on big stillwaters wouldn't be complete without using sedge pupa imitations fished in deep water.*

Some patterns

● **Marabou Bloodworm**
Hook: 12-14 long shank
Head: peacock herl
Body: red floss ribbed with fluorescent red floss
Tail: long red marabou.
Head: black
● **Midge Pupa**
Hook: 8-14
Head: peacock herl or black hare's fur
Body: black silk ribbed with gold or copper wire
Thread: black
● **Damsel Nymph**
Hook: 6-12 long shank
Body: dubbed green marabou or wool
Thorax: dark olive marabou
Wing case: light green feather
Tail: olive hackle fibres
Rib: copper wire
Thread: green
● **Little Red Sedge**
Hook: 12-16
Body: hare's fur, palmered red cock hackle
Rib: fine gold wire
Wing: partridge tail

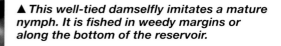

▲ *This well-tied damselfly imitates a mature nymph. It is fished in weedy margins or along the bottom of the reservoir.*

Tip Into the wind

Why fish into the wind and put up with casting and presentation difficulties? The answer is simply because the wind blows surface food (weak-flying hatching insects such as midges) into a corner. All that concentrated food means hungry trout won't be too far away.

▲ *A ravenous predator of other insects, the damsel nymph is found mainly in stillwaters – from huge reservoirs to tiny ponds.*

In still conditions when dust and other particles – combined with the surface tension of the water – make it difficult for the hatching pupae to break through, trout go on a feeding spree, and midges are picked off by the thousand.

Most major hatches occur in spring and summer, during the early morning and evening. These are prime times to fish a midge pupa imitation. Fish an artificial

▼ *The midge pupa, a staple diet of stillwater trout, has problems breaking through the water's surface tension. A build-up of dust in calm conditions may also hinder midges.*

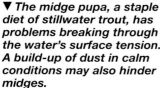

▶ *This is an artificial midge pupa (size 8), also known as a buzzer, pupa buzzer or buzzer nymph.*

A slow, constant retrieve often proves successful when using this ever-popular fly.

▲ *Stillwater trout depend upon freshwater hoglice (above) and shrimps in the early months of the year. Unlike shrimps, hoglice rarely leave the safe haven of weeds in summer.*

▼ *Corixas are generally found near weedy lake margins. They can survive in waters with low levels of oxygen. You can sometimes see them rising to the surface to take in air and then darting back down to hide.*

▲ *Though daphnia are too tiny to imitate properly, many anglers claim a small orange nymph (14-18) attracts daphnia-feeding trout.*

emerger – this has a polystyrene ball located near the eye of the hook – in the surface film, giving it an occasional twitch to imitate a struggling pupa in the process of hatching.

Darting damselflies Damselfly nymphs make up a large proportion of a trout's diet in summer. They are usually brown or green, blending in perfectly with their weedy or reedy environment. Damselfly nymphs are capable of short bursts of speed.

The nymph stage lasts about a year – though some species take up to five years to develop into an adult.

Fish a damselfly imitation in weed beds along the bottom or just under the surface in shallow lake margins. Experiment with different retrieves such as slow and steady along the bottom or short, fast strips near the surface.

Margin-loving corixas These brown beetle-like insects – known as lesser water boatmen – are found on most stillwaters near shallow weedy margins. They thrive on algae and other plant debris. Varying in length from 4mm to about 10mm, they have a remarkable ability to live in water with a low oxygen content. You can often see them rising to the surface and then quickly sinking to the bottom like a small stone. Corixas carry their air supply in a bubble between their wings and back. When the air is used up, they must leave the security of their weed or root and make a dangerous journey to collect more.

Fish the fly in shallow, weedy areas, suggesting the insect's natural habit of sinking from the surface to the bottom.

Caddis (sedge) flies Some species of caddis larvae make shelters from sand, small stones

Using a marrow spoon

Once you have caught a trout, you can examine its stomach contents with a marrow spoon to see what else it has been feeding on (in addition, of course, to your fly!).

Put the spoon into the trout's mouth and ease it back until the fish deposits its meal. You may have to look closely to discover what the trout has been feeding on. Sometimes you may not need to use a marrow spoon: some trout still have half their meal in their mouths!

Tip Acting real

To catch a trout with an imitation involves everything from how a fly or lure *looks* to how it *acts*. Looks alone won't always convince wary trout. Nymphs must be fished to act like real-life nymphs, and not like lures.

▼ *Five medium-sized stillwater rainbows display their bright silver sheen. The importance of having an intimate knowledge of a trout's favourite food items can't be overstressed.*

and plant debris. Others rely solely upon camouflage. During the larval and pupal stages the insects develop under water.

Even though the pupa is fast-swimming, it is no match for a trout. At the point when the insect is about to break its sheath and hatch into an adult on the surface of the water, it is virtually immobile for a few seconds and vulnerable to hungry fish.

To imitate the caddis larva, fish a pattern such as a Stickfly slowly along the bottom. To imitate the quick and ever-popular pupa, fish an imitation such as Goddard's Sedge Pupa near the surface of the water – particularly at dusk when major hatches of caddis flies take place. Remember, the pupa can swim quite fast, so you should retrieve quite quickly.

Fish an adult sedge imitation (such as a Little Red Sedge) static on the surface, giving it an occasional twitch to suggest life.

Crustacean magic Water fleas, freshwater shrimps and hoglice are an important year-round food source for trout. Recently hatched trout often feed on daphnia until they are large enough to tackle bigger mouthfuls. Since daphnia are so small, proper imitation is difficult.

Stillwater trout may feed exclusively on shrimps and hoglice during the lean months in spring when insect life is low and competition between recently stocked fish and overwintered trout is high. Freshwater shrimps and hoglice are much more common around weeds where they have cover. In April and early May, fish an imitation slowly right along the bottom.

Terrestrials Land insects such as hawthorn flies, daddy-long-legs, black gnats and flying ants can be blown on to stillwaters in late summer and early autumn when they are numerous. Terrestrials are in an alien environment as soon as they touch water. Many become trapped in the water's surface and then waterlogged – an easy meal for trout. Use floating line and long leaders of at least 6lb (2.7kg) breaking strain.

The flies of Britain's rivers

Pick up a rock from a clean river in summer, and you'll probably see a host of dark shapes, scurrying to safety. John Roberts, Yorkshire fly-fishing expert, looks at some of the food items that trout feast on.

▼ *Rich in weed growth and nutrients, this river is a haven for aquatic insects. In many cases river trout live almost exclusively on insects and crustaceans. Imitation and presentation are the keys when fly-fishing on rivers – use a pattern which closely resembles the natural.*

Shrimps and aquatic insects such as mayflies, caddis flies and stoneflies are important food items for most trout and grayling in rivers all year round. Terrestrial insects such as daddy-long-legs and beetles are also significant – especially from May to September.

Trout and grayling can sometimes become selective towards an insect species. This is usually because that insect is avail-able in greater numbers than others. It's not the size of the fly or nymph that attracts trout, but the numbers of insects available.

Mayflies

Trout take mayfly nymphs underneath the water, and they feed on the adult duns (recently hatched adults) and egg-laying spinners on the surface.

In some species of mayfly the egg-laying female deposits its eggs on the surface. With others they crawl into the water to lay their eggs. Weeks later the eggs hatch, and the tiny nymphs emerge. Moulting several times to grow, they reach maximum size a couple of weeks before becoming adult flies. Their life-cycle lasts about a year.

Some mayflies thrive in slow-moving water with a silty river bed. Other species require faster water with a bottom of stones or gravel, and still others need moss or weeds in moderate currents.

The body shapes of nymphs have adapted to different environments. Broad-bodied, flat nymphs cling to the sides of stones in fast water; cylindrical, fast-swimming

The mayfly dun

This is a newly hatched mayfly (a dun); it moults after a few hours into a spinner and then mates. The female returns to the water to lay her eggs and dies soon afterwards.

The mayfly nymph

Mayflies are the most important group of river insects. The nymphs range from 6-30mm (¼-1¼in) in length and have six legs and two or three tails, depending on the species.

▼ *This angler is fly-fishing upstream in summer on the River Whiteadder in northern England.*
  Caddis larva or sedge pupa patterns are effective mid-summer flies.

nymphs live among weeds. Slim-shaped, burrowing nymphs only come out from the silt when about to hatch into adults.

Nymphs become more active just before they become adults, as they wait for ideal hatching conditions. Their wing pads darken, and they reach their maximum size

(6-30mm/¼-1¼in depending upon the species). They swim busily about and even make tentative journeys to the surface. Trout begin to take an avid interest in the nymphs at this time.

When hatching at the surface, the nymph pauses while the upper sides of its nymphal

The sedge pupa

The sight of the hatching sedge pupae send trout spiralling in sheer ecstasy. The insects are fast swimming, so look for tell-tale splashes as trout chase them to the surface. Fish your imitation in the surface film.

some are free swimming. The larvae feature in the diets of trout and grayling for 12 months a year. They are most important in winter and early spring, though, when fish take more of their food from the stream bed.

When a larva matures, it seals the case or builds a shelter with sand and silk, and then pupates. When it's ready to emerge, the pupa chews through its case and swims to the surface (or crawls ashore, depending on the species).

With folded wingpads on the underside and long rear-facing antennae, the pupa is humped in appearance. At the surface the winged adult sheds the pupal skin and emerges. They can take flight immediately.

skin split. The winged dun struggles out of its nymphal shuck. The surface tension is sometimes too much for the fly, and the trauma of the change can cause many to die in the process of emerging.

Hungry trout feast upon newly hatched adult insects that are sitting on the water's surface, waiting for their wings to dry. The best time to fish is *during* a hatch when most trout are feeding. Present a dry fly such as an Adams, making sure your fly drifts in line with the trout's lie.

The sizes of the adult upwinged flies vary from 8-30mm (³/₈-1¹/₄in). Within a few hours the dun sheds a layer of skin to emerge into the final stage, the spinner. At this point the insect is much brighter and has a longer tail than the dun.

The spinners mate, and the females return to the river to lay their eggs. Both the males and females die within 24 to 48 hours after they emerge as adults.

All species have different peak hatching times in the season with preferred times of the day for emerging. Recognizing a major group of mayfly common to a particular river and knowing when it might be expected to hatch are important aspects of fly-fishing on rivers.

Caddis (sedge) flies

The segmented, grub-like larvae of the various sedges live on the river bed and among weeds. Most species build cases with the materials found on the stream bed, but

▶ *A wild brownie stuffed to the gills with midge pupae. Slow stretches of river usually have an abundance of midges – especially from May to September.*

Translucent shrimps

Freshwater shrimps thrive in slow-moving rivers which have prolific growths of starwort and crowfoot (chalk streams, for instance).

Some species of shrimps grow up to 2.5cm (1in) long and are active swimmers.

Fish an imitation such as Walker's Shrimp upstream, giving it a slight tug once in a while to suggest the natural's start-stop style of swimming.

Tip Other styles

In North America, trout anglers recommend that nymphs should be fished *on* the bottom 90% of the time. They claim this is where most of the nymphs (and trout) are found.

So try fishing your fly on the bottom for results.

▼ *With a bleak winter landscape in the background, an angler nets a 1½lb (0.7kg) grayling on the River Severn near Caersws in mid-Wales.*

The adults' wings, covered in tiny hairs, are held in a roof-shape when at rest. Many species have long antennae. None has a tail. Adult caddis flies range widely in size from 6-17mm (¼-¾in). Colouring is fairly sober in brown or beige.

The mated females return to the water to lay their eggs, and here they attract the attention of trout. Some egg-laying females stay quite still. Others skitter over the water, and a few dive or swim below the surface to deposit their eggs.

Of the almost 200 British species of caddis flies less than a handful are easy to identify, but the fly-fisher needs only to copy the natural with an artificial of the same overall size and colour.

Stoneflies

Most stoneflies prefer fast-flowing, stony-bedded rivers. Only a few species live in slow-moving water. Stoneflies are brown or black in colour and have two tails.

The nymphs vary in size from 8-33mm (⅜-1¼in). Adult stoneflies have four wings. When the insect is at rest, the wings lie flat across the back.

Stonefly nymphs usually stay close to the river bed clinging to stones or debris, and they do not swim freely along the bottom. When ready to emerge, they usually crawl ashore. Imitating the nymph stage (with a Brown Stonefly Nymph, for example) is often your best bet.

Midges and smuts

In slow stretches of water midges (Chironomids) and smuts (Simulium) can be very important. These black, mosquito-like insects are weak swimmers and poor flyers.

Small dimple rises are one sign that the trout are taking pupae in the surface film. Because of their feebleness, especially when it comes to breaking the water's surface, midge pupae are taken more than the adult. Emerger patterns fished in the surface film are highly effective during a hatch.

Dry flies: upwings and sedges

John Roberts examines dry flies, artificial flies which float on the surface of the water. They are designed to imitate newly hatched adult aquatic flies or mated female flies returning to lay their eggs in the water.

▲ *Mayflies clinging to a dandelion – notice the upright wings and tails.*

Two important orders of natural aquatic flies for fly fisherman are Ephemeroptera (mayflies) and Trichoptera (sedge or caddis flies). Mayflies have upright wings while sedge (caddis) flies have two pairs of hairy wings. When the sedge fly is at rest, the wings have a roof-shaped, triangular appearance.

Sitting pretty

Natural upwinged flies rest only their legs on the water's surface. No other part of their body touches the water. Most artificial dry flies are designed to copy this. In the standard dry fly only the hackle tips and tail fibres sit on the water – its shoulder hackle needs to be stiff enough to support the hook. With some dry flies, however, the fly body rests on the surface to imitate emerging nymphs and duns in the process of hatching from the water.

▼ *The hackle and tail keep this fly (the Dogsbody) floating on the water's surface. Only the bend of the hook is submerged.*

Hatch intensity

In the early part of the season, trout feed on nymphs (immature insects) and insect larvae which live below the water's surface. Hatches of upwinged and sedge flies are much more important on rivers than stillwaters because insects are one of the river trout's main food source. Stillwater trout feed on insects, but they also eat small fish such as stickleback and perch.

Fly hatches can occur almost every day of the trout season – except perhaps on the coldest, wettest days. But as the warm weather approaches, hatches increase tremendously, and trout feed off the surface much more regularly. In fact, trout may become preoccupied with flies on the surface.

Great challenge

An abundant hatch of a particular fly species can mean that trout become selective towards that fly, ignoring all other flies. Only an imitation of the hatching species

▲ *Caddis flies are abundant in summer. At rest they have roof-shaped wings.*

can induce trout to rise. This is *the* great challenge of dry fly fishing. You first have to recognise the natural fly, noting whether it is an upwinged fly, a sedge fly or any other species.

Try and match the natural fly with an artificial of the same overall shape and colour. If sedges are hatching or egg-laying, use a sedge imitation of approximate size and colour. If upwings (mayflies) are hatching, use a shoulder-hackled dry fly, and again match it as closely as possible in size and colour.

Wings or hackle?

It is not always necessary for the dry fly to have wings. Although the imitation looks more lifelike to the angler, trout rarely seem to notice that the wings are missing. Often the blur of the hackle, seen from

▲ *This autumn grayling fell for a fly. Not just for summer, dry flies can be used throughout the season.*

underneath, is a sufficient suggestion of upright wings. Winged sedge patterns are also effective, but many fly fishers don't use winged imitations of upwinged species because it simply isn't necessary.

Buoyant materials and fine-wire hooks help the fly to float. It is also essential to coat the artificial fly with a water-repellant grease, either solid or solvent-based, to ensure that it floats for a long time. But apply the repellant sparingly to avoid clogging the hackle fibres.

The fly leader shouldn't be greased. If it is, it floats on the surface of the water, and the trout can see it. To ensure that it sinks, rub a bit of mud on it.

▲ *From left to right, Grey Duster, Little Red Sedge and Pheasant Tail.*

▶ *The Red Tag, one of the most popular grayling flies, can be fished either wet (underneath the surface) or dry.*

Popular patterns

These are some effective dry fly imitations.
Beacon Beige (hook size 14-16) Olive imitation.
Grey Duster (12-18) Imitates mayflies.
Adams (14-16) An American pattern.
Little Red Sedge (12-16) An effective search fly when nothing is rising.
Pheasant Tail (14-16) General dun imitation.
Elk Hair Caddis (12-14) A highly buoyant fly.

Dry flies: terrestrials

Photographer and fly-tying expert Peter Gathercole examines terrestrials – a type of dry fly. Trout and grayling feed on them much more than many game anglers think.

▲ *Early autumn and summer are peak times to spot the frail-looking daddy-long-legs (also known as a cranefly).*

◄ *On this daddy-long-legs dry fly, notice the long gangling legs (pheasant tail fibres) which are vital for correct imitation.*

Very vulnerable

Most aquatic or semi-aquatic insects have ways of avoiding predators. But because terrestrial insects are land-based, they are in an alien environment as soon as they touch water. On both still and running water they make up an important part of the trout's diet, especially in summer and autumn. Most trout and grayling are opportunist feeders, ready to snap up any victim which becomes trapped on the surface, terrestrials included.

Over the years fly-tying enthusiasts have created a vast range of creative and effective patterns. They are often well hackled and incorporate buoyant materials (such as deer hair) to help them float in fast-flowing river water.

▼ *The male hawthorn fly is also called the St. Mark's fly because it often seems to appear in large numbers near St. Mark's Day (April 25). Both male and female are black in colour.*

Terrestrials are simply insects – or their larvae – that live on land. They include grasshoppers, caterpillars, beetles, hawthorn flies, black gnats and daddy-long-legs – and various other creatures such as spiders – that accidentally get blown on to the waters of a river or lake.

▼ *Most hawthorn dry flies are big and black. Use downeyed, short shank hooks in sizes 10 to 12.*

The 'daddy' of flies

Although some species of daddy-long-legs are aquatic in the early stages of life (both larval and pupal), the most common ones have larvae known as leather-jackets — grey-coloured grubs which munch away on the roots of grasses and flowering plants. You can certainly find adult daddy-long-legs throughout the trout fishing season. But as the summer comes to an end, the first cooling winds of autumn blow large numbers of these insects on to the water. It may take a little time for the trout to adjust to the daddy's size and shape, but once they do, watch out!

Tackle daddy-feeding trout with a floating fly line and a suitable imitation which includes long trailing legs and a bushy hackle.

Hawthorn fly

The hawthorn fly (*Bibio marci*) is another important terrestrial. It is a weak-flying insect, easily blown on to water by moderate spring or summer breezes. In some respects, this fly resembles an emaciated bluebottle.

During their main hatching period in April the male flies dance in loose clouds over vegetation on the waterside, looking for mating partners. Anglers generally fish with an imitation which has trailing black legs to represent the male. Trout which are feeding on terrestrials are looking for creatures trapped in the surface film (not below the water), and an imitation which fits this profile is the one most likely to succeed.

Extra terrestrials

Some effective patterns include the following.
Deerhair Beetle (size 10-12) A highly buoyant pattern good for fast water.
Walker's Cranefly (8-14) An excellent stillwater pattern.
Black Gnat (16-20) One of those essential flies to have in your box.
Black Ant (14-18) An imitation readily accepted by trout in summer.

▶ *Despite the large size of some species of terrestrials, you can use them (whether on rivers or reservoirs) as you would other dry flies.*

Hungry trout rarely miss an opportunity to feast upon such a tempting mouthful.

Tackling up

A floating line and a light leader of perhaps 2-4lb (0.9-1.8kg) are the ideal combination for summertime angling with terrestrials. But remember that when fishing with daddy-long-legs imitations, you might want to use up to 6lb (2.8kg) monofilament line as a precaution against smash takes.

▼ *A wild river brown trout in perfect condition displays its dark colours. Studies in Britain and North America have shown that trout feed mainly on terrestrial insects in summer and early autumn – so it can pay to keep a few patterns handy.*

Dry flies for rivers

Fly fishing on moving water has many challenges – fly selection is one of them. Here are a few suggestions to get you started or to add to your collection.

The following flies – twelve of the best – are well-established, some for over a hundred years. They will certainly meet almost every dry fly river situation you may encounter, forming a nucleus of both imitative and suggestive patterns which no serious fly fishermen should be without.

1. Adams This is a fly which has many devoted enthusiasts – especially those who fish on southern chalk streams.

Ray Bergman created the Adams in the late 1920s or early 1930s, the exact date being difficult to pinpoint. With its blue-grey body and light brown hackle, it can pass as an iron-blue (upwinged fly) – though it wasn't created to be an exact representation of a particular species. Some

anglers claim the grizzle-point wings are one key to its long-lived success.

2. Pheasant Tail First invented by Payne Collier in the early 1900s, this is another general, nondescript fly that has accounted for many trout. Its body is made of pheasant tail fibres, ribbed with copper wire, with a honey dun or natural red cock feather for the hackle.

▲ *One of the best times to fish rivers such as the Upper Nidd in Yorkshire is early May – when the mayflies abound, and trout are keyed up and rising readily. A Grey Duster or Grey Wulff is a good pattern for these conditions.*

Variants

Famous patterns have almost always produced a number of 'offspring'. If the patterns don't follow the creators' designs and use their ingredients, then call them variants.

Sometimes, however, variants go on to become more popular than the original flies.

Twelve dries

The following suggested flies should see you through the season quite well.
1. **Adams** (hook sizes 12-20)
2. **Pheasant Tail** (12-18)
3. **Iron Blue Dun** (14-16)
4. **Red Tag (variant)** (14-18)
5. **Grey Wulff** (8-14)
6. **Walker's Red Sedge** (10)
7. **Terry's Terror (variant)** (12-16)
8. **Wickham's Fancy** (14-18)
9. **Coachman** (12-16)
10. **Black Midge** (20-22)
11. **Beacon Beige** (14-16)
12. **Grey Duster** (12-16)

3. Iron Blue Dun Named after the natural, it is an imitative pattern which is useful from May to October. The natural iron blue nymph emerges during the daytime and is commonly found in most unpolluted, weedy, alkaline rivers. The Iron Blue's red tag gives it an extra flair that attracts a fair share of trout every season.

4. Red Tag (variant) An excellent fly which doesn't look like any natural, the Red Tag has taken thousands of grayling since its creation in 1850. To limit it strictly to grayling, however, would be a mistake: it catches many trout, too.

5. Grey Wulff This pattern is known world-wide and can easily pass for spinners of upwinged species. Lee Wulff devised a whole series of patterns with thick, beefy bodies and wings and tails made from hair (bucktail, calftail or goat hair) rather than feather fibres. He claimed the chunky flies offered trout more of a mouthful, compared with the quill-bodied flies which were being used.

6. Walker's Red Sedge Created by Richard Walker, this represents not only red sedges but also many other species. The naturals are on the water from May to the end of July. Because sedges hatch during the day, use the Red Sedge as a searching pattern if nothing is rising. The artificial's orange tag represents an egg sac on a mature female. When females lay their eggs on the top of the water, some remain motionless, while others skitter about the surface. Fish this fly according to the circumstances. Cast it upstream, and allow it to drift back drag free. If that fails, cast upstream again and when the fly is across from you, lift up the rod, skating the fly across the surface.

7. Terry's Terror (variant) Though it seems that it wasn't created to imitate a particular natural, this fly can pass for many upwinged and sedge species. The

▲ *An angler returns a dry-fly caught brown trout to its weedy, chalk stream home.*

Up or down?

It's often said that if trout are refusing your imitiation, go down in hook size. Some anglers, however, say that the opposite is true: attach a **larger** fly. This might provoke a take. Try it and see what happens.

▼ *This small wild brown trout fell for a dry fly – a Pheasant Tail, in fact.*
  For wild trout it's important to use small hooks – sizes 18-20.

original called for a hackle of a natural red cock; this pattern varies slightly in that the hackle is a dark red cock.

8. Wickham's Fancy is over a hundred years old. Veteran fly fishermen swear by it. Even its wingless derivative has many followers. As the name implies, the fly is impressive with its gold tinsel body, starling wings and palmered ginger cock hackle – though it's not overly ornate. In smaller sizes it works well as a general searching pattern; the gold flash helps to tempt fish up from below.

9. Coachman Another general utility fly that has caught hordes of trout and grayling is the Coachman. Though the fly won't pass for most naturals (except possibly a moth), many river-fishing experts agree that the white wings and the bulbous peacock herl body provide the stimulating combination which few trout can allow to drift past untouched.

10. Black Midge On occasions you need the smallest of flies to convince stream-wise trout. Enter the Black Midge. When the naturals are hatching, or when the adult female flies return to the water to lay their eggs, this pattern – fished in the surface film – is the standard choice. The naturals often hatch throughout the trout season. With small flies such as this, use a very light, pliable tippet.

11. Beacon Beige One of the all time classics, this fly is highly regarded for freestone rivers – though on chalk streams it is even more acclaimed.

The Beige was created during World War I in the West Country as an imitation of upwinged flies (especially olive duns, which abound throughout the trout season). It was later renamed Beacon Beige.

12. Grey Duster In various sizes this Welsh fly imitates midges, olives and even mayflies. It's also one of the easiest flies to tie. Blue-grey rabbit fur for the body and a badger cock for the hackle are a simple yet deadly combination.

Modern stillwater flies

Stan Headley, competitive fly fisherman from Orkney in Scotland, describes eleven of his top boat flies which have all proved themselves on stillwaters from the Midlands to Scotland.

Key to flies

Stan Headley's selection of stillwater flies are mainly for loch-style fishing.

● **Surface flies** - use in or just under the surface film.
1. Dabbler
2. Coachman Nymph
3. Hare's Ear Muddler
4. Golden Olive Bumble

● **Intermediate flies** - fish these in the top 30-90cm (1-3ft) of water.
5. Pearly Buzzer
6. Stickfly
7. Peach and Pearl Pheasant Tail
8. Hare's Ear

● **Deep-water flies** - designed for visibility.
9. Booby Nymph
10. Pearly Green Palmer
11. Clifton

▼ *This superb trout was taken from Loch Leven in Scotland, where a range of modern stillwater flies are fished alongside a variety of traditional patterns.*

The depth you fish has a direct effect on the style and dressing of the flies you need. There are deep-water, intermediate and surface-film patterns for boat fishing.

Surface flies

The flies here should suit any water and a variety of weather conditions. The style of these flies is in direct contrast to their mid- and deep-water cousins.

Top-of-the-water patterns tend to be neutral in tone, with bulky, well picked out bodies and lots of loose hackle fibres, providing motion and imitating life. Bright or flashy surface patterns occasionally catch fish, but drab flies are usually more productive.

1. Dabbler This Irish pattern has taken the wild-trout scene by storm in the past few years. It is basically a palmered Mallard and Claret. This style of straggly wet fly is best fished on the top dropper in conditions with sizeable waves. Use short shank hooks in sizes 10 and 12.

2. Coachman Nymph This is a new slant on an old pattern. When there's a hatch of dark midges, this fly can do a lot of damage. Cast it towards feeding fish; retrieve slowly, and prepare for action. Tie on size 12 emerger hooks.

3. The Hare's Ear Muddler works well during midge and sedge hatches and if there are corixas on the trout's menu. Fish it on the top dropper or the point, depending on the preferences of the fish and the

Tip The right hooks

Often mass-produced flies come with rather low-quality hooks. If you tie your own flies, however, you can use the different styles of hooks available today to enhance your patterns.
- **Emerger hooks** are light and are made from fine wire – perfect for surface patterns.
- **Sedge hooks** have a curved shank and many anglers use them for emergers.
- **Wet-fly hooks** are heavy and rugged, essential for patterns fished in deep water.
- **Midge hooks** allow you to tie that all-important curved bend.

▼ *Conditions here are perfect for loch-style fishing. Two anglers try to tempt the fastidious Loch Leven brown trout, using teams of wet flies and nymphs.*

amount of wave. Use sizes 12 and 14 short shank hooks.

4. Golden Olive Bumble Designed in Ireland for brown and sea trout, this fly is fished on the top dropper. Trout can mistake it for a whole host of natural insects. Fish it in sizes 10-14 bobbed over the waves to create maximum impact.

Mid-water flies

These patterns are used in the top 30-90cm (1-3ft) of water. They are imitative in design and suggest nymphs and pupae struggling to the surface.

5. Pearly Buzzer When fishing at intermediate depths, have a buzzer pattern on the leader. Even when no hatches are taking place, many natural pupae make exploratory trips up from the bottom. Tie this fly on sizes 12-18 emerger hooks.

6. Stickfly Although originally designed to imitate caddis larvae in their cases, this pattern does well when fish are concentrating on damselfly nymphs and midge pupae. Always tie the Stickfly on long shank hooks in sizes 12 and 14.

7. Peach and Pearl Pheasant Tail has a pearly thorax and is nymph shaped – though it could easily be mistaken for a small fish. The fluorescent head gives the trout the classic 'aiming point', and the pattern can be tied with a variety of coloured heads to suit the taste for the day. Use short or long shank hooks in sizes 10-16.

8. Hare's Ear Possibly the most successful boat pattern in recent years, the Hare's Ear is a marvellous fly. Use it at any depth, fished fast, slow or static. Tie it on standard and long shank hooks, sizes 10-18.

Deep-water flies

Trout need to be able to see flies in deep water (over 2m/6½ft deep) where light penetration may be poor. Light-reflecting and fluorescent materials can help. You can also improve your catch-rate by using materials (such as marabou) which move easily in the water, making the flies appear alive.

9. Booby Nymph When fished on a sinking line, this fly always fishes above the line. But pulling the line quickly makes it dive for the bottom, and it floats up again as soon as the tension is released. During a normal retrieve the fly swims with an up-and-down style, making it almost irresistible to fish. Have a variety of colours tied on long shank hooks in sizes 10-14.

10. Pearly Green Palmer This pattern performs well both on southern waters and Scottish lochs. Fluorescent green is a powerfully attractive colour to fish. Use size 10 for rainbows and size 12 for brown trout.

11. Clifton Devised by Martin Cairncross to be a 'halfway house' between a nymph and a lure, this pattern is a must when using fast-sinking lines. Most effective in the early months of the season, it is best tied on long shank hooks in sizes 12 and 14.

The history of North Country wets

Yorkshire fly-tying expert Oliver Edwards traces the history of North Country wet flies and provides a selection of his favourites to take you through the trout season.

Rooting through angling history trying to trace the origins of the North Country wet fly is similar to solving a good 'whodunnit'. In this case no one person 'dunnit' – the many sparsely dressed North Country patterns have simply evolved through the generations.

The beginnings

Poverty probably played some part in the creation of the flies. A Dales' farmhand, for example, earning a pittance and with a hungry family to feed, probably found it easy to fool a trout with a fly wrapped with a feather and a bit of fur.

With no fly tying vices or equipment it is likely that he could only manage one and a half or two turns of hackle. He probably also found the fly worked better if he somehow covered the remaining shank with a little rough hare's fur – this is the orgin of a simple spider pattern.

Upland peaty regions are not the best places for gathering worms, so it may have been less time-consuming to tie a few sparsely dressed flies.

A growing list of flies

By the mid 1700s the North Country wet fly was established as a fish-catcher, and lists detailing killing patterns were steadily growing. These flies were (and still are) characterized by a simple elegance – a thin, short body and a very sparse application of both dubbing and hackle.

The materials were, as you would expect, all locally obtained. Small feathers from various wild birds and game (snipe, woodcock, moorhen, dotterel, curlew, partridge, jackdaw and many others) all provided suitable feathers – as well as a meal.

There was also no shortage of rabbit and hare skins. Farmers would employ the services of the local mole catcher, so the skin of the mole was also soon added to the list of dubbing providers.

While the ultimate goal of the early fly

Ten North Country wets

1. Aphid (hook sizes 18-24) This tiny scrap of green is lethal when the leaves start falling in autumn.

2. Dark Needle (14-16) This is another good pattern in autumn when stoneflies (or needle flies) hatch.

3. Starling Bloa (16-20) This is the fly to use when light-coloured upwinged flies are hatching.

4. Snipe and Purple (16-20) This pattern is useful when iron blues (another type of upwinged fly) are hatching.

5. Brown Owl (14-16) This fly does well in low water conditions – especially during summer evenings when sedges are around.

6. Partridge and Orange (14-16) If you could only fish with one fly, choose this one – it takes fish throughout the year.

7. Spring Black (16-20) This is more of a summer or autumn fly than a spring fly, representing terrestrials of all sorts.

8. Waterhen Bloa (14-16) In spring and autumn this is excellent when large dark olives (upwinged flies) are hatching.

9. Greenwell's (14-16) A good pattern when medium olives (upwinged flies) are hatching in spring.

10. Winter Brown (12-14) A good stonefly pattern, this fly is also useful when the stream is clearing after heavy rains.

It's often said that long rods (over 10ft/3m) are best when fishing with a team of flies; the added length helps to control the fly line better than using a short rod.

Many freestone rivers, however, are heavily lined with trees, and casting accurately – an essential part of fishing North Country wet flies – with a long rod is much more difficult than with a shorter one. And anyway, the line control isn't noticeably greater, especially in the hands of an experienced angler.

▲ North Country wets work well in all freestone rivers – from Scotland to Cornwall – even if the flow is quite fast.

▼ The hackles used on North Country wets are very mobile – this added allure has been the downfall of many specimens – including this grayling from the River Irfon in mid Wales.

fisher was to fill his creel or pannier for the kitchen, it is likely that he also enjoyed the thrill of a hefty brown trout bending his simple fly rod. By the late 1700s catching trout and grayling with an artificial fly was looked on as a sport as well as a means of obtaining a meal.

North Country selection

The list of flies given here is by no means comprehensive; it's as short as possible but can be used to cover the whole season. The selection probably won't be to everyone's liking – there are many regional and even local preferences. But all of the flies listed can be used to great effect on any brisk, stony river or stream.

When tying your own flies, try to obtain and use only quality materials. For example, cheap partridge hackles which have big brown spots on them absolutely ruin Partridge and Orange flies. The partridge hackle should be speckled.

Similarly, if you use cheap thread for the body (instead of silk) on a cheap hook it shows immediately. Starting out with quality materials, you'll place a greater value on the flies that you tie – and value the fish you catch on them too.

Stillwater trout lures

Over the past twenty years the popularity of stillwater trout fishing has soared, and the range of lures mirrors this boom. Peter Gathercole describes twelve top trout lures.

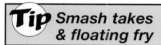

Tip *Smash takes & floating fry*

If you see a trout surface next to your imitation, don't strike right away. Wait until the fish has taken the lure and gone under before striking. As is the case when using a daddy-long-legs in autumn, use at least 6lb (2.7kg) mono to guard against smash takes when using a floating fry.

▼ *Fly fishing on Tal-y-llyn in Wales. Brown trout such as this one in the net often fall for lures, especially Goldies.*

Defining what makes a lure a lure is not an easy matter. At first glance it appears simple enough to the beginner: a lure is a large artificial fly which does not imitate or suggest a living creature.

This statement is perfectly correct for most patterns, but there are notable exceptions. Some lures are specifically designed to imitate the fry of roach and perch.

Two explanations

Why does a trout take a non-imitative lure if it isn't trying to eat it? Although no one has yet managed to obtain an answer from a fish, the two most plausible explanations are aggression and curiosity. Of the two the 'curiosity theory' is more convincing. When a trout sees something different, the only way to find out if the object is edible or not is to take it into its mouth.

Whatever the reason, the important point is that trout do take lures. On most stillwaters lures catch the largest number of fish, compared to other flies.

Types, sizes and colours

Lures range from sombre-coloured Muddler Minnows to bright orange Dog Nobblers. Sizes vary too – from ½in (13mm) to the giant 4in (10cm) long Tandem or Tube Fly. Most lures, however, fall somewhere in between. They are usually tied on long-shank hooks ranging from size 6 to size 10 and are made from a wide variety of materials including hair, feather, chenille, wool and tinsel.

Two main types of lure are hairwings and streamers. Wings of feather (cock hackles or the extremely popular marabou) are used in streamers. Marabou is the soft downy feather of the domestic turkey. The feathers are sold in many dyed colours.

You only have to see marabou work in the water to understand why it's so effective. On every twitch of the retrieve it pulses in the most enticing manner – one which trout often find irresistible.

Here are 12 modern trout lures. Each one has proved its worth on British stillwaters over the years.

Goldie Devised by Bob Church, this hairwing lure combines two colours which work particularly well for brown trout – yellow and black. The pattern fishes well regardless of depth. It is effective dressed either on a single long shank hook or as a tandem.

Viva Black and fluorescent green are perhaps the most killing combination available

to the trout angler. Although the Viva works particularly well when it's fished slow and deep during the early season, it takes trout throughout the year. The lure also catches well at a variety of depths and retrieval speeds. This is truly a lure for all seasons.

Cat's Whisker Any lure that contains marabou, either as a tail or a wing, is usually effective. David Train's Cat's Whisker goes one better: it has both! The combination of white marabou wing and fluorescent green chenille body is a deadly alternative to the black and green Viva.

Floating Fry Allowed simply to drift, this is an imitative lure which mimics a small dying coarse fish floating on the surface. During the months of August to October trout (usually really big browns) go mad feeding on shoals of small fish in preparation for the lean winter months to come. Trout rip through the shoals of fry, stunning and killing many fish. The hungry trout then return to their easy meal.

Muddler Minnow Don Gapen of the USA created this pattern in the 1950s. The Muddler has since spawned a vast range of variations. The original imitated a small

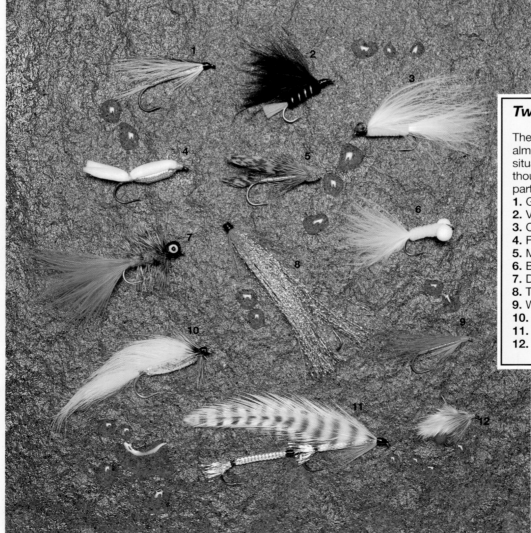

▲ *Tying some lures (such as the Baby Doll or Goldie) isn't as difficult as you may think.*

There's plenty of room to manoeuvre your fingers around large long shank hooks (sizes 6-10).

Twelve modern lures

These twelve trout lures can cover almost any stillwater angling situation that you may encounter, though each was created for a particular purpose.

1. Goldie
2. Viva
3. Cat's Whisker
4. Floating Fry
5. Muddler Minnow
6. Booby
7. Dog Nobbler
8. Tube Fly
9. Whisky Fly
10. Zonker
11. Tandem Lure
12. Mini-lure (Jack Frost)

Tip Level leaders

When distance casting isn't crucial, the most economical way of attaching lures is to use a long level leader – 6lb (2.7kg) for example.

Use a double grinner or a water knot for droppers.

Tip **Lead core fry**

Try using a floating fry pattern with a Hi-D line. You can make the pattern dive and then bob up to the surface.

Tying a Baby Doll

The Baby Doll, originally tied by Brian Kench for Ravensthorpe Reservoir in 1971, is illustrated for two reasons. It is one of the easiest lures for a beginner to tie, and it is another very popular reservoir lure, passing for a roach or perch fry.

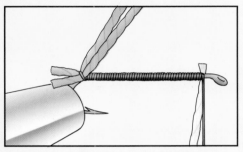

1. Starting near the eye, wind the thread down to the bend of the hook to form a secure bed. At the bend, tie in 2 or 3 lengths of fluorescent green wool, leaving tails 5-7mm long. Bring the thread 2mm from the eye. Catch in a length of fluorescent white wool (or a substitute material).

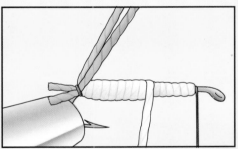

2. Wind the white wool down the hook shank in neat butted turns and then back up towards the eye. Secure the white wool 2mm before the eye with 2 wraps of thread. Cut off the excess wool.

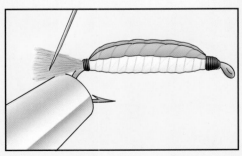

3. Bring the green wool over the back of the lure and secure with 2 turns of thread. Clip off the excess, and build a neat head. 'Pick' out the tail with your needle, forming the single tail.

fish. Today, however, Muddlers come in every colour imaginable.

All have the classic buoyant head of spun deer hair. When retrieved, the fly's bulbous head makes a disturbance in the water which really turns trout on.

Booby This style of lure, originally tied by professional fly dresser Gordon Frazer, has

▼ **With the net nearby, this angler pulls a rainbow trout close to the boat.**
Mini-lures, fished loch-style, can be good substitutes for traditional wets on many southern stillwaters.

proved absolutely deadly. The combination of marabou tail and buoyant eyes (made of Plastazote) produces a ducking, diving action similar to that of the Dog Nobbler.

Because the Booby is buoyant, use a very fast sinking line (Hi-D) and a short leader, so the fly fishes just above the lake bed. The retrieve is a slow figure-of-eight. Takes are so positive that the Booby is often swallowed.

Dog Nobbler This was *the* lure of the 1980s. Invented by Trevor Housby, the Dog Nobbler took the stillwater scene by storm. Since the early 1980s it has accounted for literally thousands of trout, many of them of specimen size.

As you retrieve the Dog Nobbler, its heavily weighted head and long marabou tail

◄ There are no definitive rules when choosing a lure. Experience coupled with trial and error are often the only ways to find a successful pattern for the time of year and the particular water.

▼ *Though imitation has gained an important place in lure design, the order of the day is still colour and flash.*

Lures take more stillwater rainbow or brown trout than any other type of fly.

Tip *Long, heavy Tube Flies*

Because of the size of Tube Flies (and the weight of the brass ones), you need a fly line in excess of AFTMA 9 and a long, powerful rod to match. Use a fast sinking line (Hi-D), and fish the Tube Fly just off the lake bed. Attach a 9ft (2.7m) leader of 6-8lb (2.7-3.6kg).

This is a deadly method for big brown trout lying off the bottom.

produce a wiggling motion. This erratic movement is the attraction of the lure. Effective colours include black, white, orange, yellow and olive.

Tube Fly This specialist lure is tied on lengths of fine plastic, aluminium or brass tubing. It has a treble hook at the end instead of a standard long shank hook. The Tube Fly can be tied either to imitate small

coarse fish about 7.5-10cm (3-4in) long or as a general attracting pattern.

Whisky Fly This hot orange eyeball-burner was devised by the late Albert Willock to catch cruising summer rainbows. Orange flies, particularly those as bright as the Whisky Fly, prove deadly when the trout are in the upper water layers.

During the warm summer months, especially when the fish are feeding on daphnia, 'orange madness' takes hold of trout. A Whisky Fly fished fast just below the surface can produce spectacular results.

Zonker The Zonker originates from the USA. It has a body of mylar tubing and a wing fashioned from a thin strip of rabbit fur, making it a very mobile and effective pattern. It's tied in a wide range of colour combinations, but grey and silver ones make great fry imitations.

Tandem Lure This is basically two long shank lures tied together 'in tandem' – one after another. Although this style of dressing is often used to imitate small coarse fish, any lure pattern may be dressed in this way. The joint between the two hooks is flexible 20lb (9kg) nylon monofilament.

Mini-lure Although lures are usually large, there are times when trout still want the pulsing movement of marabou – but in a short-shanked version. Here the mini-lure comes into its own. This style has become popular in competition fly fishing on stillwaters where there is a limit on the length and size of the flies used.

Flies for fry-feeding trout

In summer and autumn trout often gorge themselves on perch, bream and roach fry to get ready for the long winter to come. To tempt these prime trout you need large, mobile lures.

▼ *Here are some top big flies for late season fry-crashers.*
1. *Mylar Zonker*
2. *Appetizer*
3. *Blakeman's Tandem*
4. *Blakeman's White*
5. *Troth Bullhead (variant)*
6. *Ethafoam Fry*
7. *White Muddler*
8. *Silver and Gold Tubes*

Large lures, though they may seem rather crude to imitative purists, are essential for late season action. If trout are taking 10cm (4in) long roach, there is no point trying to fish with a team of size 16 Buzzers, for example. Fry patterns in sizes 2-8 account for more specimen brown and rainbow trout in stillwaters than dries, nymphs and wets combined.

Key ingredients

Colour and mobility are the common denominators in most successful fry patterns, including the following.

1. Mylar Zonker Simple patterns often perform better than overly elaborate ones. Hare's fur, pearl Mylar and a turn of grizzly for the hackle are all you need for this top pattern, the example on the right was tied by stillwater expert Peter Gathercole. The ultra-mobile hare's fur pulses enticingly with even the slowest of retrieves, and the scale-like Mylar provides a realistic impression of a roach's body.

2. Appetizer Created by Bob Church in 1972, this fly is still one of the best all-round perch patterns; it takes trout at all levels. Green and orange hackle fibres and mallard breast feather fibres form the tail and beard. The wing is made from white marabou and squirrel hair. White chenille, ribbed with oval silver tinsel, creates an attractive body.

3. Blakeman's Tandem Inventive lure-

tyer Tony Blakeman devised this pattern for Draycote Water where trout feed on large coarse fish.

Only the front hook on this fly is weighted – this causes the fly to dive nose-first in the water. Many trout take the tandem on the drop. When you retrieve in short strips, the fly zig-zags through the water, mimicking an injured fish.

4. Blakeman's White This superb lure is deadly for trout feeding on roach. The underbody has 72 turns of fine lead wire around the hookshank, so it gets down quickly. The marabou wings and tail are the key to the fly. Whereas black is a good general colour for the beginning of the season, white is the late-season killer.

◄ *Slow-moving, deep pools in rivers are ideal to try lures such as the Troth Bullhead, but make sure you have permission to use a lure on the water before fishing.*

▲ *To cast long distances with large, heavy lures, use a rod and line both rated AFTM 8-10.*

Here Jeremy Herrmann blasts out a lure with a WF9 at Blagdon, Avon.

▼ *This rainbow was stuffed with small, late-summer roach. An Appetizer fished near the surface fooled the trout into taking.*

5. Troth Bullhead (variant) Al Troth from Dillon, Montana, USA invented this pattern, a bullhead imitation. The body is white wool, and the head is spun deer hair clipped to shape. Black ostrich herls run along the back and form the tail. The ends are curled by trapping each strand between your thumb and a closed pair of scissors and pulling through.

The Troth Bullhead is an effective still-water lure, but it makes an even better river pattern. Using bullhead imitations for river fishing in Britain isn't common, but in Canada and the USA they regularly take large trout.

6. Ethafoam Fry Trout often drive a shoal of fry upwards, causing the small fish to leap clear of the water to escape. Browns and rainbows alike may not eat the prey as they pass – instead they slam into the fleeing fish and then return later to mop up the dead and dying.

If you see fry jumping frantically from the water, attach an Ethafoam Fry to imitate injured or dead baitfish. Fish it motionless, giving it a small twitch now and again. The body is dressed in white polypropylene, with an Ethafoam back, marabou tips for the tail and spun deer hair head. Adding eyes makes the fly more realistic looking and helps it to float better than a deer hair head without eyes.

7. White Muddler This is another fly you shouldn't be without during fry-feeding time. Because of the buoyancy of the deer-hair head, it's primarily a top-water pattern which often catches well in a big wave.

You can dress the White Muddler in many ways. This one has a wing and tail of marabou. Include six or so strands of Crystal Flash in the wing to reflect light and catch a trout's eye.

8. Tube Flies Silver and Gold Tube Flies are popular with boat anglers who use tubes with lead-core or Hi-Speed Hi-D lines to catch big, heavy-metal browns from the depths of waters such as Rutland. All that Flashabou pulsating through the water certainly doesn't go unnoticed for long.

Nymphs for river fishing

You need a well-balanced range of nymphs for river fly fishing – not boxes and boxes of flies. Here are nine of the best.

Ask any ten fly fishermen to name their favourite nymphs, and no two lists would be the same. However, some patterns seem to be constantly in the news, and in too many fly boxes, for them not to be justifiably famous. This selection contains well-proven fish deceivers old and new – from Victorian to contemporary creations.

Agile darting nymphs
1. Grey Goose Nymph An innovation of Frank Sawyer's – one of the fathers of chalk stream nymphing – it's slim, streamlined, fast sinking and easy to tie. He tied it for his deadly 'induced take' method – raising the nymph in a steady sweep in front of the target fish. Use it when you suspect pale wateries or spurwings are about to emerge.

2. Sawyer's Pheasant Tail Nymph This famous nymph can be found in tackle shops all around the globe. Sawyer created this simple, effective pattern to represent any of the darkish coloured nymphs as they ascended to the surface to hatch. This was the pattern with which he devised the previously mentioned 'induced take' method.

Dun copies
3. Iron Blue Nymph The natural is a very striking little dun. Like its winged form, the nymph is quite dark and equally small. In

decline on some rivers, many still hold good populations. From the vice of that great nymph fisherman, G. E. Skues, this very effective tie has stood the test of time – a must for every fly box.

4. Edwards' Heptagenid Nymph This modern pattern fills a gap unexploited since

Key to nymphs

Don't be without this selection of nine top nymphs for river fishing.

1. Grey Goose Nymph
2. Sawyer's Pheasant Tail Nymph
3. Iron Blue Nymph
4. Edwards' Heptagenid Nymph
5. Gold Ribbed Hare's Ear
6. Gold Head Pupa
7. Killer Bug
8. Hans van Klinken's Leadhead Nymph
9. Walker's Mayfly Nymph

▼ *A beautiful autumn grayling ends up in the net. This River Severn fish fell for that deadliest of grayling deceivers – Sawyer's Killer Bug – fished using the 'induced take' method.*

dressers started tying nymphs. Devised to 'close copy' the nymph of the yellow may dun, it equally imitates those of the *Rhithrogena*, *Ecdyonurus* and *Heptagenid* insects. Used 'dead drift' in popply riffles and glides, it's a fabulous fish fooler.

Old and new

5. Gold Ribbed Hare's Ear The winged form of this pattern was on the fly fishing scene in the Victorian era. Just when the wings were removed and it evolved into a first class river nymph is unknown. An excellent representation of a medium olive at the point of emergence – tie it moderately weighted or without any weight.

6. Gold Head Pupa Coming from the vice of Austrian tying ace Roman Moser, this is intended to represent a caddis pupa surrounded by its gas-filled pupal shuck, on its way to the surface to emerge. It is now used as a general pattern when no specific emergence is on. Fish it 'on the swing' or strip-retrieve it.

7. Killer Bug Sawyer devised this pattern in the early 1950s to imitate the freshwater shrimp. It is one of the easiest of all flies to tie and is deadly for grayling. Quite heavily weighted with copper wire to get down

quickly, it can be used 'dead drift' where the current is fast enough, or cast to a sighted fish with the 'induced take' method.

8. Hans van Klinken's Leadhead Nymph This modern pattern is lethal – fish literally throw themselves upon it. It could pass as a cased caddis larva or small fish. Every fisherman should tie a few.

9. Walker's Mayfly Nymph The late Richard Walker's most successful pattern, this takes thousands of fish each year. Whenever mayfly emerge this pattern scores. For best results make sure you don't tie it too full-bodied and use it with a quick figure-of-eight retrieve to imitate the fast-swimming mature nymph as it rises to the surface to emerge.

◄ *Hans van Klinken's Leadhead Nymph has a small lead shot (now lead substitute) cunningly mounted on a short strand of nylon line, just behind the eye of the hook, so that it fishes point up.*

Problems of tying the Killer Bug

The original Killer Bug used the now unobtainable 'Chadwick's No:477' darning wool. However, you can use one of many 'dirty' coloured wools or synthetics as a perfectly decent substitute.

▼ *Hans van Klinken, one of the Netherland's leading fly dressers and fishermen, is seen here fishing a nymph downstream. Upstream and downstream nymphing with the nine nymphs given here can be highly effective.*

Seven styles of midges

If you know something about the life-cycle of midges and can match the size and colour of a natural with an appropriate artificial, you are well on the way to catching midge-feeding trout. Here are seven of the best flies.

Fifty years ago fly fishermen didn't take midges seriously. They considered midge patterns of minor use only – sedges and upwinged flies ruled the clean lakes and rivers. But today, because of declining water quality, midges have taken over and are thriving.

Stillwater trout have had to adapt their feeding habits and now rely heavily on midges for growth after stocking. In fact, reservoirs with large midge populations (such as those in the Midlands) produce

▼ *A variety of midge imitation patterns (main picture, see key). The close-up (inset) is of a Suspender Buzzer. Tie the fly in various colours and sizes, but use Plastazote for the head: it is very durable and floats exceedingly well.*

Midge imitation patterns for stillwater trout

1. Shipman's Buzzer
2. Suspender Buzzers
3. CDC Claret Emerger
4. Hare's Ear/CDC Midges
5. Pearly Buzzers
6. Black Pennell
7. Marabou Bloodworm

hefty, fully-finned trout, while the slightly acidic waters in the north (with small midge and other insect populations) often contain thin, under-developed fish.

Life-cycle in brief

The female midge lays her eggs on the water surface. After hatching, the larvae sink to the bottom, finding shelter among blanket weeds or burrowing into the silty bottom where they feed on organic (even decaying) matter. They can tolerate the low levels of oxygen common on the bottom and often live in deep water.

In some of the largest species the larvae pupate after a year. The pupae remain close to the bottom, sometimes moving up into the middle layers of the water. Just before emerging as adults they pause and hang under the surface film for a while, depending on the conditions. Then the pupal skins split and the adults leave the water. Hatches can occur throughout the year, except during the very coldest days.

There are 450 or so different species of midges in Britain, the largest (producing the larva known as the bloodworm) being 2.5cm (1in) long. Midges come in many different colours, including grey, red, olive and bright green, brown and black.

Flies for all levels

There are probably as many imitation midge patterns as there are species. Here is a selection of established patterns.

1. Shipman's Buzzer (hook sizes 8-16)
Devised by reservoir angler Dave Shipman,

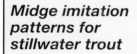

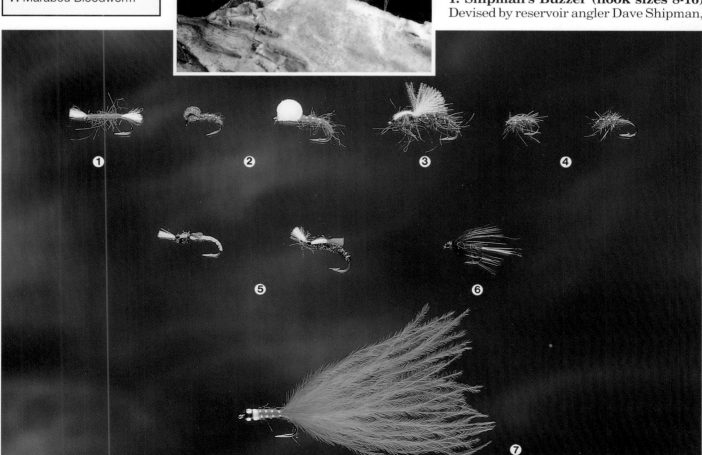

▲ *Don't always associate midges with deep water – they can also be found along the weedy shallows. Here a bank angler brings in a small, buzzer-caught brown trout.*

this emerging buzzer pattern – seal's fur substitute and white polypropylene – is highly praised by stillwater boat anglers.

2. Suspender Buzzers (10-14) Recent innovations, these were popularized by Brian Leadbetter who fishes them at all levels. They're excellent searching patterns when fished on the surface. The body is seal's fur substitute with thin Pearl Lurex ribbing. The thorax – Plastazote – is tied to the hook and folded over itself. Tie them in many colours.

3. CDC Claret Emerger (14-20) The use of natural *cul de canard* feathers (from the preen gland of the duck) is increasingly popular. Many modern patterns feature the material. The oil in the feathers makes them waterproof, and they move easily in the water – giving the impression of life.

This pattern, with the wing behind the thorax, sits in the surface film – it is devastating when trout are in the top layers of the water during a hatch.

4. Hare's Ear/CDC Midges (14-20) A very slim, sparsely dressed pattern is often deadly for trout feeding on emergers in the film and adult, egg-laying females on the surface. Hare's fur has always been the standard choice for the body. But try using natural grey *cul de canard* feathers cut up and dubbed for the body.

5. Pearly Buzzers (12-14) These colourful pupae imitation patterns are best fished from the bottom to the middle layers. Sometimes trout may be taking natural pupae (ones just about to hatch) quite a way below the surface – and the Pearly Buzzers work well for this situation.

6. Black Pennell (10-14) Stillwater boat anglers in years gone by always had a few Black Pennells in their boxes. This pattern is a reliable, midge-imitating wet fly, best used from a drifting boat. Some anglers prefer to have a sparse hackle while others tie the fly with a bushy, unkempt look.

7. Marabou Bloodworm (10-12) The silver bead head, fluorescent white collar and long marabou tail make this an excellent pattern for fishing in deep water during the early season – when the trout may be taking bloodworm on the bottom. Fish the fly just off the bottom with a slow strip or figure-of-eight retrieve.

▼ *A well-presented midge – even as small as size 20 – can fool prime, grown-on trout such as this 3½lb (1.6kg) Draycote rainbow.*

Emerger patterns

How often during a hatch have you fished a dry fly adult imitation of the natural to no avail? Perhaps the trout were feeding on the adult flies as they emerged from their nymphal skins. Tie some of these important emergers, and you won't be caught out again. Paul Losik explains.

▼ *An angler fly fishes Llandegfedd Reservoir, where midges are top of the trout's menu. Many young lowland reservoirs are predominantly midge waters.*
The CDC Midge and Misting Midge are both good choices if fish are moving on top.

A fly in the process of trading in its aquatic world for a life above water is called an emerger. Included here is only a small sample of emerger patterns. They may not be to everyone's tastes, but if you see something that you like, why not tie it and try it?

Upwinged flies

Once the eggs are deposited by female spinners, they hatch, and the nymphs mature underwater. Approaching the time of emergence, they become very active, even agitated, awaiting ideal conditions to hatch.

Some nymphs make preliminary journeys up to the surface. Once conditions are ideal, the flies hatch, most via the water's surface. The moult begins when the nymph reaches the surface film. The nymphal skin splits, and the adult or dun emerges.

The transformation from water to air is traumatic. Inevitably, some flies don't make it. Those which are unable to break through the film or cannot free themselves from their shucks are called stillborns.

Olive Stillborn Doug Swisher and Carl Richards were the first to emphasize the importance of emergers, and also stillborns. The Olive Stillborn is based on their Wet Emerger. It is really more of a river fly but in the larger sizes it can be used effectively

▼ *A selection of upwinged emergers, from left to right: Olive Stillborn; Snipe and Purple; Olive Emerger; BWO Emerger; Emerging Caenis; Waterhen Bloa; March Brown Floating Nymph.*

▲ *With the Yorkshire Dales in the background, this angler uses traditional North Country wets on the River Ure. Along with spider patterns, these are superb when trout are taking emerging upwinged flies.*

to imitate pond or lake olives.

This particular fly is tied on a size 18 dry fly hook. The tail is a soft grizzle hackle with the fibres pulled back and tied in and the tip clipped leaving three or four fibres trailing behind. It's a good stillborn imitation of small dark olives (*Baetis scambus*) and dark olives (*Baetis atrebatinus*) (agile darters) which tend to favour weedy, alkaline water.

Add a natural grey cul de canard (CDC) wing to imitate the blue-winged olive (*Ephemerella ignita*), which often suffers a high mortality rate when hatching, even though it emerges below riffles in fast water. Apply floatant to the body so the fly fishes in the surface film.

Olive Emerger The Olive Emerger, based on Marc Petijean's pattern, is a small dark olive imitation. The body of the fly fishes below the water while the wing case – natural grey CDC fibres loosely covering the thorax to trap air – is in the surface film.

BWO Emerger The Blue Winged Olive Emerger fishes in a similar way to the Olive Emerger. The CDC wing is above the surface, while the body is beneath.

North Country Wets are excellent representations of emerging flies when fished up or downstream near the surface. A popular imitation of large dark olives (*Baetis rhodhani*) is the Waterhen Bloa. The blur of the soft hackle fibres moving through the water gives the impression of a hatching upwing.

The body on the Waterhen Bloa is ultra-sparse. The thin veil of fur allows you to see

Armour-clad stoneflies

As a general rule, stonefly nymphs prefer the rocky-bottomed, fast water of freestone rivers. There are, however, a few species which are also found in slow-flowing, weedy rivers and some in stillwaters. Because the nymphs crawl out of the water to emerge instead of rising and hatching at the surface, imitating the emerger is virtually impossible. The nymphal stage, represented with patterns such as Partridge and Orange, Willow Fly and Dark Spanish Needle, and the adult egg-laying female, imitated with Jansen Stonefly or Moser-Winged Stonefly, are the two important stages for the trout and the fly fisher.

the tying thread underneath. This sparseness creates translucency, mimicking the natural's nymphal skin which is seen from below by the trout.

For imitating iron blue emergers (*Baetis muticus* or *niger*), try the classic, time-honoured Snipe and Purple.

Emerging Caenis Tiny silt-crawling caenis, referred to as angler's curse, are a common sight on many rivers and stillwaters. Species dwelling in rivers emerge in slow water – pools, glassy glides or silty margins. Once trout are keyed into hatching caenis they won't look at anything else. In slow-moving areas and stillwaters they have a long time to inspect their quarry and can be very fussy.

The Emerging Caenis is a good fly to combat difficult trout. The body floats just under the surface film while the wing is above water. But presentation has to be accurate – in line with feeding trout and free of drag on rivers.

March Brown Floating Nymph The stone-clinging March Brown (*Rhithrogena germanica*) is a large river-dwelling upwing. Imitations should be dressed on hook sizes 10-12. With the parachute hackle and ball of dubbed polypropylene, this is a robust design to keep afloat in fast water (where the naturals tend to hatch). The ball represents the crumpled wings of the fly before blood is pumped in to straighten them out. Again, the body should fish in or just beneath the surface. Apply floatant to the dubbed ball and parachute hackle to ensure that they remain above the surface.

Myriad midges

Midges are the main food source for many stillwater and river trout (exept in rivers where the water is sparkling clean). Pollution from industry, sewage and agriculture has eliminated vast populations of upwings, sedges and stoneflies whereas midges thrive in the poorly oxygenated, algae-rich waters.

During the mornings and evenings throughout the season trout gorge themselves with midge pupae hanging under the surface film. The pupae pause there momentarily before splitting their skins and emerging.

The dry fly and the emerger

The dry fly on the left, a Griffith's Gnat, sits on the surface film, imitating a fully fledged adult. The CDC Midge (an emerger) straddles the surface. The thorax and extending CDC fibres are above the surface while the body remains below.

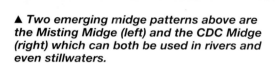

▲ *Two emerging midge patterns above are the Misting Midge (left) and the CDC Midge (right) which can both be used in rivers and even stillwaters.*

Misting Midge and CDC Midge These are both excellent stillwater and river patterns to hang in the film. Though it's essential to vary the colour and sizes of the flies, the key to their effectiveness lies with where the pattern fishes.

Both flies straddle the surface film, a bit like an iceberg; that is, the Ethafoam and CDC is in and just above the surface while the curved bodies are below – quite similar to the natural.

The Misting Midge is tied with a healthy chunk of Ethafoam or closed-cell foam to guarantee its buoyancy in strong currents or large waves. Again, the sparse body traps air and forms a transparent sheath.

The CDC Midge is a beefier fly with an added rib of Crystal Flash to brighten it up. The thorax is CDC (see tying instructions). Using polypropylene (which has a lower density than water) for the body helps to keep the thorax and extending CDC fibres afloat. The body won't soak up water and plummet the fly to the depths.

Sedge emergers

Witnessing trout feeding during a blizzard of a sedge hatch is something anglers never

forget. The fish often boil at the surface, attempting to catch the fast-moving pharate adults (sometimes wrongly labelled pupae) as they rise from the bottom to emerge at the surface.

American Gary LaFontaine and friends did exhaustive studies on emerging flies to find out just what triggers trout into tak-

Tip **Thin profile**

When you're tying small flies it's always best to err on the sparse side than to tie fat, beer-bellied bodies. Besides, you need all the gape clearance that you can get to increase the odds of securely hooking a trout or grayling.

ing. He discovered that the thin nymphal skin, when seen from below, appears to have an aura or soft glow because it was back-lit from the light above. This is what the trout sees from below.

Incorporating this halo-like (translucent) appearance in artificials is crucial, therefore, during the day – be they upwings or sedges. Towards evening, however, the back-lit sheath is less apparent to the trout because of the lack of light.

1. Wrap a base of thread along the curve of the hookshank. Tie in one strand of pearl Crystal Flash. Lightly dub fine polypropylene on the thread and form the body. Wind the rib evenly and secure, leaving room for the thorax.

2. Tie in a whole natural grey cul de canard feather. This serves as the wing case. Take another feather and strip the fibres from it. Loosely dub these on the thread and wind to form the thorax.

3. Pull the whole feather over the thorax. You may want to leave a slight gap between the thorax and wing case to trap air. Secure with two wraps of thread. Whip finish under the extending fibres.

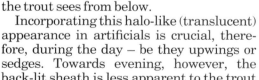

▶ *It isn't just trout which take emergers. Large grayling such as this can be very selective. Often you have to offer the suitable fly right where they expect the natural to be. Having emerger patterns along with dries and nymphs leaves no gaps unfilled.*

Klinkhamer Special and Emergent Sedge These are two superb emerging sedge patterns: the first conceived by , well-known Dutch angler Hans van Klinken and the second invented by American Gary LaFontaine. Fish both patterns dead-drift up or downstream.

The Emergent Sedge, a variant of LaFontaine's Emergent Pupa, has an underbody of dubbed golden-olive Synthetic Living Fibre (SLF) and an overbody of antron fibres tied in at the tail and loosely pulled over the underbody to represent the sheath or nymphal skin of the nat-

ural. The fly offers superb translucency for selective trout. The head and deer hair wing sit above the water while the rest lies below the surface.

The Klinkhamer Special is primarily a fast-water fly. About 80-90% of its body fishes under the surface. The white wing helps you to keep track of it in fast water and low light levels. To give the fly more translucency (and a dishevelled appearance) rub the body lightly with fine-grade sandpaper. Light tan or beige is a good general purpose colour and serves well as a search fly.

▲ *These are two of the best emerging sedge patterns to come along for quite some time: the Klinkhamer Special on the left and the Emergent Sedge on the right.*

You may want to try tying a few other sizes and colours to match the natural sedges on your local rivers and stillwaters.

Dressed to catch: the dressings of the emerger patterns

Name of fly	Hook sizes	Body	Wing, thorax and hackle	Tail and ribbing
Stillborn Olive	16-18	Olive goose herl	Olive CDC wing; olive goose herl thorax	Grizzle feather; no rib
Olive Emerger	16-18	Olive polypropylene	Natural CDC wing case; wound olive marabou as thorax	Mallard flank fibres; stretched Crystal Flash rib
BWO Emerger	14	Olive marabou (wound around shank)	CDC wing; wound olive marabou for thorax	Mallard flank fibres; stretched Crystal Flash rib
Waterhen Bloa	14-16	Yellow thread thinly dubbed with mole or rabbit fur	Marginal covert of moorhen for hackle	No tail or rib
Snipe and Purple	16-20	Purple silk	Marginal covert feather of snipe	No tail or rib
Emerging Caenis	20-22	Fly-Rite Light Hendrickson dubbing	Natural grey CDC as wing; polypropylene to match body colour for thorax.	Mallard flank fibres; no rib
March Brown Floating Nymph	10-12	Brown antron	Grizzle hackle wound parachute style around the base of cream poly dubbing ball; peacock herl thorax	Mallard flank fibres; no rib
Misting Midge	16-20	Olive deer or elk underfur	Ethafoam	No tail or rib
CDC Midge	14-18	Dirty-coloured polypropylene	Natural CDC for wing case and dubbed for thorax	No tail; stretched Crystal Flash rib
Emergent Sedge	12-16	Golden olive SLF underbody and beige antron as overbody	Natural deer hair wing; black ostrich herl head	A few fibres of antron trailing to represent shuck; no rib
Klinkhamer Special	12-22	Light tan poly yarn	White poly wing; chestnut cock tied parachute for wing; peacock herl thorax	No tail or rib

Flies for sea trout

Some of the flies which are used for sea trout are no more than scaled-up versions of traditional trout patterns, according to fly dresser Kevin Hyatt.

Fry imitations, usually more at home on still waters, mirror the shimmering colours of the sea trout's main food sources at sea – small sandeels and sprats – and are probably the most effective lures. It's no wonder, then, why traditional dressings in hook sizes 6-10, such as the Alexandra or Butcher, are so deadly and so popular among anglers.

Here are eight traditional patterns with which sea trout anglers have taken countless fish – even during the day.

Alexandra This fly is widely used for sea trout fishing on a standard single hook or often a tandem (two hooks joined by mono). The metallic green peacock sword wing, silver tinsel body and black hackle are unbeatable – especially fished quickly

across the river's surface just after dusk.

Butcher This larger-than-life version of a famous old pattern is winged with mallard blue wing quill (or sometimes crow). Like the Alexandra, the Butcher is another fry-imitating pattern; it has a silver body and black hackle with a tail of dyed red duck.

Peter Ross This fly is perhaps one of the

▶ *The Bloody Butcher (top) and Zulu (bottom) are two very old trout and sea-trout patterns. Although there are now many new fly-tying materials, these flies are still firm favourites with fly fishermen.*

Tip *Fly styles*

Carrying a range of different flies allows you to modify your technique as the night wears on. As a general guide, begin fishing when it's completely dark by using a fry-imitating pattern on a floating line. Work the fly near the surface.

Later on try fishing a lure slowly in deep pool. Also try a Rasputin or other buoyant lure.

▲ *Specialist flies, such as the Sunk Lure, Teal Medicine and Secret Weapon (top to bottom), can work wonders during a slow period. Fish the larger flies – especially tandems – slowly near the bottom.*

◄ *As night-time approaches, your prospects of catching the wary sea trout increase. This specimen was taken from the River Teifi in Wales in the dead of night.*

▼ *A brace of excellent sea trout. Some anglers argue that they don't feed in freshwater, while others claim to have seen sea trout take natural flies off the surface.*

best known, widely used sea trout flies in Scotland. Half of the body is red seal's fur substitute, while the back end is silver. A teal wing, golden pheasant tippet tail and black hackle finish it off.

Rasputin This surface lure, made from close-celled foam, is highly buoyant. It's fished in deep water on quick-sink line. The main feature of this fly is that it doesn't foul the river bed.

Secret Weapon This is simply a standard lure with a flying treble (a treble hook extended beyond the single hook with a nylon link). There many variations of the pattern, this one having a bronze mallard wing, fur body and throat hackle.

Sunk Lure A tandem with two silver bodies, a bright blue wing tipped with peacock herl and a red varnished head, this lure is an extremely popular one. Designed by Hugh Falkus, it can be 5-6.5cm (2-2½in) long and, as its name suggests, is fished in deep pools.

Teal Medicine This is another Hugh Falkus pattern. The original called for a body painted silver, a blue hackle, a barred teal wing and a red varnished head. A darker version has a bronze mallard wing.

Zulu This bushy fly is excellent for dapping – allowing the wind to drag and skate the fly on the surface of still waters to make a noticeable disturbance. Two or three hackles are used to ensure the fly floats; this is an important point if you use heavy hooks.

These are just a few sea trout flies; there are many other fine patterns such as Teal Blue and Silver, Connemara Black and Black Pennell Dapping.

Seasonal salmon flies

Stan Headley shortlists his seven favourite salmon flies and offers his experience in selecting the right ones for the right time of year.

Salmon don't feed in fresh water, yet they take lures and flies. This is surely an angling enigma. But even more of a puzzle is that salmon take some flies more readily than others, depending on the time of year and the clarity of the water.

Even though there are no concrete answers as to why salmon take, in Stan's opinion you generally need large, colourful flies fished deep in spring and late autumn when the rivers are high and possibly coloured. Small, dull patterns fished near

Headley's top seven

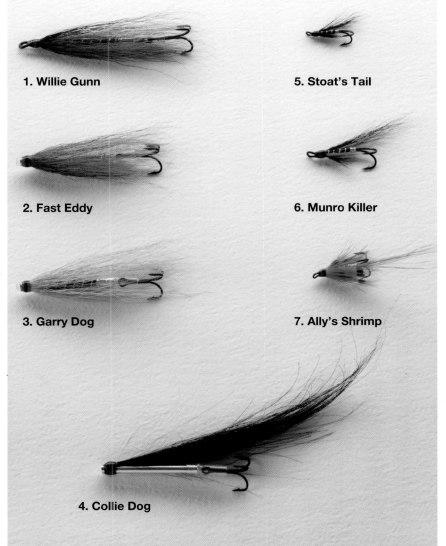

1. Willie Gunn

2. Fast Eddy

3. Garry Dog

4. Collie Dog

5. Stoat's Tail

6. Munro Killer

7. Ally's Shrimp

▲ *Low-water conditions in mid summer (such as here on the River Spey in Scotland) require small patterns fished near the surface on a floating line.*

the surface catch more fish under low-water summer conditions. At this time the salmon can be wary and often uncooperative.

It seems logical, therefore, to classify salmon flies by season rather than by their size or colour.

Spring and autumn flies

On the whole, patterns for the colder months of the year tend to be big, bright and sometimes heavy. They are frequently tied on tubes or wire shanks (often called Waddingtons or waddies) which may be as much as 10cm (4in) long.

1. Willie Gunn (Waddington) This pattern probably catches more salmon in the spring than any other. It's most commonly tied on a Waddington shank. Yellow, orange and black are good colours for early patterns. In heavily peat-stained water reduce the proportion of black hair to produce a brighter fly. In areas of clear water use a fly with more black hair.

2. Fast Eddy (tube) Stan Headley specifically designed this pattern for the River Thurso in Scotland where flies with a touch

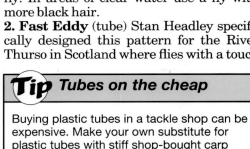

Tip Tubes on the cheap

Buying plastic tubes in a tackle shop can be expensive. Make your own substitute for plastic tubes with stiff shop-bought carp booms. Use scissors to cut tubes in various sizes and then carefully heat the end of the tube with a match to form a collar.

of green work well. Fish the Fast Eddy from mid-March to mid-May. It's also effective during a clearing spate.

3. Garry Dog (tube) is another popular spring and autumn fly. Because of its bright colours the fly is effective in peat-stained waters and in clearing floodwater. Traditional dressing gives it a mixed wing of yellow and red, but yellow and orange can be even better.

4. Collie Dog (tube) This pattern, easy to tie, has exploded on to the salmon scene in the past few years. Tied on a short tube body with a wing of hair up to 23cm (9in) long, it has revolutionized spring fishing in many areas. Versions with smaller wings work well in the summer.

Salmon may come up from great depths to take the fly, which can be fished on intermediate or floating lines. It's usually tied on an aluminium tube with no body dressing.

Small in summer

With the exception of shrimp imitations, Stan has found that summer salmon usually take dull patterns – not bright ones.

5. Stoat's Tail (double) Simple but deadly, this fly is used on floating or intermediate lines and catches a fair share of salmon. Some anglers give the fly a yellow tail.

6. Munro Killer (double) Originally tied for fishing on the Spey, this fly now catches salmon all over the world. Basically it's a jazzed-up Stoat's Tail – the dashes of colour make it supreme in the peat-stained waters of northern Scotland.

7. Ally's Shrimp (long shank treble) In western Scotland's fast spate rivers shrimp patterns reign supreme – and this is perhaps the best. Though brighter than most summer patterns it is the exception to the sombre/summer rule. Don't be without one when fishing from June to August. Ally's Shrimp is also good in large sizes when salmon become aggressive in late autumn.

▲ *This cracking, fresh-run springer took a big fly fished slowly on a fast-sinking line.*

Dressed to kill?

Overly ornate, fully dressed salmon flies like this Durham Ranger (right) are works of art – they look beautiful and take great skill to tie. But it has to be admitted that their function is rather more suited to luring fly tyers and fishermen than attracting big salmon.

Elaborate patterns such as these are hardly necessary – and can often be detrimental when it come to fishing, says Stan Headley. Far more practical, in his opinion, is a set of bare-boned, proven patterns.

Tip The humble trout fly

"Any fisherman who finds himself on a salmon river with only his trout fly box need not despair," says Stan. "There are many trout flies which tempt salmon, and the standard Muddler can catch more than most.

"Traditional wets such as the Soldier Palmer also work well."

Artificials for big trout

Spinners, spoons and lures – with their erratic actions and many colours – can take big, elusive browns and fry-hungry rainbows.

▲ *Spinners are renowned for taking specimen wild brown trout from lochs.*

▼ *You can use lures when drifting. Make sure you select the right one to cover the depth desired.*

The great advantage of spinners, spoons and plugs (or lures) is that trout pick up on their vibrations (and colour) and hit them out of curiosity, aggression or both.

The top contenders

Here are nine well-established artificials which have taken their share of trout over the years.

1. Fly spoon A simple form of spinner, the fly spoon consists of a single hook, a small, pear-shaped spinning blade and a swivel – all joined together with a wire ring. Fly spoons are normally used in conjunction with a couple of maggots.

2. Mepps Aglia Of all the spinning lures, the French-made Mepps, with its whirling, spoon-shaped blade, is perhaps the most famous. The angle and speed at which the blade spins around the wire shaft vary with the rate of retrieval. The Mepps is a spinner that performs well in slow to medium-fast moving water.

3. Blue Fox Super Vibrax This is another French design which has a bigger blade than the Mepps, producing large vibrations

---

Tip **Countdown to success**

If you are fishing at anchor, try exploring all depths of the water by casting a spoon, for example, and then counting to three before you retrieve. Recast, and then count to five (and so on) until you've skimmed the surface and scraped the bottom.

through the water. Both spinners have either a weighted shank or beads to allow the angler to cast them easily.

4. Toby Lures Tobies come in a wide range of colours – gold, silver, copper and multi-coloured ones. The weight of the lure is in the curved metal blade. Two red fins at the rear aid the balance and the wobbling effect in the water. The ones with scaled surfaces scatter light in much the same way as the scales of real fish.

5. Devon Minnows Devons are hollow, torpedo-shaped lures made from brass, aluminium, wood or plastic with fins either side. They come in varying weights and sizes and in several colours. The lighter ones need weighting to be cast well.

As it is drawn through the water, the hollow body spins around the central wire core. The two side fins make it revolve uniformly and easily when it is retrieved.

6. Flying Condom This spinner has become a sensation over the last few years. It features a conventional revolving blade at the eye while the barrel is heavy and covered with a sheath of rubber.

7. Wobbling Spoon The smaller sizes of these convex-shaped spoons are generally more useful to the trout angler than the larger versions. But light spoons are difficult to cast – though they're useful when trolled near the surface from a boat. Some spoons feature hammered surfaces that reflect light in all angles.

8. Floating Rapalas Devised in Finland,

Rapalas are made from balsa wood and are popular throughout the world. If you stop retrieving, the lure floats up. Making it bob on the surface is a great way to imitate floating fry.

9. Shad Rap Another Rapala pattern, the Shad Rap is painted to imitate the scaled body of a small bait fish. With its large, spoon-shaped lip, it dives almost vertically. And the faster you retrieve it, the deeper it dives. This lure is a must in any really deep water.

▲ *Most good tackle shops have artificial lures in many different sizes and colours to meet your needs.*

Always check that you are permitted to use artificials on the reservoir or river you intend to fish.

▼ *Lures are deadly in autumn for big rainbows which patrol the shallows in search of fry.*

CHAPTER SIX

FLY TYING

The basic fly-tying kit

Catching a trout on a fly or lure which you've created is a rewarding and satisfying experience. Here's some of the items you may need to begin fly tying.

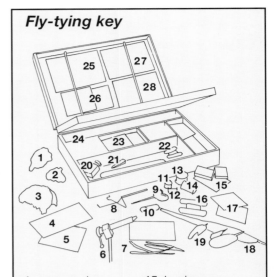

Fly-tying key

Hooks have been specially designed for dry flies (light wire hooks), wet flies (thicker and heavier to help sink the flies), nymphs (specially curved for better imitation) and lures (long shanks).

In the mid 1800s fly fishing (and tying) became really popular in Britain. Fooling a trout into taking a concoction of fur, feather and tinsel – secured to a hook by silk thread – was an art that later developed into an obsession for some anglers. Abundant natural materials such as wool, hair and a vast range of feathers were the main ingredients.

Today, however, beginners in fly-tying seem to think that they need to spend a fortune on tools, feathers, and threads, but this is simply not true. A relatively small

1. grouse wing	**15.** hooks
2. brown wool	**16.** copper ribbing
3. rabbit fur	**17.** yarn
4. golden tippet	**18.** pheasant feather
5. cock hackles	**19.** grouse feathers
6. vice	**20.** clear varnish
7. ostrich herl	**21.** clipper
8. whip finisher	**22.** silver tinsel
9. scissors	**23.** fluorescent yarn
10. hackle pliers	**24.** pheasant feathers
11. lead wire	**25.** partridge feathers
12. wire ribbing	**26.** cock hackles
13. black thread	**27.** cock hackles
14. white thread	**28.** peacock herl

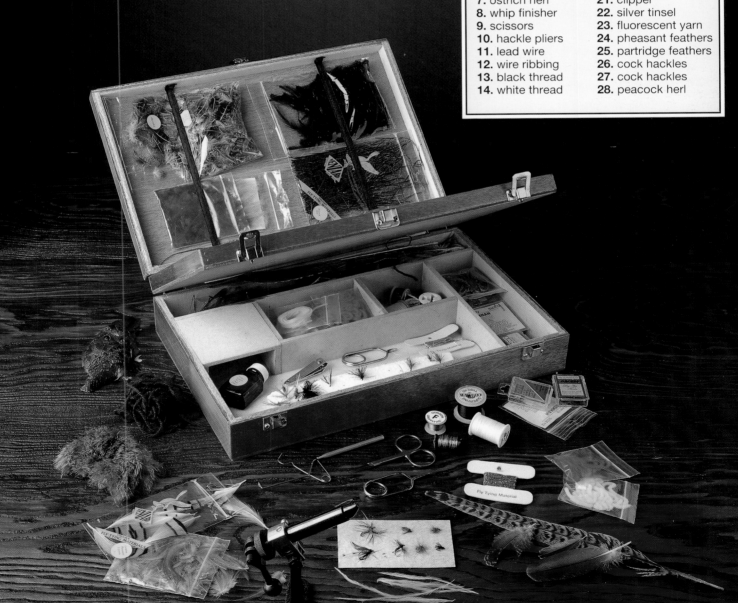

▲ Once you've acquired some of the materials in the kit, you can tie easy patterns like this Stickfly.

▲ A Red Tag, a popular and effective pattern, deceived this mottled brown trout. The Red Tag can be tied for either dry or wet fly fishing.

▼ Like most things in life the more you do something, the more your skills improve. After tying flies for a while, you'll have enough confidence to create effective patterns on the river or reservoir bank.

number of items will create many patterns.

Tools for tying

You can buy the items separately or as a complete kit in a handy case.

The vice Perhaps the most important part of any fly-tying kit is the hook vice. Buying a cheap one in the beginning usually means that you'll have to buy another one later on – the 'jaws' of the vice need to be hard enough so that they don't develop deep grooves after crimping a few hooks.

The bobbin holder holds the spool of thread, maintaining tension between the spool and the hook, so your hands are free. It also helps wind the thread smoothly and easily on to the hook by becoming an extension of your fingers.

Small scissors The scissors need to be small and sharp to cut accurately in tight places. A nail clipper is also useful.

Whip finisher Some anglers prefer to use half hitches (half knots) to finish off the head (near the eye of the hook). By using a whip finisher, you can create a 'hidden' knot which is more secure and looks neater.

Hackle pliers This tool holds a hackle feather firmly and helps you to wind it around the hook shank.

Fur and feathers

Having a variety of feathers and fur certainly helps you to tie more patterns of flies. But you don't need everything in one go. Start with some pheasant tails (cock and hen), grouse wings (or feathers), peacock herl, cock hackles, partridge feathers, pheasant tippets and ostrich herl.

You'll also need a selection of coloured wool. An inexpensive way to buy this is from end-of-line sales in a wool shop, or better yet, if you know people who knit, ask them for any bits of unused wool.

Rabbit and hare fur, which is quite cheap, is used in many popular nymphs and dry and wet flies.

Tinsels and threads

Gold and silver tinsels – in narrow and medium widths – are required in most patterns. They strengthen the fly body and give it the 'segmented' appearance of most insects. Fine wires are also used as a ribbing.

Black, brown, white, olive and yellow prewaxed threads (in a fine mono cord) are the colours that you should get first. Slightly sticky waxed threads help you keep most of the fur on the thread when dubbing (spinning fur on the thread).

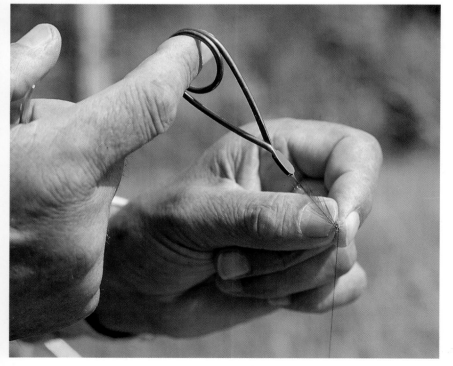

Basic fly tying: the Black Pennell

Peter Gathercole, noted fly-tying expert, explains the process of tying the Black Pennell, a simple yet effective wet fly to use when trout are feeding on midges.

For a Black Pennell you need a size 12 wet fly hook, black tying thread, black floss, fine silver wire, a soft black cock hackle and a golden pheasant tippet.

The first step is to set the bend of the hook in the vice so that its point is showing. Exposing the hook's point may cause you to catch your thread if you're not careful, but it gives you more room to manoeuvre your fingers.

A bobbin holder allows you to wind the thread smoothly and easily. Holding it in one hand and the loose thread in the other, carefully begin winding the bobbin *over* the loose thread near the eye of the hook (see *Tying a Black Pennell: at a glance* **1**). This foundation provides a secure bed on to which you can add the other parts.

Wind the thread round the hook shank five or six times until it no longer unravels

▼ *Once you have been tying flies for a year or so, you'll be confident and experienced enough to tie complicated lures such as muddler minnows and matukas.*

when the loose end is released. Cut off the loose end, and wind the thread down to the hook bend in tight turns.

The second step is to catch in (tie to the hook) three or four strands of golden pheasant tippet to make the tail (see **2**). Hold them to the hook with your left hand (or the right if you're left-handed), ensuring that the ends project past the bend by about 5-7mm. Using your other hand, wind three or four turns of thread over the strands to secure the tail.

With three turns of thread, tie in a 6cm (2½in) piece of fine silver wire at *exactly* the same point as the tail. Don't remove the waste end, though. A short length (slightly less than the hook shank) is needed to provide an even base for the floss body. Cover the waste end tightly with tying thread to about 2mm short of the eye (see **3**). Cutting the waste end off without wrapping it up the shank gives a 'lumpy' body.

The body of the fly is made of black Rayon floss. Catch in one end about 2-3mm from the eye with three turns of thread. Wind the floss down to the tail in neat turns and then back up to where it was tied in (see **4**). Secure the loose end with three wraps of thread, and cut off the excess floss.

Begin winding the silver wire (the rib-

▼ *A silver sided rainbow trout lies in the landing net. The Black Pennell is an effective wet fly for early-season trout. Fish the fly slow and deep.*

Tying a Black Pennell: at a glance

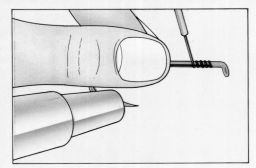

1. Wrap the loose end of the thread over the hook shank near the eye; then take the bobbin holder and wrap *over* the loose end.

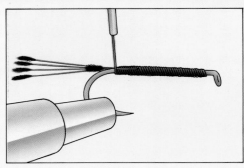

2. Catch in four tippet strands, making sure that they are even and that they extend 5-7mm past the bend of the hook.

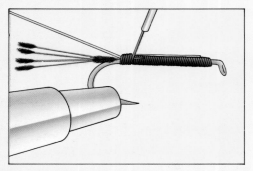

3. Tie in the wire at the same place you tied the tail. Don't clip the excess wire; tie it up the shank with the thread.

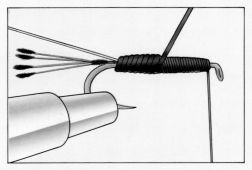

4. Near the eye, catch in one end of a 10cm length of black floss. Wind down to the tail then back up to the eye, and secure.

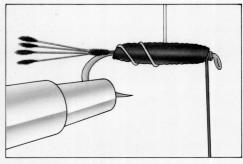

5. Wrap the wire four or five times in the *opposite* direction to the floss winding. Then secure it near the eye.

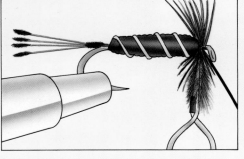

6. Tie a hackle to the hook. Grasp the tip with hackle pliers, and wind three times. Clip excess; then build a neat head.

Basics first

Often, adding fur and feathers overshadows the basic starting points of a fly. It's not worth tying complicated patterns if you don't learn the elementary skills first.

Whip-finisher

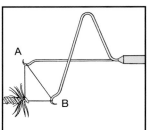

Place the arm (**A**) on the thread. Keeping tension on the thread, take the other arm (**B**) over the hook to form an upside down 4. Make sure the neat head you've built near the eye doesn't come undone.

The bobbin holder lies alongside the hook shank.

As you twist the handle of the whip-finisher, the section of thread pointing upwards (in arm **A**) winds over the section parallel to the hook shank (in arm **B**). This creates a 'hidden' knot (above) which won't unravel. Repeat this five times.

To complete the process, pull the bobbin holder so the loop tightens. As it does, slip the thread off one arm of the whip finisher. Continue to pull the thread on the bobbin holder, and keep tension on the other as it closes.

When you draw the knot to a close near the eye, slip the other arm off the loop and pull tightly. Clip the thread 1mm from the shank and add a drop of varnish.

bing) over the floss in an open spiral in the *opposite* direction to the floss. By doing this, the ribbing crosses the Rayon floss and protects it (see **5**). Four to five evenly spaced turns is usually enough. Secure the loose end of wire where the floss body ends, and cut off the excess.

For the collar choose a black cock hackle with fibres that are soft and about 1½ times longer than the hook's gape. Remove the fluff and any broken fibres from the base of the hackle, leaving a short bare stub.

With three or four turns of thread, secure the bare stub of the hackle to the hook just behind the eye. Next, use hackle pliers to grip the tip of the hackle, and wind it around the hook shank *three* times (see **6**). The Black Pennell is a wet fly

which is dressed sparsely. Catch in the hackle tip with three or four turns of thread, and cut off the excess feather. Build a small neat head just below the eye of the hook with several turns of tying thread.

The final step to complete the Black Pennell (and most other flies) is the whip-finish – creating a hidden knot which won't unravel. There are other ways of finishing a fly (such as using half hitches), but the whip finish is the most secure one. You can make the whip-finish with your fingers, or use a specially designed tool (see *Whip-finisher* on this page).

After you've whip-finished the head and clipped the waste end, apply a drop of clear varnish to the bare threads to protect and secure them.

Tying wet and dry fly wings

Tying wings on both wet and dry flies need not be a frustrating experience. Peter Gathercole explains how to attach paired slip-wings so they sit properly and look neat.

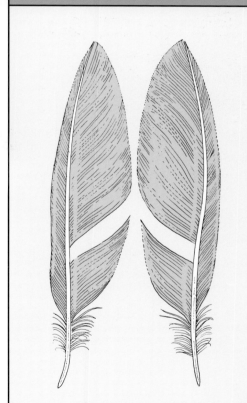

▲ These three popular dry flies (from top to bottom: Greenwell's Glory, Hare's Ear and Black Gnat) have conventional split, upright wings.
   Tying wings never comes easy at first, but with practice and perseverance, you can extend the range of your fly-tying skills.

W et and dry fly wings come in a great many different styles and forms. In essence the role of wings on an artificial is to imitate as closely as possible those of the natural insect, be it a sedge, stonefly, upwinged fly or terrestrial.

Perhaps the most commonly used form of wing is paired slips of feather taken from a

▲ Paired wings lying along the hookshank characterize classic wet flies such as the Blae and Black, Cinnamon and Gold and Blue Dun – proven patterns that should be carried by all loch-style enthusiasts.

From each wing feather

It's important that the two feathers used are taken from *opposite wings of the same bird*. Make sure the slips are from exactly the same point on opposing wings.

The correct width

You don't have to measure every slip before and after cutting. Instead, get the width by inserting into the feather a hook one size smaller than the one you're tying on. (But make sure that you don't bend any of the wing fibres.)

For example, when tying in wings on a size 12 hook, insert a size 14 to measure the width of the slips. This gives you perfect results in no time at all.

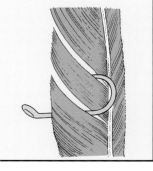

Tip Good thread

Micro thin thread can't be beaten when making small, delicate flies and when tying on wings. It also helps to use it for well-formed but not too bulky heads.

bird's primary wing quills. Popular species include mallard duck and starling – both offer shades of grey which so wonderfully mimic the wing colour of many upwinged flies (including the lake olive, medium olive and blue-winged olive).

The techniques required for tying paired slip-wings on both wet and dry flies are very similar. As the slips are paired it is important that the two feathers used are taken from opposite wings of the same bird – and better still if those feathers are from exactly the same point on opposing feathers. You'll notice that each feather has a slightly different curve, and only perfectly matching feathers give the very best results.

When you are tying a paired wing on a wet fly, selection and preparation of the slips come once you have got the body and hackle in place.

Ideally, leave a small gap of around 2mm behind the eye to accept the wing. Start by taking the two quills and removing two slips about 4mm wide – ideal for sizes 12 and 14 hooks. Judge the width of each wing so that it is exactly the same as its partner. Ensuring that the tips are even and perfectly aligned, grasp the slips firmly, with the curves in the slips facing in towards each other.

It is here that the wet and dry fly paired wings differ the most. In the wet fly it is 'curves-in', while in the dry fly it is 'curves out'. The reason for this difference is that the wet fly wing uses the opposing curves of the feathers to cancel each another out, so producing a perfectly straight wing.

Conversely, the curves in the slips for the dry fly are allowed to diverge outwards – producing the classic split-wing profile. Dry fly wings are erect rather than sloping back along the hook.

The wings on a fly either make or break the pattern. Take your time and learn to tie them well.

Tying wings on wet and dry flies

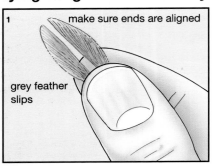

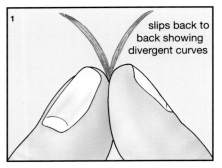

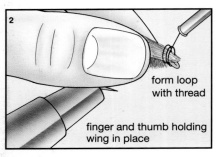

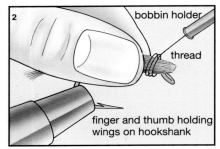

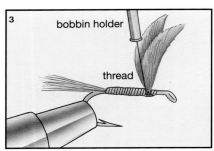

The wet fly

1. Cut one 4mm wide slip from the same point on each of two opposing wing feathers. Make sure both are the same length and width.

2. Grasp the slips with your thumb and forefinger with the natural curves facing in (towards each other) and the tips aligned. Lay them on the hookshank 2mm past the eye so that the wing projects slightly past the bend. The first few turns of thread are important: unlike normal wraps they should all be *loose* (winging) loops.

3. With the thread hanging below the hook, draw the loops tight. Winging loops ensure that the wing sits perfectly straight on the top of the hook and is not twisted around. Cut off excess wing over the eye. Build a neat head, and whip finish.

The dry fly

1. The wing on a dry fly is set a little farther back along the hook than that on a wet, and is added before, not after, the winding of the hackle feather. First of all, select two equal feather slips, and place them together back-to-back so the curves diverge or do not face each other.

2. Carefully but firmly hold the wing slips between finger and thumb above the hookshank so that the feather tips project back no farther than the bend. Catch it in neatly with two or three winging loops.

3. Add a few more turns of thread to secure the wing. Finally, remove any excess feather with a small pair of nail clippers before throwing three turns of thread under and behind the wing – this makes it stand upright (vertically).

▲ *When the flow is slow, the water clear and the trout finicky, imitative flies with life-like wings are often the most successful in deceiving wise old trout such as this River Test resident.*

The Pheasant Tail Nymph

Learn a few basic fibre-twisting techniques, and you are well on your way to making one of many variations of the Pheasant Tail Nymph, a pattern responsible for fooling thousands of trout.

▼ *Twitched directly along the bottom, a Pheasant Tail Nymph lured this 3lb (1.4kg) rainbow trout.*

Adding movement to a nymph by twitching it or drawing it slowly often convinces cautious trout, hovering off the bottom in deep water.

M ost river and stillwater fly fishermen have some form of Pheasant Tail Nymph in their armoury of favourite flies. It's one of those patterns which has proven itself over the years and has hundreds of variations. Some have fluorescent thoraxes; others have legs; and still others are tied on long shank hooks.

Frank Sawyer, a river-keeper on the Upper Avon, invented the pattern in the late 1940s. It was one of the few flies he used all season. The brilliance of the fly is its simplicity. Sawyer didn't use tying thread, only copper wire and cock pheasant tail fibres.

The Pheasant Tail represents upwinged nymphs (olives and iron blues) but can pass for a variety of other nymphs as well. Sawyer's original didn't have legs, in line with his beliefs about agile nymphs – the natural doesn't use its legs when swimming. The version without legs also falls through the water faster than one with legs (usually pheasant tail fibres).

The pattern below is similar to Sawyer's in most ways. However, thread is used to make the nymph more secure, and the copper thorax isn't covered with pheasant tail fibres. To tie the pattern, you need brown or black thread, a cock pheasant tail, thin copper wire and hooks from size 10-16.

To fish the Pheasant Tail on a river, use the dead drift or induced take methods of upstream fishing. For the dead drift, cast upstream of the intended trout, and allow the nymph to drift freely in the current towards the fish. The induced take is similar to the dead drift. However, when the nymph reaches the trout, lift the rod to move the nymph, imitating a fleeing insect.

▲ *Just a bit farther... and it's over. The rainbow is safely netted.*

▲ *The fly that tempted the trout – a Pheasant Tail Nymph tied on a size 14 hook.*

Tying a Pheasant Tail Nymph

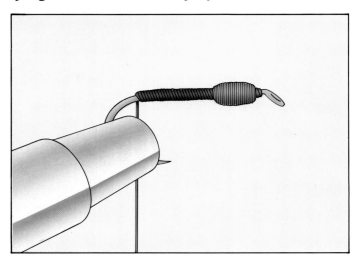

1. Wind the thread down the shank of the hook to the bend. Using thin copper wire, form an egg-shaped thorax 2mm behind the eye of the hook.

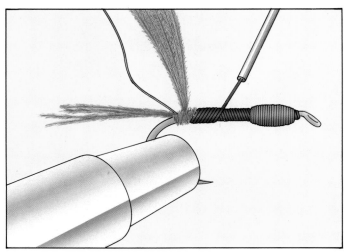

2. Using the thread, tie in 3-4 cock pheasant fibres as the tail, a 7cm (2¾in) length of copper wire as a rib, and 5-7 fibres as the body. Bring the thread to the thorax.

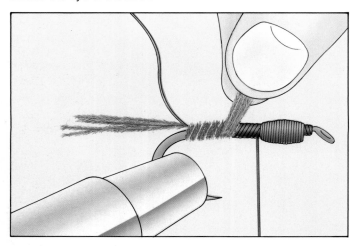

3. Begin wrapping the tail fibres along the shank of the hook, stopping at the thorax. Secure them with 2 or 3 turns of thread, and trim the excess.

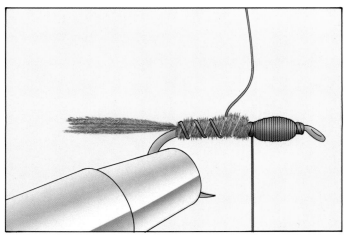

4. Wrap the copper ribbing in the *opposite* direction to the fibres. This helps to secure and protect them. Secure the wire with 2 turns of thread.

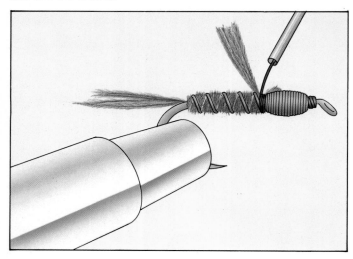

5. Catch in 4-5 more pheasant fibres with 2 turns of thread and finish with 2 half-hitches. Clip the thread. Then make another bed of thread near the eye. Bring the fibres over the thorax and secure. Remove excess fibres. Build a neat head. Whip finish. Clip the thread and add varnish to the head.

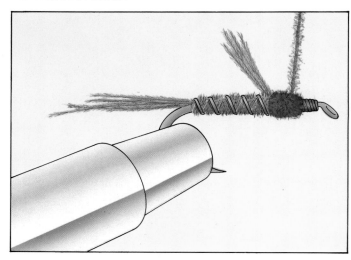

6. By substituting fur (or other materials) in different colours you can make myriad variations. Pinch a fingernail full of fur and spin it in one direction on to waxed thread. Wrap a few times to form the thorax. Bring fibres over the thorax. Secure. Finish off as usual.

The Adams: a multi-purpose dry fly

Many beginners don't include wings on their dry flies, claiming they're too difficult to tie in properly. But tying the Adams – with its grizzle point wings – is easier than you think.

The Adams, created by Leonard Halliday in 1922, came to Britain from North America decades ago, but it didn't receive much acclaim. One possible reason for this is that tight-knit groups of fly fishermen had an established canon of imitative flies which were not only effective but devised by celebrated and revered anglers of old.

Today, however, the Adams has a profound impact on chalk-stream and freestone-river anglers. Many river fly fishermen are convinced of the importance of a general, nondescript pattern, tied in a variety of sizes, to represent everything from midges and upwings to big stoneflies and sedges.

Perhaps the Adams' success lies in the combination of key colours – blue, grey and brown. Perhaps it's the grizzle wing tips.

Whatever the source of its allure, the Adams is successful both when searching the water and when a hatch is underway – especially in small sizes (16-20).

To tie the fly, you need grey thread, grizzle and brown cock hackles, blue-grey fur (rabbit or muskrat) or wool, and a range of hooks in sizes 12-22.

Fish the Adams as you would any dry fly. Here are a few suggestions which may increase your chances of catching a rising trout.
● Fish upstream and across.
● If possible try to establish the 'rising rhythm' of the fish so that you put your fly on a collision course with the trout.
● Make your first cast your best one.
● Try to show the trout *only the fly*, not the leader.

▲ *An almost-finished Adams. Some anglers prefer the traditional up-eyed hooks for dry flies; others, however, claim that you stand a better chance of hooking your trout with down-eyed ones. But the choice is yours.*

▼ *A grayling thrashes near the bank of the Upper Avon in Wiltshire, courtesy of a size 18 Adams.*
    Small flies (16-22) work particularly well for chalk stream trout and grayling.

Tying an Adams

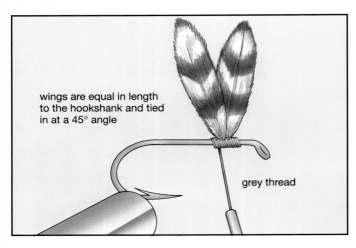

1. Take two well-marked cock grizzle hackles, and clip the tips so that they are about as long as the hookshank. Tie them in a 'V' at a 45° angle to each other.

wings are equal in length to the hookshank and tied in at a 45° angle

grey thread

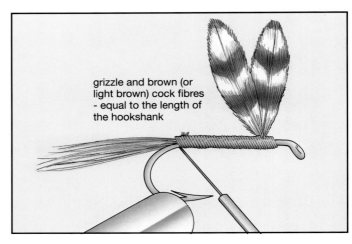

2. Wind the thread down the shank. Tear out twelve fibres from a brown and grizzle hackle. Make sure that they're as long as the hookshank. Mix together, and tie in.

grizzle and brown (or light brown) cock fibres - equal to the length of the hookshank

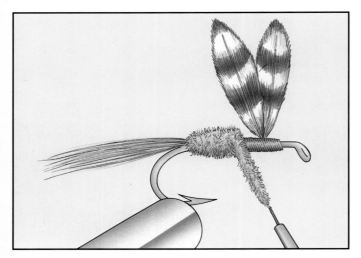

3. Take a small amount of fur and dub it (spin on the thread). Wind up the hookshank. Make either a straight or slightly tapered body.

4. Tie in one grizzle and brown cock hackle in the same place at the same time just behind the wings. Bring the thread up the hookshank just behind the eye.

one grizzle and one brown (or light brown) cock hackle tied in together

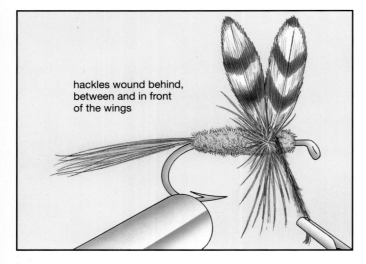

5. If you wind one feather then the other, you'll get an untidy hackle. Grasp both hackles with the hackle pliers, and wind two turns behind the wings, two turns in between the wings and two turns above the wings. Alternatively, wrap the hackles twice behind, once in between and once in front of the wings for a smaller hackle.

hackles wound behind, between and in front of the wings

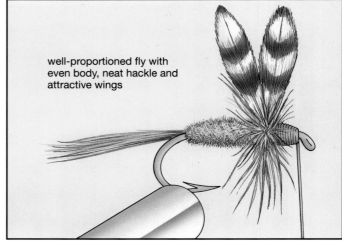

6. Once you've finished winding the hackle, secure it; then clip the excess. Form a head; whip finish and apply two thin coats of varnish. This is one pattern where you can experiment with the hackle (and tail thickness) to suit your fishing situations – e.g. in fast water, a fly with a bushy hackle floats better.

well-proportioned fly with even body, neat hackle and attractive wings

Tying the Booby

When lethargic, early season trout are down deep, hovering just off the debris-covered lake bed, the Booby is unbeatable – as anglers all over Britain can testify again and again. Here's the recipe.

Created in 1982 by Gordon Fraser, the Booby 'Nymph' really revolutionized stillwater fishing – especially from the bank. Coupled with a Hi-D line and short leader, the fly rides up off the lake bed – so no more worries about catching decomposing weeds or debris on every cast. You can fish the lure as slow as you like – some anglers fish it static. They just leave it there until a fish takes!

When you retrieve the Booby, the big bulbous eyes cause the marabou tail to wiggle enticingly: few trout (both overwintered and stockies) have the will-power to resist. They often commit themselves fully and take the fly deep. The reason for the Booby's appeal to both brown and rainbow trout is possibly that it suggests coarse fry such as roach, bream, perch and pike.

Over the years the Booby has undergone dozens of changes. The lure can be tied with many different types of body and wing material. One of the more recent improvements is the use of closed-cell foam (Plastazote) for the eyes instead of polystyrene (which isn't as buoyant and tends to get waterlogged easily).

▲ *The hot orange Booby. Notice how the hookshank bisects the eyes.*

 Let it sink

A common mistake when using the Booby is not allowing the fly to sink all the way to the bottom before you retrieve. Be aware of how fast your line sinks and the depth at which you are fishing.

▼ *An overwintered rainbow comes to the net on Blagdon Water in Avon. Though the dam wall can be productive, drop offs and points are also worth a try.*

Making the eyes

To form the eyes, cut two 5-7mm squares from a piece of Plastazote. Impale them through the centre on your dubbing needle. Now, with a sharp razor (be careful!) cut off the edges so that the blocks are more or less round. When encased in a small square of nylon stocking and tied on the hookshank, the edges compress, and the eyes become round. But if you want perfectly rounded eyes, use fine sandpaper to shape them into exact spheres.

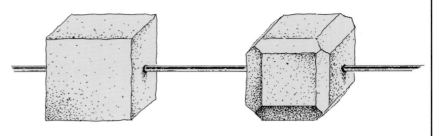

Four steps to tying a Booby

1. Trap both eyes in nylon stocking and tie them just behind the hook's eye with figure-of-eight turns. They should sit across from each other with the hookshank bisecting the eyes. Secure with instant glue.

2. Tear off a generous bunch of marabou fibres and secure above the hook bend. Make sure the tips of the marabou are aligned. Trim away the excess stalk and then tie in the ribbing material (oval gold ribbing in this case).

3. With more marabou cut from the stalk, form a rope by twisting the marabou on to the thread in one direction. Some people like a straight body; others prefer a tapered one. Wind up the hookshank in neat, even turns.

4. Wrap the ribbing around the body of the fly, and secure it just behind the eyes. Whip finish twice. Dub a bit more marabou on the thread. Turn once around to form a collar and whip finish just behind the eyes.

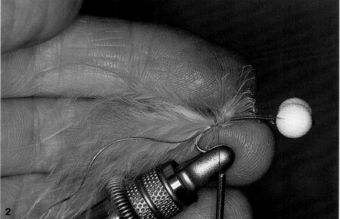

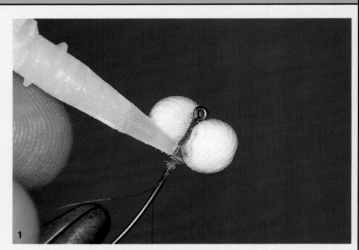

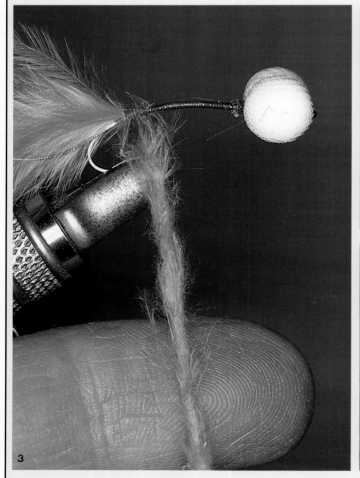

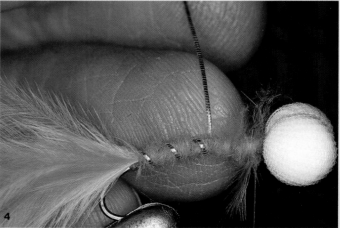

Tying deer-hair flies

The ability to spin deer hair well completes a repertoire of fly tying skills. You can master the tricky business in a few simple steps and, with the right equipment, can soon be tying densely packed deer-hair flies.

▼ *Here is a good selection of flies tied with deer hair. 1. Bubble-gum Dalberg Diver (with weed guard); 2. Muddler (body is dubbed deer hair, head is spun hair); 3. Gilled Roach (the gills are red marabou fibres wound around hookshank); 4. G & H Sedge.*

Deer-hair flies come in myriad styles and shapes and can be used to catch many species of fish throughout the world. Examples include the G & H Sedge and the Muddler Minnow for trout, the Water-Walker for steelhead, the Dalberg Diver for pike and largemouth bass and the Canadian Bomber series of dry flies for Atlantic salmon.

Deer-hair fibres contain air spaces, making the flies naturally buoyant – superb for fishing near the surface (up to about 0.9m/3ft deep). Muddler-styled lures, for example, displace a great deal of water, and trout and other predatory fish pick up this turbulence with their lateral lines and home in on the source.

Quality deer hair is spongy and flares easily when under thread tension. Most good fly fishing tackle shops have different colours and lengths available. Short hair is excellent for sedges and mini muddlers (because you trim a lot of the hair away). Long hair is suitable for large fry-imitating flies – the extra length helps to provide the right imitative dimensions.

▼ *Even fastidious river browns – such as this fine specimen – can be fooled with deer hair flies such as G & H Sedge, Muddler Minnow and Troth's Bullhead.*

Tip Fuzz busters

If you don't remove the fine underfur near the deer skin, you can't pack the hair tightly. In addition, the fur absorbs water, making the fly rather heavier than normal.

A clean mascara brush is excellent for removing unwanted deer-hair underfur. For a lot of hair work, use either a fine-tooth comb or a poodle brush – both are available at pet shops, and both do the job equally well.

After combing the underfur from the hair, save it in a small plastic bag. It is extremely fine and makes an excellent dubbing material for nymphs.

TYING A MARABOU MUDDLER

Hair and other bits and pieces

1. Short-fibred natural deer hair
2. Long hair dyed yellow, olive and black
3. Natural white hair from the belly
4. Size A rod wrapping thread (or size A mono-cord) – using strong, thick thread allows you to exert a lot of pressure on the hair, ensuring it spins well and the fibres flare properly; also you don't have to worry about the thread breaking
5. Tiemco curved scissors – these scissors are super sharp, and the curved tip is useful when clipping different fly shapes
6. Hair stacker – for lining up tips of hair when forming a collar
7. Hair packer – allows you to compress the hair a lot better than with your fingers or a Biro tube; it's an essential item for forming really tight bodies and heads
8. Marabou
9. White polypropylene

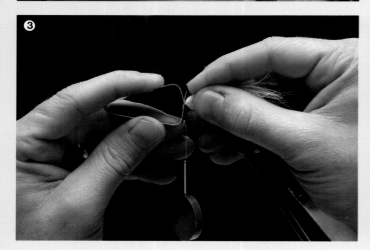

1. First make the tail, body and wing of the fly. Then grasp a small clump of deer hair by the tips and upper portion of the hair, and remove it as close to the skin as possible. (Don't handle the hair too much after cutting from the skin since you may displace the fibres and end up with a mess.)

Clip off the tips and butts; then lay the hair on the hookshank *at an angle*. Catch it in with two loose wraps of thread, making sure the thread is in the middle of the hair.

2. As you pull the thread down, release the hair a little at a time. It should spin around the hookshank. Make another wrap or two

through the spun hair. Then tighten by pulling the thread down while holding a few of the fibres.

3. Pull all the hair back. Wrap the thread two or three times in front of the fibres. Then push the hair back towards the tail with a hair packer. Advance the thread 2mm or so, and repeat the entire process until you come to a point just before the eye.

4. Pull all the hair back again, and then whip finish just behind the eye. Apply a drop of varnish to the thread for protection. Clip the head to the desired shape with sharp scissors.

Tying a white deer-hair Diver

A lot of flies look like small fish but have little action. Though the Diver doesn't look like anything natural, its action in the water is second to none. Tying a good diver isn't difficult if you follow the instructions.

Divers: colour and flash

As a general rule, use dark coloured flies – brown, black and grey – in clear water. Bright colours with a lot of Flashabou or Crystal Flash are suited to murky water.

For pike, the brighter the better: fluorescent yellow, green, red and white (with Flashabou) are the top colours.

Many people use two or even three colours of deer hair to make up the head, giving it a striped appearance.

The Dalberg Diver was created by Larry Dalberg for smallmouth bass fishing on the St. Croix River, Wisconsin, USA, in the mid 1960s. Since the early 1980s (when it was much publicized) the fly has spread across the continents and caught dozens of species – from huge pike to prize rainbows.

So what makes the Diver so special? How is it different from the Muddler? Though it may not look like a natural food item, the fly is unique because as you retrieve, it dives under the surface of the water and undulates up and down, its marabou or zonker-strip tail pulsing wildly. Stop, and it pops back up to the surface.

▼ *A Booby-hooked trout crashes on the surface near the bank of Farmoor Reservoir. Mini Divers are good substitutes for Boobies and Muddlers too.*

You can tie the Diver in many sizes and styles – from 2/0 pike flies with long marabou tails (on short shanked sea fishing hooks) to tiny river trout Divers with small zonker-strip tails (tied on size 12 hooks). For stillwater and river trout, use size 6-12 short shanked hooks.

Fish a brown or grey mini Diver in free-stone rivers by casting up and across. Allow the fly to drift downstream while giving it a few strips now and again to imitate an injured fish.

For stillwaters, why not use a size 8 Diver instead of a Booby? Grease the fly well to keep it buoyant. Attach a short leader of 60cm (2ft) and use a Hi-Speed Hi-D line. Cast and let the fly line and fly sink and then retrieve with a slow figure-of-eight.

You can also fish the fly on a medium sinker or floating line. It takes trout at all levels. But the Diver doesn't work well if you retrieve it really quickly. A slow strip and figure-of-eight are the most effective.

If you're using a floating line and the fly is skating across the surface instead of diving, grease only the top of the fly. This allows the bottom to soak up water, helping the Diver plunge under the surface.

To tie the White Diver, you need the following: a hair packer, size A white rod wrapping thread (or size A monocord), natural white deer hair, silver Flashabou and white and red marabou (or zonker strip). For more information about spinning deer hair, see pages 217-218.

Tying the White Dalberg Diver (size 6)

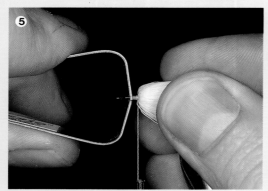

1. Start the thread above the hook point and lay down a bed of thread to the end of the hook shank. Bring it right back to the point and tie in a clump of white marabou to form the tail.

Double a few strands of silver Flashabou over the thread (as shown). Make sure some strands are on each side of the fly. Coat the area with instant glue or varnish.

2. Now catch in several red marabou fibres, and wrap them over the varnished area. Secure with a wrap of thread, and add a drop of varnish to help hold the red marabou.

3. Cut off a clump of white deer hair, removing tips and butts (it forms the collar, so you need long hair). Lay the hair on the shank *at an angle* (this helps it to spin). Make two loose wraps of thread around the middle of the hair.

4. Pull down with the thread, releasing the hair a little at a time to spin it right round the shank. Make another wrap or two through the spun deer head. Then bring the thread in front towards the eye.

5. Make a few wraps around the shank in front of the hair to stand it upright. Then with a hair packer (or biro tube), push all of it towards the tail. This compresses the hair so that you tie densely packed heads which float well.

6. Continue the process towards the eye. When you tie in the last clump of deer hair, wrap once or twice through the spun hair, but *don't* move the thread in front of it as you did previously.

To increase the density of the head even more, take another clump of hair, and make two loose wraps of thread around it while flattening the clump over the head with your thumb and index finger. Pull down firmly on the thread. Don't allow the added clump to spin; it should flair and fold over on top of the head.

Bring the thread to the eye. Pack the head. Whip finish twice and varnish. With a razor carefully flatten the bottom. Then clip the top to shape with sharp scissors.

Index

Page numbers in *italics* refer to illustrations

ACKNOWLEDGEMENTS

Photographs: Allsport (J Nichols) 37; Heather Angel 139(t); Angling Photo Service (Bill Howes) 39(t), 63; Aquila 152(c); Bob Church 61(b), 62(tr); Bruce Coleman 117(b), 207(t), (John Burton) 172(t), (Frank Lane) 153, (John Shaw) 173(t); John Darling 21; Eaglemoss (Eric Crichton) 18(c), 27, 30(t), 77-80, 104(b), 123, 219, (Ian Christy) 24(b), 122, 213(b), (Peter Gathercole) 23(t), 34, 41, 42(b), 44(b), 46-47, 57, 60, 121(t), 163-164, 182, 186(t), 188(t), 192(t), (Mike Helliwell) 203, 206(b), (Dennis Linley) 124, 194, (Patrick Llewellyn-Davies) 19(b), 24(t), 24(c), 28, 31(b), 33(b), 40(t), 58, 67(t), 70(b), 102, 116, 166(t), 166(br), 177(b), 179(l), 181, 187(t), 189(t), 191, 193(b), 195(tl), 196, 199(b), 209, 217(t), 218, (Martin Norris) 14, 20(t), 20(c), 205, 211(br), (John Suett) 11; Explorer 15; Peter Gathercole 3, 6, 9, 10, 13, 16, 19, 22(t), 23(b), 25, 26(b), 29, 31(t), 32(t), 33(t), 35, 36, 40(b), 43, 45(t), 49(b), 50, 52(t), 53, 55, 56, 59, 61(t), 62(tr), 64(b), 65, 66, 67(b), 68, 69(b), 70(c), 72(b), 81, 82, 84(r), 85-88, 91, 92, 93(t), 94(t), 95(b), 99, 100(t), 101, 103, 106, 108(b), 117(t), 120(b), 121(b), 127-128, 130(t), 140(tr), 142, 144(b), 146, 150, 152(t), 154, 165, 166(c), 166(bl), 167(b), 168, 170(b), 171, 172(b), 173(b), 174, 175(t), 175(b), 176(b), 179(br), 180, 183, 184(b), 185, 188(b), 189(b), 198(c), 198(b), 201(t), 202(b), 204, 206(t), 207(b), 210, 215(b), 217(b); Mike Helliwell 133(b), 135, 136(t); Neil Holmes 139(b); Trevor Housby 12, 71(b), 73(t), 75(b), 76, 132; Kevin Hyatt 93(b), 125(t), 197, 198(t), 200(b), 202(t), 213(t); Paul Losik 18(t), 44(t), 48, 54, 97(b), 100(b), 104(t), 131(b), 192(b), 193(t), 195(r), 195(b), 220; Mike Millman 17(t), 71(t); Natural Science Photos 42(t), (N Barltrop) 167(t), (P Sheehan) 26(t), 160, (D Smyth) 17(b), 111(t), 178(b), (A Spence) 22(b), 144(t), (P&S Ward) 131(t), 175(tr); Nature Photographers (Paul Sterry) 137(t); NHPA (Stephen Dalton) 170(tl), 173(t), (John Hayward) 137(b); Ian Neale 200(t); Arthur Oglesby 45(b), 113, 114, 129, 130(b), 141, 143, 145, 177(t), 199(t); Oxford Scientific Films (Colin Milkins) 170(tr); Planet Earth Pictures 156(b); Jens Ploug Hansen 73(b), 111(b), 211(l), 211(rc); John Roberts 84(l), 89, 90, 95(t), 98, 105, 110, 115(t), 125(t), 126, 169, 178(t), 187(b), 190,; Scotland in Focus 140(tl), 140(b); Swanpix (Graham Swanson) 20(b), 64(t), 69(t), 72(t), 97(t), 107, 108(t); Barbara Swanson 32(b); Swift Picture Library 119(b), 120(t); Russell Symons 39(b), 75(b), 184(t), 215(t), 216; Dave Tait 94(b); Mick Toomer 148; Jim Tyree 30(t), 49(t), 52(t), 176(t), 186(b); Bruce Vaughan 83, 201(b); Phil Williams 109, 112, 156(t), 162; John Wilson 133(t), 136(b), 158.

Illustrations: Peter Barret 78-79; Peter Bull 38, 47, 50-51, 58-60, 66, 70, 88-90, 92, 96, 98-99, 102-104, 110-111, 114-115, 122-124, 126, 128-129, 132, 134-135, 150, 152, 158, 160, 185, 190, 208, 209-210, 212, 214; Wendy Brammall 54-55; Dave Etchell 74-75, 82-83; Peter Etchell 62-63; Mei Lim 148; Mick Loates 147, 149, 151, 153, 155, 157, 159, 161; Denys Ovenden 142-143, 194; John Ridyard 118, 138-9.